Elazar Ste

Struggling Over Israel's Soul

An IDF General Speaks of His Controversial Moral Decisions

Translated by Yoram Kislev

Originally published in Hebrew as *Masa Kumta*
by Miskal – Yediot Ahronoth Books and Chemed Books, 2009
Photographs by permission of IDF Spokesperson's Unit

COVER DESIGN: Pini Hamou
TYPESETTING: Benjie Herskowitz, Etc. Studios

ISBN: 978-965-229-576-7

1 3 5 7 9 8 6 4 2

Gefen Publishing House Ltd.
6 Hatzvi Street
Jerusalem 94386, Israel
972-2-538-0247
orders@gefenpublishing.com

Gefen Books
11 Edison Place
Springfield, NJ 07081
516-593-1234
orders@gefenpublishing.com

www.gefenpublishing.com

Printed in Israel

Send for our free catalogue

Library of Congress Cataloging-in-Publication Data

Stern, Elazar, 1956-
[Masa kumtah. English]
Struggling over Israel's soul : an IDF general speaks of his controversial moral decisions / Elazar Stern ; translated by Yoram Kislev.
p. cm.
ISBN 978-965-229-576-7
1. Stern, Elazar, 1956- 2. Generals–Israel–Biography. 3. Orthodox Judaism–Israel–Biography. 4. Draft–Israel–Religious aspects. 5. Judaism and state–Israel. 6. Israel–Armed Forces–Religious life. 7. Israel. Tseva haganah le-Yisra'el–Religious life. I. Title.
DS125.3.S76A3 2012
355.0092–dc23
[B]

2012025677

In all the horrific, soul-destroying events of my life, one thing was never destroyed. I never stopped believing. Even when I was struck the hardest, my belief did not collapse.

I was just a week in Israel when I visited the Western Wall – known as the Kotel – in Jerusalem. My late mother did not leave with me any instructions for such a moment, for I did not have the chance to take leave of her before her death. I was standing a few steps away from the wall and its ancient stones, and felt completely out of place. I felt like a total stranger, like I did not belong. I did not dare walk the few remaining steps, but then someone pulled at my sleeve and asked me to join and participate in a minyan – a prayer quorum. I covered my head with a kippa *– a Jewish skullcap – and joined the minyan. I prayed the afternoon service and knew that I had arrived.*

It is a Jewish thing – possibly one of the most unique aspects of being Jewish – to participate in a minyan. Knowing that the nine needs a tenth, just as one needs the nine. This might even be the most significant aspect of Judaism.

I pray to remain forever one of a multitude, so that the words I whisper may unite with the words whispered by the crowd. Even the leader of the prayer is but another praying man and no more.

Life has no meaning in isolation. Only when connected to the larger experience, to the words that reach you – coming from afar – is there a meaning to one's persistent struggle.

One – but one of a community.

Abba Kovner
renowned poet, World War II partisan leader,
member of Kibbutz Ein Hahoresh

To my parents, Sara Eisner and Levi Stern

To my wife, Dorit

To Liron, Ilan, Adi, Hodaya and Amichai

Who deserve all the credit

Contents

ACKNOWLEDGMENTS

First, thank you to Dovi Aichenvald, CEO of Yediot Sefarim, without whom this book would not have seen the light of day. When Dov originally suggested that I publish an autobiography I refused, as I felt that I was still young and it wouldn't be modest. But when I asked him why he had approached me specifically, he told me that he wished to show through my life what had happened to religious Zionism, and with it, to the identity of the State of Israel in the past thirty years. His answer changed my position. I agreed to his proposal, as I share his sense of missed opportunity, and I believe that it is never too late to change.

To Professor Elie Wiesel, winner of the Nobel Peace Prize, who advised me and recommended that I translate my book into English. Aside from serving as guidance, for me his advice was a great compliment.

To Ilan Greenfield, director of Gefen Publishing House, and to all his dedicated staff, particularly Lynn Douek, project manager, and Ita Olesker, who edited the English edition of this book. When it came time to choose a publisher for the English edition, all roads led to Ilan – and after some months of working together, I understood why.

To Sue Singer, whose intelligence and feeling lent deeper meaning to my relationship with her son Alex, *z"l*, who fell in battle in southern Lebanon. My relationship with Alex began when Alex was under my command, and continued to deepen even after he was laid to rest.

This is the opportunity to thank the editor of the Hebrew edition, Shachar Alterman. When I told Dan Margalit that Shachar would be my editor, Dan replied that I must have prayed hard. Once we completed the manuscript, I realized I should recite Hallel.

Thank you to my wife Dorit – how do I express that I owe everything to her without falling back on the same trite phrases? Words fail me.

To our children Liron and her husband Shimon Abuhatzeira Mannes, Ilan and his wife Liat (Zeiderman), Adi and her husband Daniel Kesselman, Yaffa, Hodaya, and Amichai. Individually and collectively, they provide additional proof that when there's a good mother in charge, even when the father isn't around, it's possible to raise a family to be proud of.

To my parents, Sarah and Levi Stern, who survived the horrors of the Holocaust and developed infinite reservoirs of strength, which they invested in their three children – my sisters Tzipi and Batya and myself.

To Rina and Shlomo Mannes, the parents of Bracha, Ilan, *z"l*, and Dorit, who passed on to their children the importance of memory, and the even greater importance of life.

To all the bereaved families who gave me the privilege of meeting with them. I may have strengthened them, but they strengthened me still more.

To Surin Hershkow, a friend who has become part of the family. He returned home paralyzed from Operation Entebbe, yet his faith and his smile have taught us that the spirit always triumphs.

This book has no index of names. It would be impossible to list all the hundreds of my commanders, teachers, and friends, and the thousands of my soldiers. I am grateful to all of them – to those who agreed with me, more so to those who didn't agree, and also to those who criticized.

INTRODUCTION

On the night before Israel's unilateral withdrawal from the Gaza Strip – known as the disengagement – in the summer of 2005, I found myself driving through the streets of Jerusalem on my way to the Kotel, the Western Wall, one of Judaism's holiest sites.

It was August 13, 2005, and the corresponding date on the Hebrew calendar was the terrible evening of the ninth day of the month of Av, the day Jews around the world commemorate the destruction of both Jewish Temples, which used to stand with all their glory on the great platform behind the Kotel.

Like most nights, the plaza around the Kotel was crowded. Everyone sat on the ground chanting lamentations amid a mood of impending destruction, although this time the destruction was to occur elsewhere – in Gaza.

The next time I visited the Kotel was after the evacuation of the ten thousand Jewish residents of the Gaza Strip had been completed. This time I came in uniform as a general in the Israel Defensev Forces (IDF) and head of its Human Resources Directorate. My job had been to oversee the reburial of the bodies that were removed from the single Jewish cemetery in Gaza.

Forty-five civilians were buried in Gaza's small Jewish cemetery, alongside three IDF soldiers. Moving the graves outside the evacuated area was the most sensitive part of the entire withdrawal and was accompanied by days and nights of deliberations and discussions regarding how such a mission should be carried out.

Under the circumstances, I thought that the option of a military burial for both the civilians and the soldiers was the most dignified solution and would slightly ease the renewed trauma for the families. While I pushed strongly, the Military Rabbinate opposed my idea, claiming that it did not want to take responsibility for reburying civilians; it maintained that it was only responsible for soldiers. In the end, my proposal was accepted and the difficult task was imposed on the Military Rabbinate, mainly because no civilian burial society was willing to take up the daunting challenge.

Once the decision was made, I instructed all the relevant authorities to treat the families with the utmost sensitivity, exactly as they would treat the family of a recently killed soldier. This was to be the case from the time of the first announcement made to the family to the actual reburial in a substitute cemetery.

Official military delegations, including representatives of the Military Rabbinate, met with each of the forty-eight families and arranged the reburial process. The location of a new grave had to be chosen, the time to hold the funeral had to be set, and other procedures had to be reviewed.

I insisted on making personal contact with the families of the three IDF soldiers who were buried in the Gaza cemetery. With the families of Yohanan Hilberg and Elkana Gobi this turned into a very painful and difficult experience.

One of the preliminary discussions with the Hilbergs took place in their home in Netzer Hazani, a small agricultural community in the northeast corner of the Gush Katif settlement bloc. Once the technical side of our discussion ended, I asked Yohanan's father to walk with me to the memorial room they had built for his fallen son inside their community. Yohanan was one of the twelve commandos from the navy's elite Flotilla 13 – known as the Shayetet – who were killed in a Hezbollah ambush in southern Lebanon eight years earlier.

His parents were reluctant at the beginning to meet with me. I succeeded in setting up a meeting with the help of Yoaz Hendel, another navy commando, whom I had met several years earlier and who had served together with Yohanan. The father met with me in the garden of their house while the mother completely ignored my presence.

That day, we wanted to see how we could move the memorial room for Yohanan with the least damage possible. Those were days when the Gaza Strip was still open to the general Israeli public, and supporters of the settlers flowed into the settlements. As we walked to the memorial room, located next to Netzer Hazani's cultural hall, hundreds of boys and girls from religious high schools who were sitting on the grass outside started to curse me. They demanded that I, as a senior IDF officer, refuse to obey army orders to participate in the evacuation. Some of them spit in my direction.

I ignored the youth and continued walking toward the hall along the flower-lined paths, accompanied by a small group of bodyguards.

One of the rabbis in charge of the group tried silencing his students. He ran after me attempting to apologize. At first I ignored him, but after he continued to apologize, I decided to answer him. Just before stepping foot in the hall, I turned around and said, "I accept your apology as long as you remember that education is not like using a joystick. You cannot drive your flock in one direction and then, all of a sudden, turn them in the other direction. If what you are apologizing for is the shouting, I will not forgive you. If, on the other hand, you are apologizing for the mistakes you have made in the way you educated these youngsters that led them to behave the way they did, I will forgive you."

The Gobi family was from Neve Dekalim, the largest settlement in the Gaza Strip and home to approximately five hundred families before the Israeli withdrawal. Elkana Gobi was killed in 2001 under tragic circumstances. He was a soldier in the IDF's elite Duvdevan Unit when, on furlough one day, he was driving into the Gaza Strip and spotted a terrorist opening fire at passing cars. Elkana jumped out of the car and fired back. Since he was in civilian clothing, a security team spotted him and, thinking he was the terrorist, ran him over. He later received an IDF medal of honor for his act of courage.

Despite a number of requests, the Gobis were adamant not to meet with any military representatives. Then I learned that, due to an illness in the family, the parents were spending their time at Hadassah University Hospital in Jerusalem. So I decided to drive to the hospital to meet them. When I arrived, Moshe, the father, agreed to meet me in a hospital room to discuss the evacuation. But just as had happened with the Hilberg family, when he called his wife to join us, she replied, "How can you sit with him? He should leave!" It was a painful moment for the both of us.

I promised Mr. Gobi to personally assist him during the upcoming evacuation, and on the day it took place I was inside the Gobi home with my staff, packing their belongings into boxes. On the day of Elkana's reburial, Moshe called to invite me to attend. Since the family had to observe only one of the seven days of Jewish mourning – known as the shiva – Moshe wanted to spend the day in the plaza opposite the Kotel so that large crowds could come and join him. I promised him I would do all I could to help fulfill his request.

Shmuel Rabinowitz, the rabbi in charge of the Kotel, rejected our request. He said that many people had offered him large sums of money in the past to be able to sit shiva at the Kotel but that he had always turned them away. This case, he explained, could not be different. I then asked Motti Elon, a well-known rabbi from Jerusalem, for his advice. Together, we were able to arrange for Moshe to sit in a corner of the Kotel plaza together with others who were coming to sit with him, under the pretext that they were going to hear a lecture from Rabbi Elon.

I decided to attend the funeral, which took place on Mount Herzl, the site of the State of Israel's military cemetery in Jerusalem. It is named after Theodor Herzl, founder of modern political Zionism, who is also buried there. Those were still the days when I traveled without a security detail. While escorting the coffin I could hear people behind me whispering. At one point, someone turned to me directly and said, "What are you doing here? Leave now!" I don't know why I bothered responding but I said, "You better ask Elkana's father. He asked me to be at his son's funeral."

From the funeral, the family drove to the Kotel, and I made sure that food and drink would be there for the mourners. I then approached the family to say the traditional Hebrew words of comfort spoken at a shiva. I kneeled at their side to speak, and Moshe held my hand for some time and wouldn't let go. Behind me, I heard a man ask his friend why he doesn't go up to the family to pay his respects. He responded: "I am waiting for this scumbag to leave."

Even at this hour of pain and sadness, people could not contain their evil.

The day after the first Yom Kippur following the evacuation, I again visited the Kotel, this time with the Teichmans, friends of mine from the United States. It was Friday evening, and after we visited my daughter Liron in her home in the City of David – a small Jewish enclave located just outside the Old City walls – we walked together toward the Kotel for the traditional Shabbat evening prayers. We were a small group – me, Sidney and Dubby Teichman, my son-in-law Shimon, and my son Amichai, who was ten years old at the time. The Kotel, as on most Friday nights, was crowded and lively. We joined one of the groups at the entrance to the plaza for the evening prayer service.

A few minutes into the service, a crowd began to gather around me. Someone yelled: "Yeshiva abolisher! Oppressor of Jews!" I turned away and ignored him.

When the service was over, Rabbi Tuvia Lifshitz from Yeshivat Hakotel, who I knew well from my dealings with Hesder yeshivot – the programs that combine advanced yeshiva learning with active military service – came over to say hello. As we shook hands, the man who had yelled at me just a few minutes earlier started shouting again. "How can you shake his hand," he yelled out, this time at Rabbi Lifshitz. "He intends to shut down your yeshiva!"

Other people in the crowd joined in, following the example of Rabbi Israel Ariel, a known extremist right-winger. Ariel came over and started pushing me while yelling: "Go away! You have nothing to look for here! The Kotel belongs to me!"

I replied calmly that the Wall was mine just as much as it was his, and that I had no intention of leaving. The rabbi and his followers tried pushing me away from the Wall, but I continued to push forward, refusing to concede to the violent mob. By then the mob was significantly larger, swelled by people who probably had no idea who I was but wanted a piece of the action. They joined the campaign against me, a person they were now treating like the biblical Amalek.

Some people tried to protect me, including the family and friends who were with me, but they were few in the face of many. I held Amichai's hand firmly but after a few moments we suddenly got separated.

Police officers began moving into place as stones started flying in our direction. One of the officers asked that I leave the Kotel plaza. I said that the only place I am going is in the opposite direction – closer to the Wall. I asked the screaming Rabbi Ariel if the *hilul Shabbat* – the desecration of the Shabbat – he was personally causing did not bother him.

"Don't you hear the police sirens?" I asked him. "They are driving here now because of what you are doing." About the defilement of the name of the God I did not bother to say a thing. He might have the title "rabbi" but I can say for certain that Israel Ariel does not have a God!

When the pushing and cursing grew more intense, the policemen begged me to retreat, but I refused. I told them that I would not leave the place without putting my hands on the Kotel, as the ancient tradition requires. Finally, after they promised me that when reinforcements arrived they would escort me back to the Wall, I agreed to retreat toward the back of the plaza. The officers tried to convince me to take shelter in their nearby headquarters, but I refused.

I explained to the policemen that if I hid because of the criticism against me for participating in the evacuation from the Gaza

Strip, these people would have achieved their goal and would continue to prevent soldiers from visiting the Kotel in the future.

There were, as I said, a few good people who tried to help us. One was Rabbi Aharon Bina, the son of my old *rosh yeshiva*, who came down to the Kotel plaza to see what the commotion was all about.

Another was Soli Elihav, director of the Western Wall Heritage Foundation, who found my lost and frightened son Amichai and protected him. Only after large police reinforcements arrived, however, did we begin to feel safer. Needless to say, my son and guests from the US were deeply disturbed and shocked by what was happening. As I was being pulled by the police to the back of the Kotel plaza, my wife Dorit and my pregnant daughter Liron also arrived. When the police refused to let them join us, Liron identified herself as my daughter. After learning who she was, the mob started to curse her as well. They even cursed the baby she was carrying inside her womb.

After a few minutes, once the police reinforcements got into position, we started moving again toward the Wall with the intention of finishing our prayers. Rabbi Ariel stopped me and asked if he could say something. The policemen instinctively pushed him away but I asked them to let him through the ring around me, hoping that such a conversation might calm the situation. He approached me, put his hands on my shoulders, and whispered to me: "Promise me that you will release all the soldiers who refused their orders during the disengagement from Gaza and I will let you approach the Wall!"

I replied that even though most things in this world are negotiable, the right of a Jew to approach the Kotel is unconditional. He immediately resumed his howling – "Criminal! Villain!" – while I continued walking toward the Wall with the tight ring of policemen around me.

After that weekend I was put under tight protection.

The years have passed, and the security guards were called off a long time ago, but the stones hurled at me that day at the Kotel and the venom I felt sizzling behind my back over the fresh grave of Elkana Gobi still disturb my peace.

It is not the private insult and certainly not the personal fear. It is the horror of looking into what we have become as a society and even more what we might so easily turn into in the future. A direct line connects the voices that called on IDF soldiers to disobey their orders during the disengagement, to the soldiers who in 2009 during their swearing-in ceremony at the Kotel raised banners announcing that their unit does not evacuate settlements. A similar line connects the aggressive attacks against me and other officers during the evacuation of the Gaza Strip, to the ugly attacks against Pinchas Wallerstein, a veteran settler leader, after he dared to criticize the refusal phenomenon among his people. Those fresh recruits who called on their comrades to refuse orders do not understand what the real nature of an army is in a democratic society.

I often think about the older and more experienced spiritual leaders of these young soldiers, some of whom went as far as to offer financial rewards to those disgraceful soldiers who raised the banners at the Kotel. Don't they understand what they are endangering? Is it possible that they don't see the damage they are causing to our delicate social fabric? Are we at the end of this frightening process, or is it only the tip of the iceberg?

For decades, ever since Israel became an independent state in 1948, the IDF was kept out of political disputes. Criticism was freely expressed from across the political spectrum and sometimes it was even strong criticism. But there was never a dispute regarding the legitimacy of the IDF's role as the "army of all the people." During all these years the IDF served as a melting pot, integrating all facets of Israeli society – left and right, religious and secular, city folk and farmers, poor and rich, Jews and people of other religions. Only in the army, could they learn to live together and get to truly know one another. When necessary, they were prepared to sacrifice their lives for their friends, ignoring their differences and supposed social gaps and boundaries.

This idea is best demonstrated by the story of Major Benaya Rhein during the Second Lebanon War against Hezbollah in the summer of 2006.

The war caught Benaya on a furlough, one of the first he had taken since enlisting into the IDF in the late 1990s, but he immediately caught up with his battalion and received command over a Merkava tank. Throughout most of the war he worked vigorously to rescue soldiers injured in the battlefield. On August 12, two days before the war ended, Benaya's tank was hit by a Hezbollah anti-tank missile. All of the crew members were killed.

The makeup of the crew in the tank tells the Israeli story. Benaya was from a Jewish settlement in the West Bank. With him in the tank were Uri Grossman, son of the famous and award-winning Israeli novelist David Grossman, from the Jerusalem suburb of Mevesseret Zion; Adam Goren from Kibbutz Ma'abarot; and Alex Bonimovitz from the town of Netanya, who left behind him a grandfather who never had the chance to properly learn Hebrew, since he was forced to stay home and baby-sit Alex's young brother so that the parents could go out and work.

When I arrived to pay my condolences at the Bonimovitz home, the grandfather brought out his grandson's backpack and pointed his finger at the inscription on the front. Alex had drawn there a symbol of peace and love, and next to it he wrote in big black letters "It is good to die for our land," quoting Joseph Trumpeldor, an early Zionist hero, who is believed to have said these words moments before dying in a battle with Arabs in 1920.

The differences between Benaya, Uri, Adam, and Alex would have kept them apart in regular life. But not in the IDF, where the mission – defending the State of Israel – is capable of bridging almost any social gap.

Such encounters and the ensuing camaraderie is essential for our continued existence here, and it will not be found in an army composed of militias in which each unit listens to a different authority – such as a rabbi or another spiritual leader – with various beliefs and ideologies.

If the soldiers of the Shimshon Battalion will not evacuate settlements and the soldiers of the Egoz unit, for example, will refuse to guard settlers in Ariel or defend Palestinian olive pickers or search a Palestinian woman at a military checkpoint, it will be the end not only of the IDF but of Israel as a democratic Jewish state. Ultimately, this could mark the end of our existence in this part of the world.

I would like to believe that this is not the goal of those leaders in the Religious-Zionist camp when they deliberately escalated the conflict as they did, but I must say that I am not completely convinced.

That is why, when writing this book, I was filled with a feeling of great concern. This is a book about my experiences throughout decades of serving as a regular soldier and officer, as the commander of Bahad 1 – the IDF's Officers' Training School – as head of the IDF's Education Corps, and as the commanding officer of the Human Resources Directorate. But it certainly is not an autobiography. I did not write this book for the sole purpose of telling my life story, but rather to be able to tell the story of the challenges and encounters during my military service and the lessons that I derived from them that reflected on Israeli society in its entirety.

If this book happens to have an autobiographical dimension, it is because I held a somewhat unique position as a religiously observant officer serving throughout my career in different units in which the majority of soldiers were secular.

I have always believed that my personal background prepared me to combine religion and military service, and to bridge the gap, as far as possible, between those who wear a *kippa* on their heads and those who don't. As long as I was fighting to strengthen Jewish identity among regular soldiers by sending military delegations to visit Nazi death camps in Poland, or distributing Bibles to soldiers and taking them to walk along the winding, stone-paved streets of Jerusalem's Old City, the religious establishment embraced me. But once rabbis began issuing religious edicts on questions regarding the evacuation of settlements, I learned that because of my *kippa* I was often first in the line of fire from my own people.

It was as if those rabbis expected me to act as their personal representative in the army, and all of a sudden I stopped "delivering the goods." But I did not join the army to represent this rabbi or that yeshiva. I always did my best, though, to represent, among other things, the spirit of the Religious-Zionist movement I knew from my childhood and on whose principles and ethical standards I was raised.

I am sometimes attacked for certain acts and sometimes praised for others. Those who attack me fail to understand that both the praised acts and those that are violently criticized cannot be separated; everything is linked. People need to understand that seminars on Jewish identity in the military can only be held if "Jewish identity" does not become a justification for disobeying orders. Conversion to Judaism for non-Jewish soldiers cannot happen if the Military Rabbinate's religious court opposes the enlistment of female soldiers into the IDF. Ensuring that the IDF observes the Shabbat and keeps military kitchens kosher for all soldiers can only be achieved if the units are mixed with religious and secular soldiers and there are no segregated units. Tours in ancient Jerusalem with soldiers carrying Bibles in their hands cannot happen if the soldiers are also forced to wear *kippa*s on their heads. Someone who criticizes people who are conscientious objectors and refuse to serve at military checkpoints in the West Bank is a hypocrite if he does not condemn with the same vigor a refusal of orders to evacuate Jewish settlements.

As long as Judaism is considered the property of one political side, even if it is considered the property of all those wearing *kippa*s on their heads, Judaism will lose its place in the IDF. Those dilemmas are what worry me and are what this book is about.

Some readers might come to the conclusion that I bear a grudge against the Religious-Zionist movement and its members. Nothing could be farther from the truth. As a citizen of this state and as an officer in its army I haven't the slightest doubt that this movement's contribution to the state and the army is vital.

The fact that I keep sending my children to its institutions, and pray with all my heart that my grandchildren will graduate from the same institutions, is the best proof of my true attitude. After saying that, I have to admit that in recent years there is a minority within the Religious-Zionist camp, and unfortunately it is not a very small minority, which believes that our ways have parted. This compels me to always be on alert and when needed to correct the falsities that our children may encounter in the movement's education system.

As I mentioned earlier, in my final years in military service I served mainly in roles that combined both command and education. I was commander of the Officers' Training School, I was head of the Education Corps, and in my last post I served as head of the Human Resources Directorate. I regarded education of the next generation of soldiers to be a revered mission. This led me more than once to raise a clear and decisive voice on controversial issues that wiser people probably would have stayed away from.

These included the issue of draft dodging in Israeli society, the conversion of non-Jewish soldiers, the evacuation of the Gaza Strip settlements, the Hesder yeshivot, the enlistment of ultra-Orthodox youth into the IDF, and the declining numbers of youth from Tel Aviv in combat units.

Too often I was surprised at how a complex statement I made turned into a falsified one-dimensional headline in the newspapers. Being tagged the "Provocative General" proved to be a double-edged sword. On the one hand it made it easy for me to reach the press to get my message out, but those same journalists hardly ever bothered to listen to what I really had to say.

If I were to go through all the newspaper clippings quoting me in the past decade, I probably would not recognize the man quoted. I certainly would not agree with most of what it was claimed this man had said. That is one of the reasons why I wrote this book. It is, among other things, an attempt to clarify my views on many of these issues, and to invite you, my reader, to an open and sincere debate – an opportunity missed so many times because of the newspapers' pursuit of sensational headlines.

But it was not only anxiety that motivated me to write this book. I was also inspired by the love and gratitude I feel for all the people I have met during my service, who reminded me daily what we fight and sacrifice our lives for.

It could have been the squad commander in my basic training who did his utmost to erase the smile from my face but failed, or my commander and friend David Lipitz who commanded me to shine my boots on Shabbat – the Jewish day of rest – but refrained from noticing my disobedience.

It could have been Ilan, my soldier, neighbor, and good friend, who died in a training accident, and his sister Dorit, who demanded to serve in his unit and in time became my wife. It could have been Yoaz Hendel, the navy commando who taught me that someone who walks around with his head uncovered might sometimes be more pious and religious than people who wear a *kippa*, or my friend Pnina Kenishbach, a Holocaust survivor and bereaved mother who taught generations of bereaved parents how to find consolation even in the darkest of moments in their lives.

It could have been Rabbi Haim Druckman, who agreed to join my efforts to convert soldiers even when the Military Rabbinate was too scared to touch this issue, or Bracha Zisser, with her grace, who persuaded me to break down military red tape and allow recruits, on their very first day in the military, to voluntarily join the national bone-marrow donor bank. These people, and hundreds and perhaps thousands more, make up the true face of Israel, and they are the true heroes of this book. I wish to dedicate this book to each and every one of them.

Chapter 1

Who I Am

I was born on the eighteenth day of the Hebrew month of Elul in the year 1956 in Tel Aviv. Since then I have lived more then half my life in the pastoral town of Hoshaya in the Galilee. The two places and dates all played roles in shaping my life: the Hebrew date of 18 Elul and the secular date of 1956; the secular town of Tel Aviv and the religious community of Hoshaya.

My parents, Sara and Levi Stern, came to Israel soon after the State of Israel was established. They were survivors of the Holocaust and had been to Auschwitz and Mauthausen. Mother came from the Eisner family; she was born in 1928 in what is today Ukraine. Father was born in 1923 in southern Slovakia, not very far from the border with Hungary.

Father worked as an engineer for a big construction company for more than thirty-five years. Mother also stuck to the same job for many years – being a full-time mother and wife. Both of them are, in their different ways, genuine role models that no one will ever be able to duplicate.

My mother tells two stories about my childhood. The first is that when she would take me out for a stroll as a toddler, the neighbors would always get scared because of the strange choking sounds that came from my stroller. She had to assure them that it was a baby with asthma and not a dog inside. The second story she tells is that when people would peer into the stroller and comment how beautiful I was, she would respond: "Say to me whatever you want – tell me he is smart, tell me he is sweet – but don't say he is beautiful."

Mother tried to instill in us modesty, and she never stopped trying. For example, my parents were once invited to attend my niece Einat's graduation ceremony from the course that qualified her to become an education officer in the IDF. I was also there as the IDF chief education officer. When the sergeant asked everyone to rise before I entered, everybody stood up except for my mother, who was clearly heard reprimanding my father: "Sit down Lipo, it's only our Eli!" Immediately after that, I canceled the procedure of standing up in honor of the entrance of a high-ranking officer.

My parents, my two sisters, Tzipi (Zinger) and Batya (Arieli), and I lived in a spacious one-bedroom apartment. I say that with no sarcasm.

When my parents reminisce over the simplicity of those days in our simple residential project where everybody knew one another and the dirt roads were used for a playground, I remind them that every Friday my sisters and I used to receive ten agurot, the equivalent of about three cents, to buy a lemon-flavored popsicle or two pieces of bubble gum. On Independence Day they gave us twenty-five agurot to buy a chocolate-covered ice cream. I recall, with even greater longing, the days when friends from secular houses could ask to learn in a religious school and the school was more than happy to accept them.

In addition to father's work at the construction company, he also took many side jobs that forced him, most days, to sit down and calculate numbers until the late hours of the night. To this day he considers going out to restaurants to be unnecessary. "Those activities are for the children," he would say.

He shops till this day in the neighborhood open market. The shopping, like everything else he does, is a carefully calculated operation. The shopping bag, with the detailed list in it, is ready for a couple of days in advance, lying next to the apartment door. He has done that for decades – except for a short break when one time at the age of seventy-five he came back from the market and called mother to come down and assist him with the shopping bags. Mother came down, of course, but instead of helping him carry the bags, she immediately took him to the nearest hospital, a visit that ended in open-heart surgery, a quadruple bypass. At that time, I was serving as the deputy commander of a division and was stuck deep inside Lebanon without any possibility of leaving. I saw him only a few days later, after his surgery.

We were brought up to be productive and good people in the simplest meaning of the words. We were also brought up as part of the Religious-Zionist camp, but we never had to tackle the question of which should be more dominant in our lives, Zionism or religion. While this question was important for other people like me, it did not have a place in our home. I hope that my children will see the subject in the same way my parents did.

Every time one of the neighbors' children threw away his *kippa*, our house mourned a little for his poor parents. When one of our neighbors' sons didn't go to the army and instead joined an ultra-Orthodox yeshiva, there was condemnation in our house both for him and for his parents, since my parents believed that such a decision was also done with the support of that child's parents.

In 1964, my father got his first car from the company – a Susita – one of the first cars made in Israel. The license plate number was 212-925. Every vacation I had, I would accompany him on drives throughout the country to various construction sites. From those numerous excursions I developed an extensive familiarity with Israeli geography. On holidays we usually visited my Grandpa Yosef, who lived in Kiryat Shmuel up north near Haifa.

Grandpa lived there with Grandma Rozi, whom he met after World War II. He had lost his first wife and four of his children in the war. My mother and my uncle Itzo were the only ones left. From this new marriage my grandfather had one more daughter, Aunt Esther, who is naturally a very young aunt to me.

The long road to Haifa was usually spent singing Israeli songs per mother's orders. "Look and see what a pretty land we have," was usually her opening line. The long road to the north was just another excuse for my mother to sing. She always sang and enjoyed listening to Israeli music, as she does till this day. At times, she is also known to enjoy non-Hebrew songs as long as those non-Hebrew songs are sung in Yiddish.

After graduating from elementary school I went to the Netiv Meir Yeshiva High School in Jerusalem. Netiv Meir was regarded in those years as the premier Religious-Zionist high school in all of Israel. It was expensive compared to other high schools, and I was allowed to visit home only every third Shabbat. Looking back though, from my position as a father today, I feel an even greater gratitude to my parents for sending me there.

Our timetable in yeshiva began every day at 6:25 in the morning and ended at 8:00 at night, when it was time to do homework. The first half of the day was devoted to religious studies – especially the Talmud – and the afternoon was left for secular studies like every other high school. Bible lessons were also in the afternoon, as part of the secular studies division. I majored in science, but a story I will tell will show this does not mean that I was a serious student.

BREAD BALLS

I am a devoted disciple of Netiv Meir and of many of its rabbis. The yeshiva strongly emphasized that being a good person came before anything else, including Torah leaning.

This unfortunately did not save my father from having to make frequent trips to the head of the yeshiva's office, until one day when he said to me: "When will I get the chance to travel to Jerusalem because I want to and not because Rabbi Aryeh told me to?" Rabbi Aryeh was the late Rabbi Aryeh Bina, the venerable *rosh yeshiva* – otherwise known as the principal. He was and still is regarded as a mythological figure mainly due to his understanding of the scriptures and his wisdom as a teacher, but no less for his humanism and moderation.

Soon after the end of the Six-Day War, when Yeshivat Hakotel was hurriedly being established in the Old City of Jerusalem, which had just been liberated by Israel, some students came to borrow beds from Netiv Meir. One of those students wanted to seize a donkey from an Arab and load the beds onto it to take them to the Old City. Rabbi Bina said to him: "A man who will use his strength to grab a donkey from an Arab will end up slaying an Arab." Of rabbis that were known to be especially stringent and make unreasonable demands from their students, Rabbi Bina used to say: "From being so straight, they have become crooked."

I managed to put Rabbi Aryeh's legendary moderation and humanism to the test on numerous occasions. Many times I was faced with what seemed like a definite expulsion from school, but I sincerely want to believe that even though the rabbis threatened me time after time, they never really meant it.

One of the times my parents were summoned to the yeshiva was after the so-called "meatballs incident." We used to say about those meatballs, served quite frequently for lunch, that they were 95 percent *broit* (bread in Yiddish) and 5 percent bread. All our complaints were ignored.

One day I asked my friend Dovi Zinger – who later became head of the Makor Chaim Yeshiva High School – to help me collect all the untouched meatballs. We each took two large trays and passed them between the tables, explaining our plan. We wanted to show the cooks that no one was eating them. Within a few minutes we had more than three hundred meatballs on the two trays: almost all of the meatballs served that meal. We carried our cargo to the kitchen and there, most unfortunately, bumped into the institute's dedicated administrative director – the late Meir Halbertal – who was at that exact moment giving a tour of the yeshiva to a group of potential donors, emphasizing the excellent conditions the yeshiva provided for its students!

After the meatballs incident, the invitation to my parents arrived together with a personal note from Rabbi Aryeh suggesting that while my parents had a fine son, Netiv Meir was just not good enough for him. Furthermore, the rabbi wrote that he would be extremely happy to write a letter of recommendation on my behalf to any institute they might choose as his next school. Thankfully, that letter was never required.

ERASING MY SMILE

After graduating from the yeshiva, I enlisted into the 890th Battalion of the IDF's Paratroopers Brigade. It was November 1974, and I was sent directly to basic training. Due to the heavy rains, we quite frequently had our morning inspections inside the barracks.

One morning, the inspection was directed by a young team leader named Eli Yakobi, who had just been assigned to our unit two months into basic training. When he reached my place he asked me if I noticed the "elephants" – he was referring to sand – inside my rifle's barrel. I answered that I didn't see them and then smiled because I knew that not only did I not see them, but due to poor lighting in the room Yakobi also could not see them. I also smiled because I liked smiling and I still do.

Yakobi finished his round and returned to his post at the barrack's door, took out a pencil and a piece of paper from his pocket, and asked that all of those who needed to undergo the inspection process again raise their hands and state their names. When my turn came I told him my name, still with a big smile on my face.

For Yakobi, my smile was against everything he was trying to be as a commander. He dismissed the platoon and ordered me to wait outside the barrack wearing my full combat gear.

He then ordered me to run to the bathrooms and back within ninety seconds. I knew it wasn't possible to run that distance in such a short time, but of course I ran and returned to him, smiling as usual. He ordered me to run again, which I did, returning though after ninety seconds and of course with a big smile on my face. He repeated his orders; I ran and smiled.

After a few more runs, I started to feel a little short of breath and found it difficult keeping my smile. But since I realized that my smile was the issue, I ran with my head down and when I got back and caught my breath, I picked up my head with a glowing smile.

My platoon had finished eating breakfast and was already standing in a line at the door ready to go to their field training but Yakobi was not yet done with me. He gave me the order; I ran, caught my breath, and raised my smiling face. After another few rounds I noticed that another commander, Gozlan was his name, was standing next to Yakobi whispering something into his ear.

Yakobi finally gave me the order to stop, but not before saying how lucky I was. "We have to go to the field; otherwise I would erase that smile of yours even if we had to stay here all day."

Two months later Yakobi left us for some other assignment. After he took leave of the company he called me over and said: "Stern, you should know that I did not want to stop, but Gozlan explained to me what today I know as a fact. Whatever you do to Stern, he will keep on smiling."

Chapter 2

A *Kippa* under the Beret

I remember as a teenager sitting in my parents' kitchen in Tel Aviv on a Thursday evening and eating Friday's chocolate cake. The year was 1974, I was a senior in high school, and I had made the decision not to join one of the Hesder yeshivot, where most of my classmates were going. Hesder yeshivot were a fairly new invention. They combined advanced Jewish studies with military service. My father wanted me to join the Military Rabbinate, and he knew the air force's religious officer, Aryeh Shumer, who later in life would go on to become President Ezer Weizman's chief assistant.

I told my father it was a nice joke but I was not the slightest bit interested in serving in the rabbinate. Since I had just come in from my evening jog, I sat and ate my piece of cake without a *kippa* on my head. My father looked at me with a worried expression and murmured loud enough for me to hear: "I see it has already started."

The potential of becoming "ruined" in the army, falling off the religious path and removing one's *kippa*, always was and still is frightening for parents of young religious children. I use the term "ruined" since this is the term religious kids themselves use and keep using long after they have grown up. If you didn't follow Jewish halacha – law – or if you took off your *kippa*, you were ruined. I myself used this term for years until one day my non-religious assistant, Yael Wolf, said: "If becoming secular means 'ruining' yourself, then doesn't that suggest that in your eyes we are ruined to begin with?"

I thought about what she said, and I realized that this was a phrase you could use inside your own community, but once you stepped outside and repeated it in front of secular friends, it would likely offend them. If this was the case, it would probably be better not to use the phrase at all.

With time, a new phrase became popular within the religious community, a more accurate and less offending one: *datlash* – a Hebrew acronym for "formerly religious." I don't like any kind of labeling, though as an irredeemable optimist I would prefer the acronym *datla*, which stands for "religious in the future." I have witnessed over the years many people who took off their *kippa*s in the army and years later put them back on their heads.

When I was seventeen, the fear of a soldier abandoning the faith and taking off his *kippa* was great. In order to convince me to join the more protected framework of the Hesder yeshivot, Rabbi Aryeh Bina, the wonderful head of my high school yeshiva, invited me to his home almost every week – quite the privilege for any student and especially for a mischievous one like myself. The rabbi's wife served us tea. I sat there without touching my glass while listening to the rabbi try to convince me to join the Hesder program.

Ultimately, Rabbi Aryeh understood that I had made up my mind to enlist into the Paratroopers Brigade. In those days, shortly after the 1973 Yom Kippur War, all Hesder students were sent to the Armored Corps. Rabbi Aryeh promised me that if I agreed to join the Hesder program, he would use his connections so I could still serve as a paratrooper.

My ambition, however, was not to stay in the Paratroopers Brigade but to use it as a springboard to get into one of the elite commando units. These units were extremely popular among the Bnei Akiva youth movement graduates; we all knew the names of the religious soldiers in them even if we did not know them personally.

There was another reason why I did not want to go to a Hesder yeshiva. I wanted to serve together with *Am Yisrael* – the Israeli nation – and I wanted to use my service in the army as an opportunity to meet people who were not members of our sheltered religious community. Also I did not consider myself the type of person who could sit and learn Jewish texts all day and devote himself exclusively to the study of Torah, although I knew some people who were very capable of learning Gemara all day and still joined the regular army for the full three-year service. I also knew kids who were like me and not cut out for learning all day, but still served in Hesder units for other reasons.

I believe that while Rabbi Bina pressured me, he understood my decision. Later, I came to the conclusion that perhaps he even approved of my choice – at least in my case and in the case of my colleague Ishai, who shared the same ambitions and later, like me, became a general and sat with me around the table of the General Staff.

When I was drafted, a lot of people expected me to take off my *kippa*. I was the only religious soldier in my platoon in the 890th Battalion. It was a regular paratroopers platoon, made up of youth from cities, kibbutzim, farms, and the periphery. There were Ashkenazim – Jews of European descent – and kids from Morocco, Libya, Yemen, and Iraq. Some of my commanders predicted that it was only a matter of time before my *kippa* fell off, and some even tried to speed up the process. Their prediction was born out of experience since many of them had started their service religious and ended it secular. This is how people concluded that the army "ruins" religious kids.

I do not believe that the army "ruins" people. The army is simply the first opportunity these kids get to be independent and distance themselves from sheltered homes and communities. This first taste of independence comes during the stage of adolescence that involves a natural inclination for freedom. Since religious observance is not always fun and entails many restrictions and responsibilities, there are those who choose to walk a different path.

This reminds me of many debates I had with young officers who couldn't make up their minds whether or not they should remain in the IDF. Many wanted to take some time off before making up their minds. Their argument was that while they knew army life well, they were completely unacquainted with civilian life. They wanted to go out and taste the civilian world. They sincerely believed they would return afterward to the military world.

I used to tell those officers about the similarity of their dilemma to the dilemma young religious soldiers sometimes encounter during their service. They know the religious world and just want to taste the secular world. These kids figure they can take some time off from religion and then decide afterward if they will return. They always start off sincerely believing that they will one day return to religion but only a few of them ever do. The free, or if you prefer, the secular world holds great temptations for most of these youth, and this holds true of the civilian world in comparison to the military world, since only a handful who leave ever return.

For a religious soldier in the IDF, there are many temptations and challenges. A soldier who is the only religious one in his unit will at times feel alienated, like I did. I found myself in weird situations, for example, when I was on guard duty with a soldier who insisted on sharing with me in the most vivid terms all his experiences with his girlfriend. Sometimes I envied my friends who went to Hesder yeshivot, who were sitting in white shirts in a warm yeshiva building, while I was on guard duty somewhere in the freezing Golan Heights or on a hill overlooking Bethlehem during Christmas. Despite these feelings, I never once thought about leaving my unit and joining Hesder. I never sincerely questioned the path I had chosen.

My motivation to become a soldier stemmed from historical and social reasons and not religious ones. When I was debating whether or not to lengthen my army service, I used to say that the chances would be much greater that I'd decide to prolong my service if I visited the Yad Vashem Holocaust Memorial Museum in Jerusalem, than if I visited the Kotel. Nonetheless, one of the main reasons I decided to remain in the military was directly connected to my life as a religious Jew, not because religion demanded that I stay in the army, but rather because of the educational-social aspect of the service.

Being a soldier, you sort of hold a microphone in your hand, with which you can make yourself heard, sometimes with real words and at other times with the way you behave. When you serve in a platoon, the volume is low, but as you climb from one rank to the next the volume gets louder. Part of my motivation to continue climbing the ranks was because of my ambition, as a Religious Zionist, to have an impact on those around me.

During my work on this book, I found an old note I had written when I was a young captain. The note holds a list of pros and cons I prepared to help me answer the question of whether I should sign on for more years of service. Under the column of pros I found seven reasons for staying on, such as "economic security," "personal fulfillment," "all the best people resign." I also wrote in the note "The best way to help bridge the gap between secular and religious Jews."

Coercion

It was 1979 and just three days before Rosh Hashana – the Jewish New Year. I was a company commander in the 890th Battalion and my commander Arik Krausman informed me that instead of getting a furlough for the holiday, my company was being sent to the Sinai for some routine security missions.

One platoon was to secure the beach in Nuweiba, another the beach in Dahab, and the third was sent to Santa Katarina. He was astonished to find me disappointed about the news. Arik, a member of a Hashomer Hatzair kibbutz, was certain that for a religious man like me there could be nothing more tempting then spending the Jewish New Year in close proximity to God at Mount Sinai, just next to Santa Katarina. I couldn't convince him that on Rosh Hashana the natural place for me would be next to my father in our neighborhood synagogue, listening to the shofar, the ram's horn blown during the services to motivate repentance.

The alternative – staying on the beaches of Nuweiba or Dahab – also did not particularly appeal to me. For those who have forgotten the Sinai, these beaches were hardly the place a young religious officer should find himself on Rosh Hashana of all days. How do I know that? Please don't ask!

In the end, in an effort to convince me, my commander said: "Go and do things that you shouldn't do so you can watch over the people who will be there who are doing the things you shouldn't do."

If this is not anti-religious coercion, I don't know what is.

Another much more painful incident I had to deal with occurred in the early 2000s. It was the time of the second Intifada, when Palestinian terrorist attacks were rocking our cities. There was a horrific suicide attack near a nightclub on the Tel Aviv beachfront on Friday night.

In a lecture following the attack, I asked my audience to think about the religious soldier who was sent immediately to secure all of the other Tel Aviv nightclubs. It holds the same logic as my being sent to the Sinai for Rosh Hashana, though the story in this case is more painful. One of the soldiers listening to my lecture, a member of secular kibbutz, stood up and said that this is not anti-religious coercion because it is a case of *pikuah nefesh*, a principle according to which saving human life overrides Jewish law.

I appreciated his comment and told him that he was right. But I explained to him that if you believe – correctly in my opinion – that securing nightclubs on Friday night does not fall into the category of anti-religious coercion because it's being done to save lives, then you should at the very least take into account other commandments that are potentially less comfortable for you.

There are numerous such cases of tension between the religious and secular. An old joke says that common sense stops at the door of the IDF induction centers. But I don't know of any order that does not have common sense in it. When I was the commander of the IDF Officers' Training School, I used to ask the young cadets in our first meeting, "Who can give me an example of a senseless order?" One day I encountered a serious challenge. A cadet asked me what the logic was behind the order that allows them to watch regular television on Shabbat in the club on base but does not allow them to watch movies on the DVD player. Another asked me why all soldiers on guard duty at a distant ammunition bunker have to walk to their post on Shabbat.

I explained that driving to a guard post does not fall into the category of an emergency necessity since the soldier could either walk there or, alternatively, spend the entire Shabbat there and return to base on Saturday night. If we were to allow soldiers to drive there, then we would have to divide them according to their religious preference, because religious soldiers couldn't possibly be asked to drive to this post on Shabbat. If we divided the missions between religious and secular soldiers, we would find ourselves later giving one set of orders to soldiers who are right-wing and another set of orders to soldiers who are left-wing. It would never stop! That is why all the orders must be applicable for everyone.

But what made sense for the question about driving on Shabbat made no sense for the question about forbidding the use of the video player. Within their limits, military rules were aiming to enable one soldier to study the scriptures while his friends played basketball or watched a movie, each in his designated area, without disturbing one another. I suggested to the cadet who asked the question that he write a letter and we would both sign it and send it up the chain of command.

I did not tell the soldiers that when I took up my post as commander of the school some time earlier, I had tried to change this order. The rabbi of the base, though, looked at my *kippa* and the fringes of my tzitzit and said: "But sir, by permitting soldiers to watch movies we will be encouraging the desecration of the Shabbat." I told him that when I was appointed commander of the school I was expected to instruct young officers to win wars and not guarantee the preservation of the Shabbat.

In truth, though, the order that allowed watching TV on Shabbat was written before DVD players became popular. We, the religious commanders, took advantage of this carelessness and decided that television – yes, video – no.

A religious officer from one of the paratroopers' battalions told me that once he had asked a rabbi named Min-Hahar – Hebrew for "from the mountain" – if he could lend his car to secular officers who were going home for the weekend when he stayed on the base over Shabbat. Theoretically, the answer should be no, to avoid causing another person to desecrate Shabbat. But the rabbi replied that the officer should only be careful not to hand his keys to his friends directly but rather to put them on his desk, and if they are taken, then so be it. This was said with the awareness that the entire key chain would be taken, including the car keys, but the rabbi gave this answer because of the principle of *pikuah nefesh* that I mentioned earlier.

I was shocked by the rabbi's courageous decision. How did he claim *pikuah nefesh* in this case? The answer was that if the officer did not lend his car, then animosity and possibly hatred would develop between them. These negative feelings could possibly lead to a fatal incident during a future combat operation. Even though the probability that both officers would participate together in the same operation was fairly low, this tiniest possibility of future *pikuah nefesh* was enough to give someone permission to ignore the risk that they were possibly assisting in desecrating the Shabbat.

It could be that the rabbi also understood that such a positive relationship between the religious officer and his secular colleague could help create warmer relations between other religious and secular soldiers in the unit. This ruling proves to me that Rabbi Min-Hahar is a courageous interpreter of Jewish law with a deep understanding of today's reality.

When I told this story to Rabbi Avihai Ronsky, the IDF chief rabbi until 2010, he told me about another ruling, issued by Rabbi Avigdor Neventzal, a leading authority on Jewish law from the Old City of Jerusalem. The question he answered was whether residents of a certain settlement could give *mishloah-manot* – Purim food packages that Jews distribute – to soldiers guarding their community. By Jewish law, it is forbidden to give someone food knowing that they will not make the required blessing.

The question was similar to the car keys dilemma. Rabbi Neventzal ruled that good relations between the residents and the soldiers in the settlement took precedence over whether the soldiers would make the blessing.

A Special Inspection

The thread that connects tolerance and victory in combat can also be found in the following story.

It was 1976 and I was a young platoon commander in the 890th Battalion. In those days, the soldiers didn't sleep on Thursday nights. Instead, they spent the night preparing for the Friday morning inspection.

Only very few families had cars in those days, and the soldiers who went home for the weekend used to fall asleep at their families' Friday night Shabbat dinner or at the most go visit a nearby friend. There were hardly any clubs open then, and those that were open closed early anyhow.

Years passed and nowadays almost every family owns at least one car. Recreational options are endless for young soldiers on leave, and the army has unfortunately become familiar with the many injuries and deaths in car accidents that are apparently caused by the fatigue of driving soldiers. As a result, we decided to abolish the old practice of not sleeping Thursday nights and instead instituted a rule that on the evening before a soldier goes home, he needs to sleep for at least seven hours. Today commanders are more stringent about these seven hours than about the seven hours of sleep required by military regulations the night before live-fire exercises.

But getting back to the long nights of 1976 preparing for Friday-morning inspections, we used to take apart every piece of equipment and clean and polish it until all our equipment was sparkling. We even took out all of the bullets from the magazines and wiped down each bullet separately. If, God forbid, the commanders found even a speck of dirt, we were immediately punished with a second inspection.

Five months after they started their basic training, my soldiers were already in their parachuting course, and Passover arrived. A day before the Seder, I assembled the platoon, a mixture of typical Israeli youths – city kids and farm boys, kibbutz members and new immigrants, religious and secular. I informed them that the next morning, at 6 a.m, they were going to have a special inspection to check that all bread had been cleaned out of their kitbags.

Gadi, a red-headed kid from a kibbutz, raised his hand and asked me with a quizzical look on his face, "What kind of inspection?"

"Elimination of leavened foods," I repeated. "Soon your sergeant will arrive and explain all the details. All other questions you might have will be answered tomorrow, after the inspection is finished."

At 6 a.m. they stood in formation for their leavened foods' elimination inspection. I found a strictly kosher platoon, and, as I had promised, I allowed them to ask questions. The red-headed Gadi asked, "But sir, why should I have to prepare for an inspection for...what did you call it? Eliminating all leavened foods?"

I answered with a question: "I know quite well that according to your set of values you are not supposed to bother with clearing out leavened foods before Passover, and that such a task contradicts your religious-like values of civil rights and freedom. At the same time, though, Zvika and Ilan, the religious soldiers in our platoon, are not allowed to remain during the duration of Passover in a room that has leavened food in it. We are doing this to accommodate their values. Would you rather prepare for the inspection so all of you can remain together, or would you prefer to skip the inspection and have separate tents?

Gadi responded to that with: "I got you, sir. I'd rather have the inspection and stay with them in the same tent."

Such a response from a completely secular kibbutznik is the natural result of true friendships that can develop almost only in a combat platoon during service in the IDF.

There are many similar types of compromises. On Shabbat, for example, secular soldiers are forced to eat cold lunches and on the other hand religious soldiers are forced to listen to the soccer matches on the radio on Saturday afternoons in the barracks. These examples demonstrate both the problem and its solution. The orders soldiers must obey often entail a form of coercion. But the relationships that are forged during one's army service lead soldiers to accept those coercions with tolerance. When religious and secular soldiers are familiar with each other they are willing to make some compromises.

This was the reason why I ultimately canceled the order prohibiting the use of the video player on Saturday. An order without sound logic behind it will create resentment, and resentment could have dire consequences.

WITH GOD'S HELP

Many times it is surprising how the smallest of acts, performed absentmindedly, can turn into the most meaningful in life. In 1984, I was appointed commander of the Paratroopers Brigade Training Base located in an abandoned Jordanian military base in the West Bank near the village of Sanur. I attributed special significance to this assignment since the soldiers who came here for basic training had just several days earlier graduated from high school. The commanders were also new at what they were doing and received their platoons for the first time after graduating from Bahad 1, the Officers' Training School.

Commanding all of these new recruits and fresh officers provided me with the opportunity to influence them in a profound way and possibly even help shape their future. This was the reason I always chose to start my earlier command assignments with soldiers in the earliest stage of their basic training, and not when they were already in an advanced training stage.

I had a sergeant major in the training camp by the name of Haviv Amitai who was truly a role model. One day, not long after I took up my new post, he came into my office to discuss the invitations we needed to send to the soldiers' families for the traditional swearing-in ceremony at the Kotel. He showed me several invitations for past ceremonies to see if they were acceptable. I noticed that the back page of the invitations was empty, and I asked him to print there the paratroopers' anthem.

In all my previous positions I came across soldiers on hikes singing the song: "lala lala lala oh oh, lala lala lala oh oh…" – they didn't know a word of it except for "paratroopers…paratroopers." I said to Haviv that maybe if the lyrics reached the homes of the soldiers some would learn them. I took a pen and a sheet of paper and wrote down the words.

I do not usually write the initials for the words "With God's help" at the top of my letters, like many observant Jews do, since I know that many of these papers will end up in inappropriate places. On that occasion however, maybe because the ceremony was to take place opposite the Kotel and since we were anyhow making changes to the design of the invitations, I wrote the initials without giving it any thought. Several days later, Haviv returned to my office and gave me an invitation. He told me that he had decided to print an additional 1,200 invitations for future ceremonies. When I opened the invitation I discovered that Haviv, probably thinking that it would please me, made the initials for the Hebrew words "With God's help" larger than the other font on the invitation.

Reading on, I discovered that he had also added the words "If God permits" next to the date for the ceremony. These he printed in large letters, larger than those I had used on my wedding invitation. I realized that the way the invitations were printed was going to be controversial, but it was too late to do anything about it. The soldiers, like any IDF unit, came from families from all over the country and with political views from across the political and religious spectrum. I knew, for example, that the father of one of my soldiers was a member of the Knesset, the Israeli parliament, from a party that was not sympathetic toward religious circles.

Two weeks after the invitations were sent out, I heard that discussions were being held in the Knesset on the issue. While I laughed, I was also slightly sad.

While putting the initials at the top of the invitations stirred controversy, I followed the advice of the commander of the Paratroopers Brigade at the time, the late general Nechemya Tamari, and chose to ignore the noise. These invitations continued to be sent until I left the base.

My next assignment was command of the 202nd Battalion of the Paratroopers Brigade. We were stationed in southern Lebanon and were busy chasing a terrorist cell when the chief of general staff, Lieutenant General Moshe Levi, visited division headquarters. Coming back a few hours later, I found the chief of staff had left and the division commander asked me why I had caused him problems. I replied that I hadn't, and that if I had, the chief of staff knew how to rebuke me himself. Then he asked me, "What made you write 'With God's help' on the invitations to the swearing-in ceremony?"

I hadn't been commander of the Sanur training base for more than a year by then but the new commander had decided to continue sending the same invitations that I had printed, with the enlarged letters for "With God's help" and "If God permits."

I answered the division commander Ilan Biran, partly to annoy him and partly to start a discussion on the subject, that I add those initials to everything I write. He replied that the invitations were not mine personally but belonged to the position. I said he might be right but that the people who chose me for the assignment knew that when I run quickly and my hat falls off, a *kippa* will appear on my head – and that if I run even faster the fringes from my tzitzit will pop out of my pants. The same happens with invitations I write. If I am not very careful, then the initials for the words "With God's help" might also escape my attention.

Ever since then, Biran, with a smile, started calling me "With God's help."

But there were those who didn't smile. Several months after my conversation with Biran, the subject was still being debated in the media. I was by now on leave, waiting for my first discharge from army service. The chief of Staff General Moshe Levi was replaced by General Dan Shomron. The latter summoned me to his office to discuss the matter. I told him I was ashamed to be summoned to his office to discuss such an issue. I said that in my judgment the whole issue should have remained outside his office.

A *Mikve* on an Air Force Base

Years after the storm over the invitations subsided and I had returned to active duty, serving as head of the Human Resources Directorate, the IDF's chief rabbi came to meet with me one day. He said that he had received a number of complaints from husbands and wives living on the Uvda Air Force Base in southern Israel that they did not have a *mikve* – a Jewish ritual bath. The nearest *mikve* was in the city of Eilat, eighty kilometers away.

The rabbi submitted his request to build a *mikve* to air force headquarters but it was rejected. The air force officers treated his request as a sign of religious extremism and connected the issue, incorrectly, to the question of female integration into the IDF and in particular to the regulations of "appropriate dress" for female soldiers. Israeli air force bases are, to a large extent, small tight-knit communities where families raise their children. Guidelines regarding modesty and behavior of female soldiers that were written primarily for infantry units were considered to be much too strict by these communities. They regarded the request to build a *mikve* in their base as another sign of religious coercion and refused to comply.

I was on friendly terms with the commander of the Israeli Air Force (IAF) at the time, Major General Elazar Shkedy. I can honestly say that I don't know many commanders who have such a positive approach to Judaism as he does. I witnessed it every time we worked together on issues that concerned the Holocaust, and I would often see the tears well up in his eyes when I brought him to meet soldiers who had chosen to participate in the military conversion seminars I had founded.

I tried to speak with Shkedy several times about the *mikve* but I did not convince him. I explained the central role a *mikve* plays in the life of a religious-observant couple, and how difficult it must be for them to drive one evening a month to Eilat to immerse in it, as Jewish law stipulates married women must do after their menstrual cycle. Some of his aides suggested, out of good will, to arrange a monthly shuttle for all the women. A nice offer – and evidence of their ignorance, as they didn't know the basic fact that every woman has a different cycle and therefore goes to the *mikve* on a different day.

Every conversation I had with Shkedy moved him a little closer to understanding the importance of building the *mikve*. I told him that for religious women and their husbands the importance of the *mikve* is larger than the importance of a synagogue and that even in my hometown of Hoshaya, which Shkedy was familiar with, the *mikve* was the first stone building we built. "You know I am listening," he said to me. "Let me think it over." I knew we were advancing toward a solution.

Finally, the construction of the *mikve* was authorized. The chief military rabbi called to thank me and wrote me a warm letter as well. A few weeks later, I received a request from an officer in one of the field units to authorize the construction of a *mikve* in their basic training camp. I refused his request. The officer told me that both the base commander and the brigade commander supported construction of the *mikve* but I refused to reverse my decision. I explained to the commanders that I supported the *mikve* on the air force base only because the base is a home for a large number of families, and due to the large distance between the base and the nearest town where a *mikve* can be found. Their base, on the other hand, was very close to several communities that have a *mikve*. Families also did not live on the base and there were, as a result, no married women there.

I told them that if we built a *mikve* on their base, within a month we would have to allocate extra time in the morning for religious soldiers to immerse in the waters. In a very short time, I said, thousands of soldiers would adopt the immersion ritual, exactly like thousands of soldiers who fanatically adopt the non-shaving custom of religious soldiers during the period after Passover, even though many of them do not have a *kippa* on their heads. We can't make them shave for fear of appearing as if we deny them religious rights.

I also warned that if we allowed people to adopt religious customs just because they could gain some small benefit during their military service, it could lead to a religious desecration. Also, those who do so just to gain these small benefits cause those who do the same for sincere reasons to be despised and degraded.

I think they were convinced.

One morning, toward the end of my military service, I received a telephone call from Rabbi Shlomo Aviner, a leading national-religious rabbi from the settlement of Beit El. Aviner told me that he was always searching for reasons to speak with me and this time his reason was that he met the contractor who was building the *mikve* in the Uvda Air Force Base. The man told him that the *mikve* was being built due to my persistent lobbying.

Rabbi Aviner congratulated me and I told him, after he finished, that on the other hand I was also responsible for denying a similar request to build a *mikve* on a combat training base. The rabbi told me that he always tells everyone that General Stern is a rabbi and has a beard, and if you can't see the beard it's because it is on the inside. He then told me the following story:

One day, the great rabbi of the Satmar hassidim received a beardless visitor, an activist belonging to a group of so-called secular heretics. When the meeting was over, the rabbi's followers were shocked to see him accompany his guest out of the room and bid him farewell with a hug and kiss. One of the hassidim gathered his courage and asked the rabbi, how could he treat a beardless Jew – not to mention a heretic – so warmly?

To that, the rabbi answered: "When this beardless man will come before God, after 120 years, the Lord will ask him: 'Jew, where is your beard?' But when you will face the Lord," the rabbi said to the hassid, "He will probably ask: Beard, where is your Jew?"

HEARING WOMEN'S VOICES

One of the major challenges an observant soldier faces during his or her military service is finding a so-called path of compromise. I clearly remember one cold Saturday night in the winter of 1997, when two rabbis from a pre-military school – called a *mehina* in Hebrew – came to my home. I highly respected both of them.

Their visit came a week after a school in Beersheba – a large city in Israel's southern Negev Desert – told fathers of seven-year-old girls that they could not attend a class ceremony since the girls were going to sing and it was forbidden according to Jewish law for a man to hear girls' voices. I asked the rabbis if they were familiar with the story. They looked at each other and confirmed the story. I was amazed.

I asked them how many of their own students, who serve now under my command in the Officers' Training School called Bahad 1, would leave the hall if I invited Chava Alberstein, a famous Israeli female singer and lyricist, to perform on the base. They considered the question for a moment and replied that it would probably be about 60 percent. I said that in my opinion it would be less then 20 percent.

"So what do you want us to do?" they asked me.

"Stop teaching that," I said. "I do not recall a single rabbi of mine from my high school who ever taught me that it is forbidden for a man to hear a woman's voice."

One of the rabbis was surprised. "Elazar Stern," he said. "You are the one who has continuously told us to raise our standards. Now, you tell us to stop teaching this halacha?"

I replied that the level to which you raise the standard is an art in and of itself. If the average for a two-kilometer run in physical tests done before being accepted to Officers' Training School is nine minutes, and on the following morning you assemble the cadets and announce that they are going to run with you in less then six and a half minutes, you will soon find yourself running all alone.

The oversimplifying interpretation of this Jewish law regarding a woman's voice may lead some students to demonstratively leave a performance by Chava Alberstein. But a much larger group might conclude that if the voice of a sixty-year-old singer or an eight-year-old girl presents a religious challenge that forces these students to leave, then we are not of the same religion.

And of course there are the opposite cases. When I was the IDF chief education officer, I was invited to a certain formal celebration that included a show put on by female soldiers who danced and sang while wearing costumes that revealed more than they hid. I walked away. The next day I summoned the commanders of that particular base and rebuked them. I told them that I expected their observant soldiers to feel comfortable at such events even though I knew that for many of them it would be difficult. That is why, I said, I expected the organizers of these evenings to understand that the participation of observant soldiers demanded extra sensitivity and common sense. In this incident, I thought, the standard was too low, far too low.

Religious by Appetite

On October 10, 2011 (12 Tishrei 5772), a memorial ceremony was held in Hoshaya for Ori Ettinger, marking the thirtieth day after her death. Ori, who was in the same youth group as our son Amihai, died at age sixteen of cancer. When we gathered in the cemetery on the thirtieth day following her death, no eulogies were said. A few chapters of Psalms were recited, as were other verses of Psalms beginning with the letters of her name, the traditional chant *El Malei Rahamim* ("God, full of mercy"), and a song or two. I stood together with many members of our community, most of whom were there only because they were part of the community and not because they knew Ori, and the power of the ceremony did not fail to move each of us.

After the ceremony, I said to a few friends who stood beside me that this sad event, with its restraint and power, gave additional significance to our presence as a religious community. To a certain extent, again I was glad to belong to this way of life. I say "again" because the last few years I have not always been so proud of my membership in our camp.

To me, the first strategic mistake of Religious Zionism was that instead of focusing on its central role in forming the image of society in the State of Israel, it focused on the dispute over the exact location of the border between us and our neighbors. Another mistake is that Religious Zionism, ironically, has not been able to allow room for Jewish pride for one who would say, "I do not believe in the existence of God, but I am still a proud Jew."

Maybe this will come as a surprise to some people, but even in the bastions of Religious Zionism and the closed ultra-Orthodox communities – in the most elite yeshivot – there are those who do not believe or who hesitate regarding the existence of God. They are in those places, and even follow a religious lifestyle, only because of the inherent advantages – such as the powerful idea of Shabbat, even if one does not observe it in all its stringencies; the community solidarity; membership in a community or synagogue; the Hebrew calendar and its holidays; the learning; the Talmudic debates; and the Religious-Zionist education. Even these individuals are an important and vital layer in the community. Continuing extremism, such as the insistence on prohibitions like the "immodesty of a woman's voice," only serve to push them away and preclude thousands of Jews from wanting to learn about these values.

When I shared these thoughts with the director of one of the Religious-Zionist yeshivot, he looked at me and said, "Elazar, at my yeshiva there was a rabbi, who today is the head of a religious institution, who told me that he did not believe in the existence of God. When I asked him, if so, then why are you doing what you do and behaving the way you behave, he looked at me and said, 'I'm religious by appetite.'"

The power of this expression hit me. I knew that religious Jews use the recognized phrase "secular by appetite" to describe Jews who believed in God but were not careful in their observance of many mitzvot, the better to enjoy the vanities of this world – such as issues of food and relations between men and women. I did not imagine that this expression might be borrowed for its exact opposite meaning, and that one could be "religious by appetite."

Unfortunately, we are also missing the opportunities to adopt this viewpoint, and through it, perhaps even to reach a point where through practice without intention, such individuals achieve practice with intention.

Religious People and Drawers

I learned through personal experience that quite often, the hardships a religious soldier faces during his service in a mixed combat company stem not just from the challenges he faces but also from the suspicious looks he gets.

In the summer of 1997, I was appointed to a post in the IDF's Ground Forces Command that enabled me to come home almost every evening. At the time, soldiers were still allowed to hitchhike, something that was later forbidden because of the danger of kidnappings. I made a habit of picking up soldiers on every possible occasion and "interviewing" them during the ride. One day, shortly after the botched navy commando operation in Lebanon in which Yohanan Hilberg and eleven other commandos were killed, I stopped the car to let a soldier out, when I noticed a young commando officer leaning on a pole and waiting patiently for a bus.

I called him over and offered him a ride. He turned down the offer and said he was fine. I called him over again and said: "Come on, I am going to your destination."

Finally he agreed and climbed into my car, and I started asking him questions. His name, he told me, was Yoaz Hendel and he was a navy commando team leader in Flotilla 13. He said that he lived in a small town on the Carmel Mountains not far from the commandos' base but that on the weekends he went to his parents' house in the West Bank settlement of Elkana. After a few more questions, he said he recognized me from his days at the Officers' Training School, which I used to command.

I asked him why he initially turned down the ride, and he said that he never hitchhikes. He usually drives in his own car but today he had to return a jeep for a friend who was killed in the botched operation. He said he was irritated by the media's exaggerated interest in the operation and particularly the breakdown some reporters did of the dead and whether they were secular or religious. He hated the labels.

"I don't understand how they dare to label us," he said. "Yohanan and I, for example, didn't wear *kippa*s most of the time, but we were called the 'religious ones' in our unit."

They prayed, kept kosher, and observed Shabbat even though most of the time they were without *kippa*s on their heads.

"Why didn't you wear a *kippa*?" I asked. Yoaz told me that most of their time was spent in places that did not fit a *kippa*. I completely sympathized with him and with his emotions.

Several weeks later I recalled my meeting with Yoaz, took out the phone book, and found the number for the Hendel family in Elkana. His mother answered the phone, and I said, "Hi. My name is Elazar and I gave your son a lift recently."

"That is impossible," she said. "My son never hitchhikes."

I insisted that he had caught a ride with me because of a special situation, but she was adamant that he never hitchhiked and threatened to end the conversation. "Maybe he never hitchhikes but on the day I gave him a ride, he had just returned a car for a friend who was killed and he had to hitchhike," I answered back.

"Hold on a second," she said. "Which Elazar are you?"

"Elazar from Hoshaya," I replied.

"You are the Elazar who used to be the commander of the Officers' Training School in the south?"

"Yes," I confessed. She immediately apologized and for the first time in the conversation relaxed, but pressed me that she did not understand the reason for my phone call. "I just wanted to tell you that I would be extremely pleased if your son would marry my daughter," I said.

She was naturally taken back but recovered quickly and said: "But of course you must know that..."

"Know what?" I asked.

"You certainly know...that here in our settlement they say about him some things that are not good...that sometimes he walks around without a *kippa* on his head."

I asked her if she really thought that all mothers of young soldiers I took in my car received calls from me with an offer to give them my daughter's hand in marriage. I explained to her that I had made this call because I could imagine how difficult this harsh social labeling must be for her. I said to her that unfortunately this phenomenon is a central part of our way of life whether we are members of the religious community or whether we are members of any of the other communities in Israel. We label each other into banal categories – religious or secular, left-wing or right-wing, black or colored. We label every one, and it is impossible to remain unlabeled since it will throw off our balance.

We label, stuff in a drawer, lock the drawer, and throw away the key. You cannot move from one drawer to another. You cannot exit the drawer you were put in. You can only get out by breaking the drawer! I chose to offer Yoaz to marry my daughter not because I feel bad for him, but because I respect and admire him.

And as if to prove I was right, several months later, on a Saturday night, Yoaz showed up at my door. He was in a T-shirt, was sun-burned, and together with a young girl. He stopped by, he said, because his team from the commandos – most of them already discharged – had decided to spend Shabbat on the banks of the Jordan River. It was terribly hot there, so his friends had decided to leave early Saturday morning, leaving Yoaz and his friend alone in the heat to wait for Shabbat to end.

I asked myself who sacrificed more for Shabbat. Me, with my white-pressed shirt in Hoshaya, or Yoaz, with his T-shirt on the steaming riverbank after his comrades left and drove home. I pondered which of the two of us achieved more points up in heaven for sanctifying God's name.

My next meeting with Yoaz was in the summer of 2005, a few weeks before the evacuation of the settlers from the Gaza Strip, when he offered to help me talk to the Hilbergs, the family of his fallen good friend Yohanan. The family couldn't bear the idea that their son's body would be moved from his grave, and they threatened to barricade themselves inside their house.

Attempts by the Military Rabbinate to calm them had failed. Yoaz and I sat in their garden with Yohanan's father while his mother ignored us completely. I sympathized with her. That was a complicated and hurtful dialogue. But at least a dialogue started, and though it is impossible to tell its direct results, I want to believe it relieved some of the grief and the pain they felt.

I already told the story about the evacuation of the graves and Yohanan's memorial room. Here, I just wanted to tell the story about a young man named Yoaz who didn't fit into a drawer. He was simply too big for them all.

CHAPTER 3

THE MILITARY TRACK

I served in the 890th Battalion of the Paratroopers Brigade as a soldier and a squad commander. When I finished my term as a squad commander I was sent to Bahad 1, the Officers' Training School. While I was on leave before starting at the school, the rest of my battalion participated in the famous July 4, 1976, Entebbe operation, the daring Israeli rescue of Air France hostages from Uganda.

When I finished my training, I returned to the battalion as a platoon commander. It was November 1976 and parental visits to the base were not permitted. What's more, parents weren't even allowed back then to know where their son served.

On a cold and wet Thursday afternoon, I was chatting with the company commander, David Lipitz, when all of a sudden Lipitz noticed that I had turned pale. Frozen in my spot, grasping my head with my hands, I muttered to myself, "I don't believe it...I just don't believe it!"

Lipitz looked at me and asked what happened. I did not respond and continued staring. Lipitz asked again, "Stern, what is it?"

And I mumbled again, "I just can't believe it..."

Only then did he spot my mother, swiftly closing the distance between us, carrying a bunch of bags in her arms and calling out, "Eli, come and see what we brought you! Warm schnitzels and a cake I just baked!"

But I remained stubbornly shocked. "I don't believe it, Mother... How did you find out where I am and why on earth did you come?"

Now it was my mother's turn to freeze after realizing that her little boy was not overwhelmed with joy by her visit. Mother exchanged stares with Lipitz, who tried to convince me to look happier and to give a few minutes of my time to my mother. She asked where she should put the food and I responded: "Take it back home!"

Lipitz did his best to remind me that this is what parents do. My mother, with a look on her face that I'll never forget, turned to leave with her heavy bags, and Lipitz again tried to get me to go after her. He turned to my mother to gain some time and said something like: "Well, he doesn't know *my* mother!"

My mother kept walking and returned to the car, where she said to my father, "Lipo, let's go home!"

My poor father, who had opened his car door with a huge smile on his face, realized that a calamity was approaching. Lipitz was still doing his best to stall them but without success. They finally started the car and left.

For months, Lipitz and I discussed the incident, and I kept repeating, "If we forbid the soldiers parental visits, how can a commander have his parents visit him?"

Ever since that day Lipitz and my mother never miss an opportunity to tell the story of how they met, while the only consolation I can find for my behavior on that ugly day is the contribution it made to the shaping of their relationship.

Stopping Terrorists on Mount Dov

In 1979 I was a young company commander. The battalion was stationed in the north, and my company was posted on Mount Dov, on the border with Lebanon. We were alerted that a terrorist group was planning an attack in our area. According to the intelligence we received, the terror cell planned to infiltrate an Israeli town along the border and either kidnap civilians or barricade themselves inside a building with hostages in order to negotiate the release of terrorists from Israeli prisons.

Due to the intelligence report, we had been on high alert for a number of weeks. Every night we laid ambushes and did everything we could to prevent the terrorists from carrying out their plans. One Sunday during this period, I drove to the battalion's headquarters to welcome Dorit's parents. Dorit would later become my wife, but we weren't together then. Her parents came as the parents of the company's secretary, which was Dorit's role in our unit, and mainly as the parents of Ilan, one of my soldiers who had been killed in a recent training accident.

Just before he was killed, Ilan wrote a very emotional letter to his parents describing the significance of his service in the IDF and particularly serving along Israel's border with Lebanon on Mount Dov. I promised his parents that one day I would bring them to the post so they could see the place where their son had written the letter, and also show them how safe it was, since their daughter, Dorit, enlisted in the same company immediately after her brother's death and served at the same post. I managed to get special authorization to bring them to the bunker.

I picked them up and we started the climb up the mountain. When they saw the fences and minefields covering the slopes alongside the road and the signs prohibiting entrance of civilians to the area, they asked, "Are you sure it isn't dangerous?"

I showed them the border's wire fence to our north and explained that as long as we were on the right side of the fence, we were completely safe. After a few more minutes of driving we arrived at the gate to the military post at the top of the mountain. I called and informed the soldiers that I was entering. As we drove inside, Dorit's parents said to me, "But now we are on the wrong side of the fence, aren't we?"

I calmed their fears and said that there was a military post just up ahead and that we would reach it in a few minutes. I promised them that it was completely safe.

We reached the company headquarters, and I invited them into my office. Two or three minutes after we sat down, I was informed by the one of the soldiers on reconnaissance duty that a terrorist cell had been spotted entering a small Lebanese village on the slopes of the mountain. I jumped up and ran to the observation post above the bunker. I was told that the terrorists were currently out of view but that soldiers had positively identified them entering the village.

I issued several curt orders into the radio, alerting all the necessary people – and forgetting all about the guests in my office, who sat there in front of the radio receiver listening to the incident unfold.

I drove into the Lebanese village, mobilizing along the way all of our available assets. The company's bunkers were left almost completely empty. I reached the observation post near the village and spotted someone with a backpack jumping from one sheltered place to another less than a kilometer from the post. Realizing this must be one of the terrorists, I sent forward the first armored vehicle that arrived to block their possible escape route. It was commanded by Shmulik Avraham, one of my platoon commanders.

At some stage, when he passed under a nearby United Nations post, Avraham called to me on the radio: "Chief, this is Number 1...they are shooting at me!" The UN soldiers shot in front of the vehicle, trying to stop it. They did not understand why all of a sudden the Israeli army was invading Lebanon.

I asked Shmulik over the radio if the shooting was endangering any of his men and when he said that it wasn't, I ordered him to move forward. A short time later, when he radioed me again and said that the bullets shot in his direction were starting to hit dangerously close, I ordered him to stop and stay put.

When I reached the post on the edge of the small village, my battalion commander radioed and ordered me to stop where I was since we had not yet received authorization from the North Front Command for the operation. The division commander was at the time busy talking to the head of the command, going over plans for some future commando operation, and since our actions included an invasive entrance into Lebanese territory, we required special authorization to continue. I wasn't permitted to move any farther, even though I could see the terrorists with my own eyes.

Arik Krausman, my battalion commander, arrived at the post a few minutes later, and when he received all the information from me, he said, "Go for it!" Even though he had initially told me to stay put, he changed his orders and said he would take full responsibility for ignoring orders to wait for authorization from above. I admired his resolve.

In the meantime, another one of my platoon commanders arrived from a second bunker. I said to him, "Kobi, we will divide our force. I'll trail the footprints and you will cover us from above."

He climbed to his post and informed me that he could see one of the terrorists at a distance of about eight hundred meters. I said, "Good. Open fire!"

He repeated his message in case I misunderstood him, thinking the distance was too great. I said that I understood and repeated my order to open fire. He shot at them and informed me that when the shooting started they immediately laid down. "Excellent," I said. "Make sure they stay with their heads down, and point the way for me." I took six soldiers and was off.

We were advancing cautiously, with Kobi directing us on one side – and Arik the battalion commander yelling at us that we were going the wrong way and were going to get ourselves killed. He thought that we should be more cautious, and I thought we should hurry before the terrorists escaped. I did my best to calm Arik down and added that the things I could see from where I stood were impossible to see from where he stood. At this time I suddenly remembered that Dorit's parents must still be in my office and were probably hearing everything on the radio.

We advanced, and suddenly Kobi warned me that he had lost eye-contact with us. I shot up a flare, and he said I should turn left. Arik started to warn me again when Kobi broke in and said we were extremely close to the terrorists.

He hardly finished his sentence when a red-headed terrorist stood up in front of me, aiming his Kalashnikov assault rifle. I shot first and he fell down. His colleagues tried to shoot at us but we were on higher ground so their bullets didn't hit us. We shot with our guns and threw several hand grenades at them. I threw another grenade, gave an order to storm them, and within seconds it was over.

I took the radio transmitter and said, "Chief, this is commander of the Mount Dov post. We have three terrorists who have stopped moving – they are dead. These are the people we have been searching for."

Arik replied, "Don't be cocky; this is no the time for that. There should be four of them. Keep the search on!" I replied that I believed there were only three but that I would keep searching. I searched a little more, found nothing, and returned to the fence.

Meanwhile, soldiers from the South Lebanese Army (SLA) – our allies at the time – appeared on the scene. They came as soon as the shooting ended, and I remember one of them going over to one of the bodies and taking a wristwatch off of him. When I saw that I said, "Give that to me!"

I put the watch on a rock and smashed it with my rifle. I didn't want any looting.

Arik asked on the radio, "What were they carrying with them?" I said that from what I could see they had explosives and assault rifles, and I could also see some electrical wires sticking out from their bags. "I am on my way!" he said. I waited and meanwhile secured the perimeter. I said to him that we will need a bomb squad, and he replied, "What do you think *I* am?"

In his past, Arik had served as a company commander in a Combat Engineering Battalion. We didn't have the pleasure of witnessing his expertise, though, because the UN forces, quite alarmed by the shooting and the grenade explosions they had just heard, did not let him through. I told him on the radio that I would try to inspect the bodies myself. I tied a long rope on to one body, and after we all took cover, I pulled the rope and turned the corpse onto its back. Afterward I did the same with the other two bodies. They all carried bomb belts on their bodies and wires with detonators, but they were not connected. Since the UN did not allow any more Israeli soldiers into the area, Arik asked me if perhaps we could bring the corpses to him. We put the three bodies on stretchers and carried them on our shoulders.

I remember this journey vividly since it was the first time I ever carried a corpse. Corpses are much more difficult to carry than live bodies. First, live people balance their bodies while being carried. In addition, the fact that they are dead itself entails some inconvenience. We didn't tie the dead terrorists' hands, and when I carried the front of the stretcher the soldier behind me complained that the dead man's hand kept swinging back and forth hitting his face. After we let the UN soldiers see the terrorists we were carrying, they finally understood what was going on and let us go on our way.

Coming out of Lebanon, we met Major General Yanush Ben-Gal, who was at the time head of the Northern Command. He did not bring up the fact that we had disobeyed his order. We then returned to headquarters, where Dorit was waiting with her parents. They still remind me to this day how I assured them that it was a completely safe place.

A few weeks after the battle with the terrorists, I received a call from the Central Command, notifying me that I had to drive to Northern Command Headquarters to accept a commendation signed by the general. I was busy at the time and did not go. My company was then sent to the Sinai Peninsula for a training session and, surprisingly enough, the commander of the Central Command showed up there too. His assistant came over to me and said: "Stern, now it's an act of insubordination on your behalf. You simply have to drive to the Northern Command headquarters and accept the document!"

I did not go. Every time I thought about going, something else important came up, and most of the time I was in the Sinai, which is far from the Northern Command headquarters in Safed. A few months later we returned to the Golan Heights for another period of routine border patrols, and I remember standing on the roof of the bunker on the Hermon Mountain when Major General Ben-Gal came for a visit. While questioning one of my soldiers about potential targets, Ben-Gal turned to me and said in his picturesque style: "Stern, I hear you get drunk from stepping on the lid of a toothpaste tube. Tomorrow at noon you will get drunk at my office from drinking whiskey!"

I went the next day at noon, received the certificate, and drank the whiskey. As far as I remember this was the first whiskey I had ever tasted. The certificate still hangs on a wall in my parents' house.

The battalion was sending groups of soldiers across enemy lines to operate in Lebanese territory. Usually the veteran company – being the most experienced within the battalion – would get all the action and the younger companies would mostly fill supportive roles. My company, being the youngest in the battalion, was last in line. Actually we never took part in any of those operations.

One day I came to Arik, the battalion commander, and asked him when my company would be sent on a combat mission into Lebanon. He said that we had already done our part, a reference to our battle with the terrorists several months earlier.

I said to him, "What has that got to do with anything? Our company's soldiers haven't gotten any leave for six weeks now! The veteran company's soldiers get leave all the time, the other companies too, and they spend their evenings in a nearby coffee shop in the town of Kiryat Shmona! Only we stay all the time on the mountain, waiting for action. So at least we should have the benefit of being on the mission rotation. My company should be the next one that goes out."

Despite my persistence, Arik wasn't so easily persuaded and said calmly that I had done my share for the near future.

"Okay," I said. "I hear what you are saying, but remember that if I do not participate in future operations, I will not participate in future staff meetings at the battalion either."

Soon afterward I went to see a dentist at the Tel Hashomer military base near Tel Aviv. As I arrived, I bumped into Colonel Doron Rubin, who was then our brigade commander. When Rubin saw my long face he asked me what had happened. I told him that I was being kept out of missions because of the terrorist incident. Rubin thought I should fight for what I wanted. I said I already argued as much as I could, and now I decided that if they don't want me, I will remain on Mount Dov and perform my obligations there, but the battalion will not be of any interest to me anymore.

"Stern," Rubin said. "It's not like you to give up without a fight! Go pound your fist on your commander's table!"

"I don't intend to see his table again!" I said.

I returned to battalion headquarters, and the deputy battalion commander told me that they had just scheduled a company commanders' meeting. I said, "Forget it. I'm not coming to any more meetings!"

He looked at me surprised and said, "Stern, I'll be frank with you. You know I appreciate your abilities. In time, you could become the best company commander in our battalion. But this is something you are not supposed to do."

"I will do it anyway," I answered sharply.

"Do you realize what the consequences will be?" he asked, hinting that I might find myself discharged and out of the service for such an offense. I said that I had considered my options, and then I bid him farewell, returning to my mountain bunker.

A week later I got a call from the battalion commander's secretary informing me about another scheduled commanders' meeting. I thanked her for the information. Another week and she called again with a date for another meeting. I thanked her once again politely. She asked me, "Why do you thank me? You do not intend to show up, right?"

I said that it was none of her business and that it was her job to inform me about the meetings and nothing more. I continued with my boycott.

I felt a little sorry for my battalion commander. It was a very blunt statement on my behalf. But you see, soldiers live for those assignments. It is true that guarding Mount Dov was a very important mission, but the real action occurred on the missions that we weren't getting. I suspected that the other company commanders persuaded the battalion commander that we had received our share and could be erased from the mission rotation list.

Weeks later, on a Saturday morning, the guard of the bunker gate came running to me, saying that a civilian was at the gate and he thought it might be our battalion commander. It was indeed Arik. He was on leave at home for the weekend and decided to come and talk to me dressed in civilian clothes.

Before we started our conversation I said to him, "Arik, I want you to know that I really appreciate what you are doing. I am not sure I could have done the same."

It was a very extraordinary idea, to come to me wearing civilian clothes, as a friend and not as my superior officer. He came to me from his home, at the expense of free time with his family. "After this," I said, "I don't think I can maintain my boycott any longer and I will come to all the meetings as I did before the boycott started. But," I added, "I can't promise that I will not be forced again to take such steps if we remain out of the mission rotation."

The bottom line was that Arik and I operated afterward with perfect cooperation in all professional, social, and authoritative aspects. It's a story about two men – Arik and me – his resolution as a commander to take risks and let me attack an enemy when it was required, while aware of the price of failure. It is also a story about his tolerance toward a challenging company commander, as I must have been.

* * *

When I finished my assignment as a company commander I was offered a trip to a military exhibition in Paris, if I'd agree to continue my military service for two more years. I didn't intend to commit myself to two years of service for a trip to Paris, and I refused the offer. I was offered other assignments commanding other units within the Paratroopers Brigade, but since my discharge was around the corner, I rejected them all and preferred to serve the remaining time as a platoon instructor at the Officers' Training School. The commander of the school at the time, Yoram "Ya-Ya" Yair – who later became a major general – became a good friend of mine.

Dorit and I got married while I was at the school, and we bought an apartment in Ramat Gan, near Tel Aviv. I was under a lot of pressure to remain in the army, and among the offers I received was one for a house in the town of Yavneh, in the south. In exchange, I would need to commit to eight more years of service. I refused. I couldn't see myself remaining in the army for another eight years. I wanted to remain my own master and control my own future.

After that, I agreed to commit myself to six years, but those six years included two years of college, paid for by the military. I had just started my studies when I was offered an assignment with the IDF's most elite commando unit, called the General Staff Reconnaissance Unit, and known by its Hebrew name, Sayeret Matkal. I was asked to serve as the head of training in the unit and replace Moshe "Bogie" Ya'alon, who went on to command the unit, become IDF chief of staff, and serve as deputy prime minister in 2010.

Messengers came and went, but I couldn't bring myself to accept the offer. One evening, sitting in my car at a red light near Tel Aviv, Ya'alon himself drove up, stopped his car next to mine and said me, "Stern, you have to make up your mind. Give me a final answer before the light turns green. I gave him a negative answer, and I confess that ever since, I have felt that this was one of the biggest mistakes I made during my military service.

I took courses at Bar Ilan University in economics, history, and geography and immensely enjoyed my studies. The main benefit of those years as a student was that I learned to ask questions. It was especially relevant for me, a graduate from religious and military institutions, which naturally discourage their students from questioning authority.

That year, Dorit and I were also busy organizing the first group of men and women who would form our soon-to-be home – Hoshaya.

Moving to the Galilee

After we were married, my wife and I lived in Ramat Gan. Those were years when dozens of settlements were being established throughout Judea and Samaria in the West Bank. Several families from our social circle added our names to a list of people who were preparing to start the settlement Yakir. Those friends kept prodding us to come to the meetings of the founding families. We never did. I have nothing against Yakir, but I always said that when I have guests for Shabbat in my house, I want to sit and converse with them about Judaism and not about politics and the motives behind my decision to live in one controversial location over another.

I truly believe that the commandment of settling the Land of Israel is important, but I never felt that my Zionism was any feebler when I lived at 81 Pinchas Street in Ramat Gan. You can be a good Zionist wherever your house may be.

We received a call to tell us that a group of people were getting together to establish a new community in the Galilee in northern Israel. The idea fell on fertile ground because of an incident I had witnessed several days earlier. I was talking with one of my neighbors in the street when I heard her six- and seven-year-old children fighting. They cursed each other using some of the vilest words in existence.

"Don't you intend to interfere?" I asked the embarrassed mother.

"Stern," she said, "just wait until your children are six years old and you will see that they will also sound like that."

Dorit and I didn't have children yet, but I promised myself that when we did, they would not attend any school where children learned to curse like that.

It was always Dorit's dream to live in the Galilee, not far from where her brother's fatal training accident took place near the Israeli-Arab town of Sakhnin. (Today she works in Sakhnin.) So we decided to join the group and started promoting the idea along with several other families already actively involved. They invited us to meet them on the shores of the Kinneret, the Sea of Galilee, in northern Israel. They intended to interview us. They always laugh when they tell how we hardly allowed them to ask us any questions; rather, we started interviewing them.

In 1982, the First Lebanon War broke out. I suspended my studies, reenlisted in the army, and served as the deputy commander of the 202nd Battalion of the Paratroopers Brigade. One evening, during the Jewish holiday season around Rosh Hashana, I left Lebanon to attend a meeting of families planning to move to Hoshaya. I was told that we had a limited opportunity to settle ten families in the community, and if we missed the opportunity it would not repeat itself. Most of the time I was in Lebanon; Dorit was on the verge of giving birth to our first child and studying at nursing school near Tel Aviv. We looked at each other, and Dorit announced: "You can count us in!"

There weren't enough houses in the place for the ten families. They brought us used mobile homes from one of the settlements recently evacuated in the Sinai after the peace treaty Israel signed with Egypt in 1979. When people talk to me about the evacuation of settlements, I tell them that we built a new community out of the remnants of an evacuated one. We lived for six years in a house that was dismantled and carried away during an evacuation. It's an interesting technique for creating continuity. When we came to live in Hoshaya, there were no roads leading to the place. There was only one rough dirt road that passed through the community of Tzipori. There was basically nothing there.

Five more families joined us the following summer, and since then Hoshaya has never stopped growing. Today it includes hundreds of families that add up to thousands of men, women, and children.

For our meetings, we assembled on the open porches of the houses. During one of the meetings we discussed the question of whether the community should be mixed with religious and secular residents or should be strictly religious. I have a strong conviction that if I hadn't spent most of my time then in Lebanon and could have participated in more of the meetings, Hoshaya would have stood a good chance of becoming a mixed community, since I believe strongly that we should accept secular members alongside the religious ones.

When we celebrated our son's bar mitzvah on a Shabbat, we invited, among our guests, a very old lady and several people with disabilities. They came in two cars, and the cars brought them all the way to the community's front gate. A week later the news leaflet printed in the town published an appeal that driving on Saturday into the community should not happen again. Though the request did not mention names, I could not ignore it and called the settlement's chairman. He told me that several people had complained. I said that from the wording of the request one might think that people with cars constantly toured the streets of the community, when the truth was that an elderly lady and several men with disabilities were brought a little closer to the synagogue so they could attend the bar mitzvah.

I asked him how this disturbed anyone, when the road in question doesn't even enter the town. He replied that several citizens had complained and that the complaints were much harsher than the language he used in the newsletter. I asked him: "Why should people who complain anonymously have their complaint printed with the settlement chairman's signature under it?"

I considered this incident a sign of the sad fact that we somehow had failed. In my opinion, the best thing we could do was pave a circular road around the settlement so that non-religious visitors and relatives could drive on a Saturday and come as close to the homes as possible without harming Hoshaya's beautiful and unique Shabbat atmosphere.

I look with great pride at Hoshaya of today. It is a wonderful village from many aspects and a splendid place to live, but I must admit that as far as integration with fellow Israelis is concerned, I am not completely satisfied with our achievements. I think I have made very clear statements over the years on this issue in reference to the military and to Israeli society as a whole.

We have in Hoshaya families that keep many different standards of religiousness, but unhappily, we are not a "mixed platoon."

PERHAPS MY GREATEST MISTAKE

I mentioned before that there were ten families that settled in Hoshaya in the beginning but that wasn't completely accurate. I should have said nine and a half families since I wasn't really there.

Toward the end of my first year in university, the First Lebanon War broke out, and I was asked to serve as a senior member of Division Commander General Amos Yaron's staff. A few weeks after the war ended I was released and returned to my studies.

Toward the end of the summer, Arik Moran came to visit me at our home in Ramat Gan. He was a deputy commander of the Paratroopers Brigade and he came to ask me to stop my studies and come back to serve again as the deputy commander of Battalion 202, although this time as a full-time job.

When I hesitated, he asked me to come to Lebanon and meet General Yoram Yair. I arrived there during one of the bloodiest days of fighting in Beirut's refugee camps. Yair and I walked in the center of the camp, surrounded by smoke and flying bullets, and I was trying to make him realize why it was all wrong for me to become at that moment a deputy battalion commander. I was busy with other things, I explained, and there must be other good candidates for this assignment. Yair stopped me after some time and said: "Stern, this is all bullshit; I need you here and that's it."

I said to him, "Look Ya-Ya," calling him by his nickname, "if you conclude our discussion saying that you need me, I will leave everything and come. But I want you first to hear me out to the end." We met later that night in a nearby villa where the battalion had set up its headquarters and I began listing my different considerations.

First, I said that since I grew in Battalion 890 I didn't see why I should go now to Battalion 202. I told him about the settlement we were trying to build in the Galilee. I said I shouldn't stop my university studies now, and told him about the youth groups I was counseling in Hoshaya. I told him Dorit was in the third trimester of a very difficult pregnancy. Ya-Ya heard me patiently and said, "Stern, I promise you I'll consider all you said and get back to you in a few days." A few days later he informed me that he did his thinking and he still needed me. I enlisted.

I began my assignment as deputy commander of Battalion 202 a few days after the massacre at Sabra and Shatila in September 1982. The battalion commander was spending his time preparing his testimony before the state-appointed inquiry commission. This of course made my job even more demanding. I spent almost the entire period in central Lebanon, around Beirut.

A few weeks after I enlisted, David Lipitz suggested that I replace him as deputy commander of Sayeret Matkal, the elite commando unit, a post I had already been offered and had turned down. "Now, though," Lipitz said to me, "if you are already serving as a deputy battalion commander, you'd better come and be the deputy here."

I explained to Lipitz that with all due respect to his unit, our headquarters suffered a direct hit by a mortar shell three days earlier, and I just couldn't abandon my soldiers at such a time.

Of all the bad decisions I made during my service, this might have been the greatest one, although in hindsight it is difficult to tell. On the one hand, I gave up the opportunity to serve in Sayeret Matkal in a senior position and be exposed to other worlds and other ways of thinking. On the other hand, ultimately I attained very high and satisfying positions that I otherwise wouldn't have if I had taken up the offer.

A few months after I returned to active service, our first daughter, Liron, was born. I flew in our division commander's helicopter from Lebanon, directly to the hospital, to join Dorit during her delivery.

During the following winter, Dorit, accompanied by our two-month-old Liron, climbed the hill with nine more families and without me, and settled in Hoshaya. I spent most of that year in the vicinity of Beirut. Dorit, a mother of a two-month-old baby and a nurse in a Haifa hospital, survived this period with the support of our dear friends in Hoshaya.

There is no doubt that our comrades in the unstable mobile homes, who for six years shared with us the same plaster walls, played a major part in my early military service. At times, during ceremonies celebrating a new rank or a new assignment, Dorit used to say that the flowers should go to Miriam and Binny Shalev, or to Yehuda and Yona Zusman, who showed up at our mobile home every day to babysit our daughter, so that Dorit could reach the hospital in Haifa by 7 a.m.

When I finished my term as deputy commander I asked to go on unpaid leave in order to finish my university degree. The only military post I was interested in was commanding the Paratroopers Brigade's training base, called "Camp 35," and since I knew that this assignment was given to officers who had already served as battalion commanders, I thought that I did not stand a chance. I wanted to retain my freedom of choice to resign if I chose to do so, and I wanted to complete my studies.

The late Shmulik Arad, who was by then my brigade commander, couldn't see a fault in my reasoning and sent me to speak with the IDF's chief infantry officer and later Israel's defense minister Itzik Mordechai. The general looked at me and said: "I had here yesterday an officer who said that if the army does not send him to study abroad he will resign. A week ago, I had here an officer who said that if he doesn't get free housing in an officers' project, he will resign. You are offered a year of studies paid for by the army and you turn it down?!"

Instead, he said, go study and when you are finished, I will make sure that you are appointed commander of the training base. If not, Mordechai said, then you can resign.

A year later, in the summer of 1984, I was appointed commander of Camp 35. A few months later, in the autumn, our son Ilan was born.

I now planned to resign from the IDF the moment I finished my assignment as commander of the training base. In the spring of 1985 the chief of staff visited Camp 35. During his visit, the commander of the Central Command Major General Amnon Lipkin-Shahak, later to become the chief of staff, suggested that I join the chief of staff in his car for the ride to the training fields. I blushed, thanked him, and said I'd better go in my own jeep. Shahak insisted and said: "You must go with the chief of staff!"

The result of that unexpected ride was that a few weeks later I left the paratroops training camp and joined a battalion commanders' course, after which I was immediately appointed commander of Battalion 202. During this time our daughter Adi was born.

What the Battalion Needs

Hagai Mordechai was by far the best platoon commander in my battalion. I was close to completing my term and again getting discharged from the army but was naturally concerned about the way the battalion would look after I left.

One day I summoned Mordechai to my office. He had already commanded his platoon for eleven months by that time, and I told him that he was a candidate to serve in the future as a company commander. But, I said, before that he needed to serve as the incoming battalion commander's chief operations officer. To become a good operations officer though, I said, he needed to leave his platoon and start the company commander course now.

Mordechai was taken aback. "What do you mean?" he asked. "I just recently started to enjoy my soldiers and now you're telling me to leave them and go to a course? I want to be a company commander and I'll go to the course in due time but let me first remain with my soldiers till the end of the term."

"What did you say when you enlisted?" I asked him. "Didn't you say that you want to serve the state and give from yourself to the paratroops? Well this is the service you spoke of, and this is the reason why you have to go to that course."

He said to that, "Okay. Are you asking me if I want to go?'

"No," I replied, "I am not asking you. I am telling you that you are going to that company commanders' course!"

"I don't want to and you cannot force anyone to go to a company commanders' course," he said. Theoretically he was absolutely correct.

I explained to him that each of us gets tested in life. "If you refuse to go to the course and you fail to understand that you should go, you will be expelled from the battalion."

Eitan Zilberman, Hagai's company commander, supported his position. A few hours later, Benda, another company commander, came to see me and said, "Stern, you can't force him to go. There were days when people were forced to go to officers' school, but no one ever forced anyone to go to a company commanders' course."

"I didn't force him," I said. "If he doesn't want to go he can do as he wishes, but he will not remain in my battalion."

Gadi Shamni, my deputy, came to me and said, "Stern, what are you doing? You can't do such a thing!"

We were stationed on the border with Lebanon, sending out daily patrols. I stuck with what I said to Hagai and told Shamni, "Gadi, you have known me for a bit longer than fifteen minutes. You know that I am going through with this all the way!"

My relationship with Hagai was special. Throwing him out of the battalion was the last thing I wanted to do, but my mind was set. But so was his.

We met for additional discussions, usually during patrols or when I came to his post or he to my office. We would talk about life and about his approaching course and each time he insisted that he would not go. One day he returned from a furlough and said to me, "I have a distant relative who told me you cannot do this."

I knew the relative wasn't distant and that it was Itzik Mordechai, the chief infantry officer. I said to Hagai: "Look, I don't know who your relative is, but tell him that maybe he can't make you go to a company commanders' course, but your battalion commander can. As we agreed, either you go to the course or you are out of the battalion."

He asked me for permission to set up a meeting with the brigade commander. "What kind of a question is that?" I replied, "You are an officer in the brigade. Of course you can."

Shaul Mofaz, later the chief of staff and Israel's defense minister, was our brigade commander. He was scheduled to come to the battalion headquarters for an inquiry, and we agreed that he would first interview Hagai. He informed me that he planned to use my office for the interview. I was about to leave when Hagai entered. Mofaz asked me to stay. I said that this was a private interview and I didn't know what Hagai wanted to say about me. Mofaz asked Hagai if it was all right and Hagai replied that he didn't mind my staying. I guess that the way things were, he would have found it difficult to say something else, but I believe he really did not mind. I sat next to Mofaz, Hagai sat opposite us, and Mofaz, with his usual half-smile, asked him: "How are things, Hagai?"

"'Fine," he said.

"So, why don't you want to go to the company commanders' course?"

"I never said that I don't want to go. I want to go, but only when my soldiers finish their training track. Why can't I finish with them? It's customary! Afterwards I'll gladly become an operations officer."

Mofaz turned to me and said: "Well?"

"What do you mean?" I asked him.

"The boy is right."

"You hear the commander Hagai?" I said. "This is exactly what I said to you. If you think like that, you can be an officer in the brigade headquarters but not in my battalion. Either you go to that course or you go to the brigade headquarters."

Hagai and I kept discussing the subject in vain. The course was due to start on Sunday, and on Wednesday I summoned him to my office and asked him what his decision was. He said he wouldn't go. "On Sunday," I said, "either you are in the course or you are at brigade headquarters."

He replied that he did not intend to leave. I said: "Listen Hagai, tomorrow at 4 p.m. I will come to your post and listen to you give your final briefing to your soldiers. If you don't brief them, I will."

As a commander, I was worried that I was about to lose the best officer in my battalion. I did not want him to leave but I knew that if he didn't attend the course I would have no alternative but to throw him out of the battalion. I didn't insist on this course out of shear stubbornness. I was thinking about the incoming battalion commander and the good of the battalion, which must come before our own aspirations and desires.

I came to the mountain post at 4 p.m. The platoon stood in formation. They were all very good soldiers. I asked Hagai to go and stand in front of them and he asked me why. I said that this was his final briefing. The soldiers were confused and I asked Hagai again to speak to them. He refused.

I walked to the front and said: "Listen. You are a wonderful platoon and you had the best platoon commander in the battalion but he is leaving today. You were together in your basic training, you conducted border patrols together and everything you did was commendable. Does anyone have questions?"

Hagai stood a little away from us. All the soldiers were embarrassed. I said, "Well, no questions?" and then someone at last got the courage to ask what was happening. I explained to them what it was that I expected from them, soldiers and commanders alike. I said to them: "I demand from your commander to give all he has. I believe that he can do it, that's what he needs to do, and that's what the battalion needs. He may think otherwise, so on the coming Sunday he will no longer remain your commander. Thank you and have a good day."

On Sunday Hagai went to the course. After he finished the course he returned to the battalion. Today he is a brigadier general and besides our personal relationship he brings me a lot of satisfaction. Maybe he agrees with me now, or at least understands my motives.

In 1989, two years after my discharge from the army, I returned to take up the position of deputy commander of the Eastern Brigade on the Lebanese border. It was during this time that our daughter Hodaya was born.

Toward the end of 1993, I was appointed commander of the Officers' Training School, called Bahad 1.

Chapter 4

Always an Officer

When I became commander of Bahad 1, the IDF Officers' Training School toward the end of 1993, I said that there was no possible promotion from this assignment. I meant that this was the most significant, influential, and satisfying role an officer could ever wish for. Years later I still think the same.

When I was offered the assignment, Dorit and I decided to temporarily leave Hoshaya and move our family to Mitzpe Ramon in the Negev Desert, a good five-hour drive from Hoshaya. We were the first commanders' family to make such a move. Dorit says to this day that I told her a lot of fairy tales in order to convince her to agree to the move, but I honestly believed that the move would allow me to spend more time at home.

Of course this never happened, but we never regretted our move there. For two years we had the delight of living among people we had not met before, whose uniqueness and beauty was impossible to grasp from a distance. And if you add to this our acquaintance with the Negev, the proximity to all the wonderful hiking routes in the desert, and the involvement of my family in the school experience, I think it was a very beneficial move for us all.

While we were there, Dorit gave birth to our son Amichai in the hospital in Beersheba. Since Mitzpe Ramon is quite far from Beersheba, Dorit arranged her schedule ahead of the birth so that most of her time would be spent in Beersheba in case she suddenly felt like she was going into labor. She was smart, because on one of her walks there one day, labor kicked in and she immediately checked herself into the hospital.

I was alerted by the hospital at once. This was the second time she had to check into the hospital without me. Dorit told me that on her way to the hospital for her first birth, she had to stop her car beside the highway for every contraction and wait until the pain subsided, and then continue driving. At that time I was in Lebanon. Now, I was a little closer.

For many officers, commanding Bahad 1 is like coming full circle. Returning to the officers' school – the place you left as a junior officer – and coming back as the commander in charge of instructing and training the next generation of commanders, gives one a sensation that is too difficult to describe in words. I will not deny that this post is also considered one of the most prestigious in the IDF and a fairly certain step toward a position among the military's top brass.

Somehow for me, the assignment signified primarily the final turning point from a combat soldier into an educator. These two characters – the fighter and the educator – should be present side by side in every officer and in every commander from the first day he is appointed to command his first squad of soldiers. In Bahad 1, without my noticing at first, the balance inside of me started to shift. The following stories might help explain what I mean.

Guarding the Public Telephone

Soon after I arrived at Bahad 1, I noticed a weird phenomenon. A fully armed cadet would patrol around a telephone booth, right in the center of the base. I asked him what he was doing, and he replied that he was guarding the public telephone. I was dumbfounded.

I asked my operations deputy why he assigned a guard to the public telephone, and he told me that this was a requirement made by Twito, the camp's legendary sergeant major. I called Twito and asked him why he issued such a requirement, and he told me that there were too many incidents in which unhappy cadets, encountering a broken telephone, poured their frustration out on the telephone. The telephone company had announced that the next time the telephone would be broken, they did not intend to come and fix it. If this happened the cadets would not be able to call their homes. This was, of course, a long time before cellular phones.

I asked Twito to cancel the public telephone guard. He said he would not know what to say to the parents when their kids didn't call home. I told him to put all the blame on me, since I did not know how to run an officers' training academy that needed a guard on the public telephone.

The guard was cancelled and the phone, if you are wondering, is just fine.

A Platoon Commander Never Fears

One day I entered a class during a history lesson. I sat quietly in the back of the class until I felt an irresistible urge to intervene.

My urge was awakened when I heard one of the cadets say he knew for a fact that several of the cadets who were to become officers would not have the courage, when they were tested, to stand up and run straight toward an enemy. I asked the cadet if he knew anyone like that in his squad or his platoon and he said he didn't. I told him that if he personally felt that way, or if he knew someone else who did, he should report it to the school and we would expel this individual from the course.

I went on and asked him how *he* would act when facing the enemy. He said he knew he would be frightened but he hoped that he would overcome the fear and perform his duties as expected of him. I said to him that if by the following morning his answer remained the same – and he only "hopes" – he should come to my office to be dismissed from the school, like every other cadet who recognizes his personal handicaps and reports them to the school authorities.

The discussion then continued until it reached the question of what is the right way to speak to one's subordinates. One of the cadets said that they should say: "Even I, your platoon commander, feels fear, but I know I will overcome it."

I considered this to be the kind of openness that deteriorates very easily into a striptease show. I told the cadets that in my opinion a commander should always avoid any remark that might instill fear into his soldiers' hearts, even if it is a temporary fear, since this could prove fatal at a time of real combat.

Is a platoon commander immune to fear? Of course he isn't! Should he share his fears with his subordinates? Of course he shouldn't! Such a foolish exposure would undermine his soldiers' confidence and could create a legitimate case for soldiers to refrain from storming enemy positions. It could produce a situation in which people will feel comfortable enough to say: "All right, we both were afraid – you overcame your fear while I simply didn't."

A short while after the lecture, I sat in on another class of cadets who were debating the ongoing combat operations in Lebanon. The question was whether standard procedure demanded that immediately after a unit launches a massive attack, including heavy gunfire, does it need to immediately storm the enemy position – as we teach it should – or is there room for a commander's consideration based on each situation.

During the debate one of the commanders, who was trying to defend the standard procedure, said it was important to be done by the book, since if a commander waited, he could go into a state of shock, and the soldiers would find themselves without a commander.

"A platoon commander enters a state of shock," I wondered to myself. This was a horrible example. This should never have been said before future officers who might come to accept this option as legitimate. A platoon commander will never enter a state of shock, even if he enters a state of shock! And a platoon commander will never be too afraid to lead an attack, even when he is afraid to lead an attack.

I issued a paper on the subject and I called it: "What will never happen to a platoon commander, even if it happens to him."

What I meant to say was very simple. A platoon commander who was not tested under fire, which is the ultimate test, isn't really a platoon commander. All his record, including the excellent leadership he might have demonstrated during training, may serve him in other professions. The platoon commander has a completely different *raison d'être* – if he is afraid to storm an enemy position and lead the attack then he is not a platoon commander, and he graduated from the school by mistake.

During a commando raid in the early 1950s, someone asked Meir Har Zion – a legendary Israeli soldier – what it was that made him rise every time and attack. He nodded toward the soldiers behind him and said: "They do!"

A real commander feels this kind of responsibility toward his soldiers, and the suggestion that he will not live up to the ideals he was raised on shames him. The responsibility and the shame are enough to make the commander overcome any fear he might feel. Fighters and commanders were born for the moment of the attack. Any other attitude, which may fit into a dialogue with a psychologist, will only weaken the values of our army and could lead us to paralysis in battle.

Lesson from a Lost Weapon

One night, during a navigation exercise in the Negev desert, one of the cadets lost his weapon. He fell asleep at one of the rest points, and when he woke up and continued his navigation he suddenly noticed that he had left his weapon behind. When he returned he did not find it. Several platoons combed the entire area very thoroughly but did not find the gun. After many hours of futile search the cadets returned to the base and the military police were notified.

It was an early Thursday morning. In the afternoon the whole company was scheduled to participate in a ceremony to commemorate the thirtieth day after the murder of Lieutenant Shachar Simani, a member of their platoon who was killed while on furlough from the base. I asked the battalion commander what his plans were after that, and he answered that the following day the company was to go on leave for the weekend. I suggested they go out again to search for the lost weapon.

My suggestion was not welcomed by the staff of the company. I said that there were several practical reasons for a second search after a cadet loses his gun. Someone might have found the gun and later became scared because of the possible consequences, and gotten rid of it. He could have met friends who told him he must be insane not to know that the Jews will not rest until they find their missing gun. And maybe when those who found the gun see the cadets combing once again in the area, they will get rid of it. And lastly, maybe the gun was never taken and lies there unseen.

The company left before sunrise to search again for the gun. Several hours later, the gun was found, lying on the ground. I felt that my initial reasons were on the mark; whoever had taken the gun was probably afraid of getting caught, after seeing the numbers of soldiers out looking for the gun and knowing that the army was not going to give up. On Sunday, the deputy commander of the battalion showed up in my office and declared: "Sir, I came to salute you. I did not believe the gun would be found."

On the evening before a class's graduation I met with the cadets who graduated with honors. I asked them what, in their opinion, was the most significant thing they had learned in the course. One of the cadets said that searching for the gun was the most monumental experience of the course.

I asked him who gave them the order to go out and search. He replied that the staff issued the orders but when they asked why, they were told that the order came from the top brass command. Apparently, the staff was concerned that their soldiers would criticize them for giving an order that seemingly had no logic, since they did not believe the gun would be found, so they put the responsibility for the order on the top brass.

I asked him what he and his friends said about the order when they were on their way to the field. He said they said it was done to cover the base commander's ass, and he added that some very unpleasant words about me personally had been thrown around as well.

"What did you say on your way back, after the gun was found?" I asked.

"We were silently digesting the true meaning of the incident," he responded.

Afterward I met the whole company and its staff and asked them what they had learned from the second search. They all said they learned the importance of persistence. I added, "As a commander, when you say to your soldiers that 'those are the orders from above,' you will lose a priceless opportunity to show leadership."

Educator against My Will

Whenever I had to demonstrate what my expectations were from IDF officers or other leaders, I always turned to an example from my experience as a high school teacher.

Two teachers teach the same class of kids. One, the class educator (special and important role in Israeli schools), tries to demonstrate and explain to his students the importance of decent values, good citizenship, and tolerance toward one another. The second teacher, a geometry teacher, speaks to them about triangles.

After the educator finishes his hour of education, the second teacher enters the classroom and starts explaining the different angles of the triangle. In the middle of the explanation, one of the kids yells at another boy: "Shut up, you Russian maniac. It's a pity they ever let you come here. You only cause trouble!"

The geometry teacher has two ways to deal with what is happening in front of him. He can slam his hand down on the table and say, "Excuse me, this noise disturbs me. Please concentrate on the blackboard!" Or he can stop the geometry lesson and say, "Forget for the moment about triangles. Let's talk about what just happened here."

In which of the two cases did the geometry teacher pass on to his students a real educational message? My answer is that he would be delivering messages in both cases. Someone who ignores his educational vocation and dodges his responsibilities is delivering these kids a loud educational message even if he doesn't intend to do so.

This is the profound responsibility that is tied to the vocation of teachers and military commanders. Education and the instruction of human values cannot stop with the recess bell. If the geometry teacher chooses to ignore a racist outburst, his silence provides the students with what can be called negative legitimacy and sets a personal ugly example that will remain with them. The teacher thinks he is only responsible for teaching geometry, but he actually has given them a major lesson in what can constitute low-level human behavior.

And the same is true in the case of a platoon commander who just finished leading his recruits with great devotion up a hill, encouraging them all the way, and carrying the heavy stretcher far more than any of them – and now, entering the battalion's mess hall, he doesn't stop being a role model. If he absentmindedly finishes all the table's allocation of french fries before his fellow commanders arrive and join him at the table, his soldiers will carry this picture in their minds much longer than they will remember his honorable behavior while climbing the mountain. Without knowing it, the tray of french fries he devoured is an educational message he will leave with his soldiers.

It is not important what your role is: a teacher, a principal, a leader, an officer, or a parent. You should always be aware of the possibility that there will be someone who looks up to you and will assimilate the values you represent in what you say or in your behavior, even if you don't want them to.

Shortly before the evacuation of the Jewish settlements from the Gaza Strip, my daughter Liron left her college in Jerusalem and volunteered for a couple of weeks to assist the settlers. At the end of the few weeks she had planned to be there, she decided to extend her stay. I asked her why. Did she ever hear me say she should volunteer in Gush Katif? Liron answered me: "What you said isn't important; the important thing is what I understood."

A Walk in Caesarea

During the period I served as commander of Bahad 1, I took my family for a short weekend vacation to a hotel in Caesarea. On Saturday morning, since we couldn't find a minyan – a Jewish prayer quorum – in the hotel, I walked with my eleven-year-old son, Ilan, to the town's synagogue. We left just as the service was finishing in order to hurry back to the hotel to join Dorit, who was in a very advanced stage of pregnancy. As we were walking, Ilan suddenly said to me: "Dad, President Ezer Weizman is approaching us."

We had never met before. When we were closer, I greeted him; but instead of replying, he rebuked me for having left the synagogue before they said the blessing for the government. I was a little surprised that he knew that I left the synagogue early, but I said: "I wouldn't dream of doing such a thing. We already finished the part of the prayer that asks the Lord to watch over the state and its leadership. You were taken care of."

The president asked me, "Where are you from?"

"Usually I am from Hoshaya in the Galilee. But now I live in Mitzpe Ramon."

"What do you do there?"

"I work there."

"Doing what?"

"I serve in the army."

"Where in the army?"

"In Bahad 1."

"And what do you do there?"

"'I'm a commander."

"Commander of what?"

"Commander of the Bahad."

Weizman put his hand on his ear, as if he didn't hear well, and asked me again, "Commander of what?"

"Commander of Bahad 1."

"You are the commander of Bahad 1?"

"Yes."

Weizman hit his brow and said, "Go figure. I am walking down the street and here I meet the commander of Bahad1."

I replied, "Mr. President, go figure. I was just walking down the street and bumped into the president of the State of Israel."

The president turned to his guard and shouted to him, "Do you know who this is?"

The guard, who happened to know me, said he did. Then the whole show repeated itself. Weizman turned to his guard, hit his brow, and asked him, "Well, what do you say about that – to walk down the street and meet the commander of Bahad 1…"

I told him that he was embarrassing me, and he moved onto a detailed investigation of my entire military resume. When he was finally satisfied, he said to me, "I would like to come and visit you."

Three months later, the president arrived to visit our base. As usual he skipped the small talk and asked directly, "What are you doing here?"

I showed him the training charts, and when he saw a full week labeled "Jewish Identity" he stopped me and asked, "What's that? This isn't your assignment."

I apologized and said, "I have only one assignment: to prepare officers to win a future war."

"Precisely," he exclaimed. "So why Jewish identity week?"

"Mr. President," I said, "we have Druze cadets and Bedouin cadets and we are very careful to pay respect to their heritages. But beyond this, I believe that a Jewish officer who is not able to say 'I am proud to be a Jew' and give his soldiers a twenty-minute discourse on what it is that makes him proud to be Jewish, will not win the war. And I don't care what he says in those twenty minutes. One officer will say that he prays three times a day, eats kosher food, and fasts on Yom Kippur. Another officer will say that he doesn't pray and doesn't eat kosher food but he does fast on Yom Kippur. A third will say that he doesn't pray or eat kosher or fast on Yom Kippur, but he feels Jewish because he lives in Israel and his grandfather survived the Holocaust. I don't care what his explanation is, but I want him to say willingly, 'I am proud to be a Jew.' He doesn't wish to say that? He has no explanation? He will lose the war!"

"Splendid," smiled Weizman, "let's go and meet the cadets."

We entered the hall where 240 cadets and staff members were waiting to greet the president. As soon as they sat in their chairs the president went up to the podium. His first question almost knocked me off my feet. "What can you tell me about your Judaism?"

A cadet from Jerusalem stood up and said: "Well, Mr. President, all I knew about Judaism before I came to the course was how to pass my matriculation exam in Bible studies. Since I have been a cadet here I know much more."

The president turned to me and asked, "Well, commander, what do you say to that?"

"Mr. President, I'd rather not..."

But he insisted: "Speak up, speak up!"

I realized he would not let me dodge the question and I said, "Mr. President, I am satisfied that we have been successful. Nonetheless, I really don't think this should be our duty. I would be just as satisfied if the cadets would come to us with their national pride fully developed from high school so we could use the time we have here for other things. But if the cadets come here lacking Jewish identity, we have no alternative but to do what is necessary to instill within them Jewish pride."

An English Signature

When I was appointed commander of Bahad 1, I was certain of the way an IDF officer needed to look. After spending some time there, I learned quite a lot about the cadets and the commanders who run the school, and new qualities were added to that picture.

An essential device for my education was the assessment committees, whose job was to assess cadets about whom there were doubts. The committees included the staff of the school who knew the cadet – from his squad commander all the way up to his battalion commander – and me. The committees also included a psychologist who met the cadets in question, as well as a human resources officer.

The soldiers called these committees the "sack committees" since they often recommended expulsion from the school. The cadets did not believe that the committees could reach a reasonable and objective decision. They were convinced that a cadet who was called to one of the committees was doomed, that his sentence was decided in advance by the lower ranking commanders. They didn't believe that the high command could really evaluate matters without prejudice. I can proudly say that during my service in the school, both the staff and the cadets learned to consider those committees fair and open to making an honest assessment, with results that could go either way.

Once we discussed the issue of a cadet from Sayeret Matkal, the IDF's elite commando unit. The cadet was convinced that he would graduate from the course, since his unit needed him to have an officer's rank and there was no one in his unit or in the course who could step into his shoes. He and everyone else knew that he was going to graduate with good marks. He was brought before an assessment committee for behaving disrespectfully toward a staff member.

One day, while the cadet was waiting in line for the public telephone, a certain staff member cut in line. The cadet didn't like his behavior and told him what he thought about him. Some of the staff thought this proved that the cadet was vulgar and arrogant and therefore should not be an officer. I told the staff that I could easily sympathize with the cadet's rage toward the staff member who ignored the line, but the staff members said it wasn't the first time that he had behaved with arrogance.

Before the cadet entered the room, I reviewed his file. In addition to the regular documents, there were also some handwritten notes, signed by the cadet. I noticed that he wrote in fluent Hebrew and at the end of the page signed his name in English.

When he came in, I surprised the members of the committee when I asked him how many years he had spent abroad. The cadet replied that he was raised in Israel. I then asked him if his parents came from an English-speaking country. He answered that they did not. "Then, why do you sign your name in English?" I asked. He replied that when he was a child, he saw his father sign with English letters and he had adopted the custom.

I informed the cadet that I had decided that the official reason he was being brought before the committee was due to his English signature. I told him I was determined to suspend him unless he managed to convince me that it was acceptable to sign his name in English.

Our debate lasted an hour. He insisted on his right to sign his name in English. I declared that this was a direct demonstration of his lack of national pride, as if he was embarrassed to use his native language. I also considered it to be an act of arrogance – sort of a declaration that he was different, that he stood out from the rest of the class. The meeting adjourned with him thinking he had the full right to sign his name in his language of choice. I thought he was wrong.

I contacted his unit's commander. I talked about the signature and added my overall impression of the soldier and some characteristics I recognized in him that fitted with his stubbornness. I told the commander that they should hurry and search for another soldier that could be sent to the school to be qualified as an officer, because I didn't think the current member of the unit at the school was going to graduate.

The unit commander told me he was surprised that we so accurately identified his soldier's deficiency. The boy, he said, was very gifted but did have a weak spot, which they had also identified, and while they debated whether he should become an officer, they had felt his other qualities overcame his arrogance. If we decided to remove him from the course, the unit commander said he would not appeal the decision.

The cadet was brought before the assessment committee three more times. During the first two sessions he stuck stubbornly to his original position. In the third session I noticed tears welling up in his eyes. Then he admitted that I was right. I believed his sincerity and returned him to the course. I knew that after he insisted so stubbornly on his position during the first three long meetings, he wasn't deceiving me now. I thought he really understood. Therefore I believed he could become a good officer, which he eventually did.

An Officer and a Gentleman

In several discussions I led with my cadets, I returned again and again to what I had told my recruits in 1978: "We have two goals to achieve in your training as combat soldiers. The first is to teach you to hit the target, take proper cover, and then rise, attack, and hit your enemy again. Our second goal is to teach you to give your seat on a bus to an old lady. When we try to achieve these two goals at the same time we face a problem. We have abundant rocks and hideouts in our training areas and sufficient ammunition to properly achieve the first goal. The problem is with the second goal. We only get on buses once every three weeks and there are usually no old ladies on them. Therefore, you will have to learn this lesson from our overall conduct as commanders and officers."

One day, I received the assessment papers of a cadet who was a candidate for expulsion. The staff told me that during a lecture given by a Holocaust survivor in Jerusalem, the cadet put on sunglasses and fell asleep in front of her eyes. I invited the cadet into the committee's room and said to him that I had several questions that might seem a bit personal so he could refrain from answering if he wanted.

I asked where he was on the night before the lecture. He replied that he was with his girlfriend. I said that I wasn't interested in how they spent their time, but I did want to know what time he went to sleep.

The cadet answered that because they hadn't seen each other for some time, he had gone to sleep at 3 a.m.

I said to him, "In that case you are dismissed from the school."

He said, "But that is not an offense that leads to an automatic expulsion."

I asked him what offenses did lead to automatic expulsion, and he said, "Not giving your seat to an old lady on the bus, for example."

I said, "I am sorry, I didn't express myself accurately. You are dismissed from the school for not giving your seat to an old lady on a bus, and my evidence is that you put on sunglasses during a lecture delivered by a Holocaust survivor in Jerusalem."

I explained to him that first, someone who goes to sleep at three in the morning declares that he knows what it takes to become an officer better then I do. He knew he had a lecture in the morning and also knew that he would have to get up at six o'clock. He must have known that he would be tired and would not be able to remain attentive during the lecture. "What you declared by your behavior was that the content of the lecture is not important for becoming an officer and that you can become an officer without it," I said to him.

In this matter, I told him, we do not agree, and since I was in charge of the school I had decided to dismiss him. The second reason I had decided to dismiss him, I said, was because he had insulted the woman who had taken the trouble to come deliver a lecture before his class. Putting on sunglasses and sleeping during the lecture clearly demonstrated that her stories were not of interest to him.

Someone who does not give up his seat for an elderly lady on a bus is not a gentleman. "Our buses," I said, "do not carry old women; they are used either to drive you to base or home for the weekend. In civilian buses you might encounter old women but your staff is not there to report on your behavior. So why, in your opinion, did I take the trouble to explain that a person who will not give up his bus seat to an old lady can't be an officer, when I know perfectly well that we can't monitor whether the cadets obey?"

The values behind the requirement for a soldier to give his seat to an elderly lady are the same values that require him to stay awake and pay attention during a lecture by a Holocaust survivor in Jerusalem. Someone who doesn't understand this is not only not a gentleman, but is also stupid, and someone who is stupid cannot become an officer.

Years later I sat in a meeting with several other officers in the presence of Moshe "Bogie" Ya'alon, who was then the IDF chief of staff. At a certain point, we tried to find a definition for an officer. The chief of staff said: "I don't know what the definition is." He thought about the issue for a moment and then said, "Someone who doesn't give up his seat on a bus to an old lady cannot be an officer."

I smiled.

★ ★ ★

One day I received a letter from a female officer who served as an education officer at the Artillery Corps's training base, called Shivta. The officer informed me in her letter that she had ridden a short while ago on a bus to Jerusalem accompanied by an elderly man. There were nine cadets on the bus, but they all ignored the old man and didn't offer him their seat. There weren't enough details in the letter for me to discover who the cadets were so I called her. She was surprised by my call and gave me the exact date of the bus ride. I thoroughly examined the training charts, found the company that had gone on leave that day, and summoned the soldiers to the hall to discuss the incident with them.

I told the cadets about the letter I had received. "First," I said, "I want to believe that the story is false. But if it is correct, I am going to dismiss nine cadets. What will be the outcome of this? There will be debates in the army and in the general public. Headlines will be written about this, people will talk about it, and some will say that the commander of Bahad 1 has gone crazy by throwing out nine cadets over such a minor issue. Others will approve of my decision. The bottom line is that there will be a debate and we will all benefit from it. I'm sharing this with you now because

I want you to debate the issue with me: tell me whether I am right or wrong."

There was a debate that lasted for an hour and a half. At the end of the discussions, a cadet stood up and said, "Sir, I was on that bus. I know exactly what you are talking about and I completely agree with you. But we had just completed an all-night land navigation exercise. We got on the bus in Ramla and after a minute we were asleep."

I was very glad for two things. One, they agreed with the philosophy that says that someone who doesn't give up his seat for the elderly should not be an officer. Second, that the nine cadets hadn't ignored the elderly person; they had all fallen asleep!

★ ★ ★

On Rosh Hashana eve, when I was at Bahad 1, I sent the staff and all the cadets, greeting cards that said:

> In a recent meeting of company commanders, one of the officers told me that he recently rode on a bus from Beersheba to Mitzpe Ramon and an old Bedouin woman carrying heavy bags climbed aboard. In the back of the bus two cadets sat who didn't recognize the company commander sitting there. He overheard them saying: "The commander said that an officer is expected to give his seat to an old lady." Both cadets rose and let the old woman sit in their seats. I hope that each one of you, be he a commander or a future commander, will feel in the coming year what I felt when I heard this story!

Protecting a Cadet's Privacy

Before I actually began my assignment as commander of Bahad 1, I sat with my predecessor, Yitzhak Eitan, who later became a general, for a number of meetings with some of the top cadets. In those conversations, the cadets mentioned a seminar they had attended in Netanya as the highlight of their whole course. I was baffled. How did it happen that after six intensive months in the school those cadets could say that the most significant part of the course for them was a seminar conducted by civilian psychologists at a Netanya leadership school?

I decided to look into the matter. I joined a group of cadets who were participating in the course. The psychologists asked me to sit outside but I assured them that I would not use what I heard against the cadets.

A week later, one of the cadets I had met in the group came before the assessment committee. At the seminar, his friends had discussed his lack of integrity, and now I had to decide if he should be expelled from the school after I had promised not to make use of the information I obtained there. It certainly wasn't a simple situation for me.

In the meantime, after sitting in on the classes in Netanya, I decided to adopt the idea and open a self-improvement course at Bahad 1. The idea was to hold workshops where a cadet's colleagues could openly criticize and instruct him on matters pertaining to leadership and values – with constructive criticism only, never destructive. For this purpose I consulted a psychologist who told me: "Stern, if you are successful, you will deserve a PhD." I never received the PhD I was promised, but the groups were a huge success for many years.

I thought that five weeks after entering the school, cadets already knew what was expected of them and what type of officer we wanted them to be. I opened the self-improvement groups by explaining to the cadets that I did not expect them to discuss whether the maneuvers they conducted were successful, but rather to give each other feedback on how they are as officers. I had an agreement with the cadets that nothing said in those workshops would be used against a cadet. I did everything I could to allow them to speak openly without fearing that what they said would reach my ears.

Sometimes a friend's criticism is much harder to swallow than a commander's reprimand. I was afraid that harsh criticism by a cadet's friends might lead him to depression or self-destructive behavior. To avoid tragic consequences, every group met first with a psychologist who laid down the limits of the discussion.

One day, a cadet was brought before an assessment committee. I was told that his "sin" was that he had said during one of the workshops that he intended to emigrate from Israel after he finished his military service.

My first question, before he entered the room, was to the staff: "Why is something that was said in the workshop being discussed in our forum? Aren't we supposed to be completely ignorant of all that is said in those workshops?" I was told that one of the other cadets reported his statements to the staff. "Why did you bother to listen to the informant? The rules are very clear on this," I said.

The staff member said that both he and the informant were hesitant to raise the issue before me but decided to do so since I always spoke so seriously about issues of Zionism and pride in being Israeli. If the cadet said he intended to leave Israel, the commander said, he must not like the country, and how then could we make him an officer?

I wasn't convinced. I asked the staff if they had discovered that the cadet had murdered someone. I then asked them why they hadn't explained to the informing cadet that there was a pact between the school and the cadets that they could speak freely at the workshops. "Don't you realize that using any information that comes from the workshops will be a death blow to the whole concept?" I asked them. "The cadets will immediately cease speaking in the groups, or even worse, stop being truthful."

The staff nodded their heads; maybe they agreed with me, maybe they didn't. Someone pointed out that the cadet was waiting outside. I asked him to enter. I started the meeting by telling the cadet, "You are not being dismissed. Even if what reached our ears is correct, you still spoke inside the workshop and this renders you full immunity."

After that introduction, I went on to ask him to explain to me what he meant in his comment. He stood by what he said and repeated that he planned to leave Israel after completing his military service.

I turned to the staff and said, "That's what he thinks now but he has barely started officer's training. He intends to emigrate after he graduates from the school, and after he serves a year as a platoon commander, and then maybe another year as a deputy company commander. That means, in two years. Who can tell what will happen in two years? What things he will find himself doing? How much love of Israel will be drawn in and how much love he will receive from those around him. I am certain that his heart will follow his actions and keep him in Israel."

Putting a label of a potential immigrant on a cadet and expelling him for that from the school would most probably serve as the final trigger and lead him to leave the country. Keeping him in the army, turning him into an officer, can potentially lead to experiences that will convince him to stay where he belongs.

Commander, Parents, and Cadets

I refused to meet cadets' parents during my term as commander of Bahad 1. The only exception was on their graduation day. I believed, and I still do, that there is room for some relations between parents and commanders during the very first stages of a new recruit, when they are going through the changes from adolescence to adulthood and civilian to soldier.

However, there is a fundamental difference between listening to parents' opinions before making decisions on where their son will serve, and listening to their opinions about whether their son will become a commander or an officer. We certainly should not consult a parent on a question that involves putting other soldiers under someone's command.

This understanding should not reduce the gratitude that we owe parents for raising and educating their children in such a way that when we receive them they already have the necessary qualifications and abilities that allow them to graduate from Bahad 1.

This was not so clear to everyone during my first weeks as commander. Not everyone knew yet that I refrained from meeting cadets' parents.

One day I was informed that a cadet's gun was stolen from his room. The cadet had gone to the field to train as a machine-gun operator and had left his personal gun without proper supervision. When he returned, the gun was gone. Up to that moment the soldier was considered an excellent cadet by all standards. Those were days when terrorism and soldiers' kidnappings were out of control. The staff hesitated; a gun theft is a very grave matter in the IDF, but they thought that his negligence was understandable and forgivable. He was a talented cadet, and the gun wasn't left unattended somewhere in the open field. It was left in his room.

My position was completely different. I said that there are issues that are too significant to permit us maneuverability in our decisions. In the officers' school, several offenses were traditionally followed by automatic expulsion, and though I gave several of those offenses fresh consideration, I did not think the offense of leaving his gun unguarded could be dealt with differently.

In the debate that we conducted I explained my decision to expel the cadet from the school and said that the case was a blow to the sacred value of "purity of arms" – one of the key values stated in the military's official ethics doctrine.

When the cadet's commanders raised their eyebrows doubtfully, I explained to them that in my eyes, when someone takes a gun and shoots innocent people, beside the criminal offense he commits, he is also committing an offense against the "purity of arms."

Therefore, a person who allows through his negligence the misuse of his gun for the purpose of hurting innocent people is also guilty of an offense against the "purity of arms."

The staff didn't see it in the same way, but after a long discussion I think they finally accepted my view – at least I thought so until the battalion commander asked me to explain my decision to all the battalion's cadets. I was a little surprised, and a little disappointed, but I asked them to assemble the cadets.

The next day, I had several meetings in Tel Aviv. On my way back I got a call from my deputy, Lieutenant-Colonel Aryeh Itach, informing me that he had scheduled a meeting between me and the dismissed cadet's parents, upon their request. I asked him why he didn't check with me first whether I would agree to hold such a meeting, since he knew my policy of not meeting with parents. He apologized and said that it was all new to him and he was not accustomed yet to the policy, and anyway, the parents were already on their way from Jerusalem to Bahad 1.

I didn't want to embarrass Itach, and I didn't want the parents to think that the school wasn't talking in one voice, so I met with them. They were a very nice, educated couple. They didn't come to complain about the expulsion. They came to persuade me to change the reason for the expulsion from an offense against the purity of arms code. For them this was a label they couldn't live with. I explained again my line of logic and hoped they understood.

The cadet was dismissed, and due to the circumstances I said I would allow him to return to the school in the future, if he wanted, for a second course. He said that due to the reason behind his expulsion he did not believe he would return. I told him that no one was forced to become an officer.

I saw him less than a year later. He was back at Bahad 1, attending a lecture in one of the school's halls.

A Parent's Right Not to Know

Here is another story that demonstrates the many problems parents can cause by interfering with military issues. This time the problems had a smaller impact on the army's daily conduct but a greater impact on the parents' peace of mind.

One day, a cadet was brought before me. He was accused of forging the guards' list of the previous night out of vengeance; he wanted another cadet to be awakened for guard duty instead of him. The poor cadet was very unhappy when he was awakened in the middle of the night, but nevertheless he finished his unexpected duty. The next morning he complained to his commanders and gave them the name of the cadet who, he said, was definitely the forger.

The suspected cadet was brought before the assessment committee. He did not admit that he was the person behind the forgery, so I asked him to write the other soldier's name. He wrote the name, and I noticed that two of the letters looked quite similar to the letters on the guards' list. I said to him that I could see a similarity in certain letters and pointed them out.

"Please write the name a few more times."

He did as I asked, but being certain that I wanted to examine the two letters I claimed were similar, he concentrated his efforts on those two. I was observing different letters altogether and saw that the writing was exactly the same.

I then told the cadet that in my opinion he was a liar. I explained to him that since he had lied to me he could not be an officer. I usually did my best to refrain from labeling cadets who appeared before the committee as liars even if I caught them lying. Only when a cadet insisted and stuck to his lie did I call him a liar. When they quickly confessed to their actions I expelled them with the right to return to the school in a year. Many people lie from time to time, but if you told a lie in Bahad 1 and didn't confess, you were a liar to me.

I told the cadet that he was suspended from the school for twenty-five years. For judicial and administrative reasons, the commanders of Bahad 1 were not allowed to suspend a cadet forever. We had to limit the suspension within a time frame.

A few hours after this unpleasant incident I was phoned by the head of the IDF's Human Resources Directorate, Major General Yoram "Ya-Ya" Yair, who asked why I had dismissed the cadet. Every dismissal that occurs in the last two weeks of the course requires the approval of a general. In this case, Yair's signature was required.

I told Yair that the cadet was expelled for lying. Yair said, "But he doesn't admit that he did it." I explained that I had compared the handwriting and was certain it was his. He said, "How can you expel him when you don't have decisive proof?" I asked him what he meant by decisive proof, and he answered, "The military police."

I was surprised. I asked if he himself, when he was commander of the school, ever used the military police in such cases. I found it hard to believe that they would bother to investigate such a trifling matter. "I am also the commander of the military police," he said, "and I'll make sure that they give it their quickest treatment."

"And what if they do not finish the investigation in time?" I asked.

"You will give him the officer pin, and if we later find out that he forged the list, I will be responsible to take it back from him," he said.

Military policemen came to the school and questioned the cadet. He said he didn't do it. They took several examples of his handwriting and sent them to a laboratory in Jerusalem for comparison. We waited for the results. In the meantime I found out why Yair intervened in the incident in the first place. Apparently, the cadet's father was a senior officer in the manpower division. He came to Yair and said, "I know my son is not a liar."

After two weeks, the results of the comparison arrived and the military police summoned the cadet, who had in the interim received his officer pin. When they confronted him with the results, he admitted he was the original writer.

I summoned the soldier back to Bahad 1 and assembled the assessment committee with exactly the same officers who had taken part in the earlier session. I said to the cadet that I had no intention of making him go through a rank stripping like in the Dreyfus Affair, but I wanted him to return his officer's pin. He took off the pin without saying a word and handed it to me.

Before he left I asked him: "What does your father say now?" He said he didn't know. I asked him what he meant, and he said that his father hasn't spoken with him since he learned that he lied.

I called Yair and said to him: "Instead of the original situation under which the father thought I falsely blamed his son, he now has gained a son with a liar's certificate. I will not remain the boy's commander forever, but he will always be the boy's father."

I think that the lesson that should be learned from this anecdote is that there are limits to the things we should know about our children. We don't have to know how our child behaves when he is under enormous pressure, like during military service. We, the commanders, must know. The parents' peace of mind will be greater if they don't know.

Selective Motivation and the Rabin Assassination

Two and a half weeks before graduation, a Golani infantry brigade cadet was brought before the assessment committee. According to his commanders he was very talented. The problem was that ever since he passed the last test of the course, he had lost all interest in becoming an officer and behaved accordingly.

When the cadet entered the room I immediately recognized him. Four months earlier another cadet had told me about him with generous words of praise. He told me that the cadet – his name was Arik – had helped him throughout the course. In those days, my family lived in nearby Mitzpe Ramon and I used to come to the base and stroll around on Fridays and Saturdays. I remembered coming on Friday and spotting a cadet with a brown Golani beret on his head a little off mark. I called him over, fixed his beret, and asked for his name. He said Arik, and I remembered that he was the one whom the other cadet had told me about.

Now, four months later, he stood before the committee. This is the place to explain that Bahad 1 works in the following way: if a platoon commander wants to expel a cadet, he tells the company commander, who then holds a discussion about the cadet with the staff; only after he is convinced that the cadet should not become an officer does he take the case to the battalion commander. On the other hand, if the company commander doesn't agree with the platoon commander, the platoon commander still has the option of taking the case to the battalion commander, and if he disagrees, the platoon commander can then take his case to the commander of the school.

This cadet was brought to me after everyone except for his platoon commander had opposed the expulsion. The company commander, the battalion commander, and the psychologist said that though the cadet had stopped investing in the course, he was extremely talented and should graduate.

I hesitated for a long time. After all, I had also had a positive impression of Arik. At last I made up my mind, wrote in his file that he suffered from "selective motivation," and could not be an officer. He left the school.

Two months later, Prime Minister Yitzhak Rabin was assassinated. The school staff was called to secure the funeral and man the honor guard. On Wednesday after the funeral, the graduation ceremony was held at the school and Chief of Staff Lt. General Amnon Lipkin-Shahak came.

He entered my office at 11 a.m. and asked, "Stern, did the police pick up one of your cadets last night?" I said that as far as I knew all my cadets were still on the base. He asked his assistant to check with the military police. By the time the assistant returned, we were already on the ceremony plaza and I was standing a bit away. I could tell that the chief of staff was not interested in telling me what his assistant had discovered.

On Saturday night, I found out that the police had arrested a soldier whose father was a dentist and who lived in Bnei Brak, and who was suspected of belonging to a Jewish underground, for being in possession of explosive materials.

I immediately knew that this was the cadet that the chief of staff had asked me about earlier in the week. I also knew that he wasn't a cadet in the school at the time of his arrest, but a cadet who had been suspended and had yet to be reassigned within the IDF. I asked to receive all the lists of suspended cadets in the last three months who live in Bnei Brak and the immediate vicinity.

Leafing through the list I bumped into the name of the cadet I had suspended for selective motivation.

Two hours later I received visits from the battalion commander and the psychologist. Each in his turn came to salute me. This soldier was never brought to court even though the prime minister's Jewish assassin Yigal Amir confessed during his trial that he had received a demolition block from him. We were so close to a situation in which we could see headlines screaming: "IDF officer arrested in connection to prime minister's assassination."

The Suspensions That Never Were

After I was appointed the IDF chief education officer, I came one day to Bahad 1 to deliver a lecture to the staff and cadets. During the question period, one of the deputy company commanders stood up and said, "We hear many stories about the time you were commander of the school, and we would like to know if they are true." I said tell me the stories and I will say which are true and which are false.

He chose this story: "One evening, before the cadets' graduation, you called a final meeting of all the cadets and told them that if someone cheated in a land navigation mission (when soldiers go out in pairs) he should confess now, and you promised not to do anything to him."

According to the story, eight cadets raised their hands. I told them to sit down, and then I asked them who their partners were on the mission, and I told them to stand up. I asked the partners to collect their personal belongings and wait in my office. According to the story, all of the eight partners were expelled from the school for not reporting on the cheating cadets.

I said that I did not recall such an incident, and I believed that it never happened. I admitted though that the story did fit the spirit of the school in my time and that I regret that I never thought of this trick back when I was the commander.

MARRYING A COMBAT SOLDIER

Another story, this time a true one, was distorted over the years, and can be found even today on certain news Internet sites. According to the story, I had told my daughter that she could only marry a combat soldier.

Here is what really happened:

One day, I was asked by cadets whether the rumors that I gave non-combat cadets more guard duty and other menial tasks than the combat cadets were true or false. I explained to them that the opposite was more accurate because it contradicted my basic belief that an officer is an officer is an officer.

I told them that since they asked me I would say as follows: I don't know if my daughter will ever come to ask my advice regarding who she should marry but that if she did ask me about two boys who were exactly the same except one was a combat soldier and the other was a non-combat soldier, I suppose you can guess what my recommendation would be.

Human beings are never similar and the subject was completely theoretical. I only meant to pass on a message that anyone who *can* be a combat soldier *should* be a combat soldier unless we – the IDF – decide differently.

Still today, I come across people who were insulted by what I said.

One Friday night in 1996, while we were still living in Mitzpe Ramon, I came out from Shabbat prayer services and saw a soldier in air force uniform. I invited him to have dinner at our house, and he thanked me and said he was already invited by someone else. I asked him who invited him and he pointed at Yashka, otherwise known as Yishai Sar-Shalom, an officer on the staff of Bahad 1. Yashka, who was a little embarrassed, told the soldier that he should feel free to go with me.

On our way home the soldier told me that he served in a radar-control base near Bahad 1. He asked me what I did, and I said I would tell him later. I didn't want to scare him; I thought that if I told him who I was he might wish he hadn't switched dinner invitations. He asked if I was one of the operation officers, and I said that I was something like that.

When we sat down at the Shabbat table the soldier said he noticed our name on the front door resembled the name of the Bahad 1's commander and asked if I was his relative. I said I was sort of a relative. He asked, "Are you his brother?"

I nodded indecisively. By now my children were trying to hide under the table not to laugh. The soldier saw that the kids were laughing; he pressed on. "Nu...*are* you his brother?"

I replied, "Sort of."

The baffled soldier regained his composure and said, "You *are* Elazar Stern, aren't you?"

I confessed and saw that he was now a little scared. He now raised his voice and said, "But, I didn't see a Daihatsu Applause in the parking space in front of the house," the car that IDF colonels were allotted back then.

"We have a parking spot in the back," I said.

The soldier stood up, pointed his finger at my fourteen-year-old Liron, and said, "Hold it a second, so I can't marry her?"

So why do I tell this story? This young soldier never heard me speak, wasn't an officer, didn't serve in the school, didn't even know what I looked like. But, he had heard the story about my not allowing my daughter to marry a non-combat soldier. I learned from this trivial incident a lot about the significance of things you say and how they can easily get distorted. I also learned something about mass media. I know people were offended by certain statements attributed to me. I hated offending people, and I am sorry this happened. But I certainly do not regret the basic message that got through.

In Praise of Chutzpa

When I was a young company commander in the Paratroopers Brigade, I was often blamed for teaching my soldiers to be overly critical, on the edge of insolence. People told, as an example, that one of my soldiers asked his commander in a weekly discussion why the company staff entered the mess before their soldiers did.

I told my critics that I was proud that the soldier considered such conduct to be irregular. I knew that we had succeeded in impressing him with the importance of a commander's duty toward his subordinates. I knew that the soldier who asked the question would never eat before his subordinates did.

In later years, in one of my conversations with cadets at Bahad 1 about the ideal form of an officer, I told them a true story about my good friend and neighbor Binny Shalev, who was planning a trip to the United States and asked me if I would like him to buy me a cheap video camera. I agreed but insisted that he declare the camera at customs upon his return.

When Binny returned he brought me two receipts, one for $599.99, the price of the camera, and the other for double that amount from Israeli customs. I confessed to the cadets that if I wasn't an officer, I'm not sure I would have insisted that he declare the camera.

One of the cadets raised his hand and asked me, "Sir, don't you think this is hypocrisy?"

The staff that sat in the hall's front rows turned around to look at the cadet who had the chutzpa to ask such a question. They were certain that he was about to be expelled from the school. I asked the staff to turn back around. First of all, I said, I thought it was a good question, and I was only afraid that maybe I wouldn't have a good answer. Second, we have to encourage cadets to ask difficult questions, otherwise a cadet will put up an artificial figure of himself when he arrives at the school. This figure will train, it will nod its head when asked questions and laugh when we tell lousy jokes, but will refrain from asking difficult or unpleasant questions and certainly would never criticize anything or anyone.

At graduation, the cadets will throw their berets up to the sky, leave the school and their artificial figures behind, and return to their units the way they left them.

A place that does not accept criticism is a place that cannot educate or help someone advance. The cadet's development as an officer will only be in his head – and not in his heart – and that success will only hold until it is put to its first test.

The Compass and the North

Whenever people asked me, "When did you realize that you wanted to become the head of the IDF's Human Resources Directorate," I recalled the following episode:

I was still commander of Bahad 1. The media had published that there were two candidates to become head of the Human Resources Directorate: Doron Almog, a former paratrooper, and Gideon Shefer, a former pilot. A story was circulating in the media accusing Shefer of paving a road from his home directly to the air force base he commanded. While it appeared that he had misused his authority, his version was that his action was due to military operational considerations to enable him to participate in a specific mission. One of the cadets asked me how I could speak about integrity when this high-ranking officer did what he did.

I couldn't be angry with the cadet. I knew that a day earlier the chief of staff was asked the same question by colonels who attended the IDF's Staff and Command College.

The following day, the chief of staff visited the school. When I was alone with him in my office, I said to him, "Sir, it might seem strange to you, but I would like to say something about the nomination of the next head of Human Resources Directorate."

Lipkin-Shahak, with his dry humor, asked me immediately, "Stern, do you want to be the head of Human Resources Directorate?"

"I never gave it any thought," I answered. "I never thought that I would remain in the military for so long. But if you are really asking me and I'll still be a soldier, then my answer is yes. I want more than anything else to be head of the Human Resources Directorate."

After saying that I said I wanted to talk about the two candidates. I said that he probably knew that Doron Almog was my commander and a very good friend of mine. I think very highly of him and believed he would make an excellent head of Human Resources Directorate.

"I don't know much about Gideon Shefer," I said, "but from what I know, he is a good man. If he is not nominated because of that road he paved, all of us are absolute hypocrites."

Amnon looked at me surprised, maybe because he expected me to take the opposite stance.

"I understand what you are saying. Let me tell you something," he said. "From the moment I was informed that I was going to be nominated chief of staff until I actually started the assignment, I had plenty of time. I used this time to meet many different people and get their advice, including Chief Justice of the Supreme Court Meir Shamgar, who told me that even the court must be attentive to the voice of the masses, and if the court has to, the army certainly does."

I said I thought the same way, but that the voices of the masses were not necessarily the voices one hears in the media. To make my opinion completely clear to the chief of staff, I told him the following story:

At the beginning of the nineteenth century, there was a Jew by the name of Sheler who had converted to Christianity in the city of Cologne in Germany. One day, the local Cardinal called him to his office and said, "People have reported to me that you were seen hanging around various houses of ill-repute in the city. Since you are a man that has great influence over the young, I beseech you to avoid those places."

The converted Jew responded, "Cardinal, I think you do not understand. I am the compass, not the North."

I finished the story and said to the chief of staff, "I demand from my cadets that they be both – the compass and the North. But I tell them no one can really be the North; we can only aspire to get near it by moving in the areas to the Northeast or the Northwest.

What we can't afford is to move to the East and the West altogether. What Shefer did might not be exactly to the North, but it is in the range, a place many of us often find ourselves. If we do not nominate him because of this story, it will be hypocritical."

Shefer was appointed to the post, and during his term I had several bitter arguments with him, especially surrounding the IDF Code of Ethics that was composed at the time under the supervision of Professor Assa Kasher. I never told Shefer about the conversation with Lipkin-Shahak. If I had told him, I would have considered myself to be making an attempt at a very low sort of flattery.

When Shefer had almost finished his term, two years after I had left Bahad 1, he suddenly told me, "Stern, I have to tell you something. Immediately after your conversation with the chief of staff, he called me and told me everything you said to him."

"I didn't know you then," I told him, "and my appreciation for you was because of things that I had heard about you. Now I appreciate you even more for the fact that you did not say a word about this for all those years."

Fear of Justice

There are times when the compass arrow flaps nervously far away from the North, even when high-ranking IDF officers are involved. Toward the end of my term as commander of Battalion 202, after we had completed a brigade-level exercise, I was summoned to a meeting of Paratroopers Brigade commanders one Friday morning. By the time it was over, it was getting really late and close to the beginning of Shabbat. I informed Saul Mofaz, our brigade commander at the time, that I planned to race home to make it there in time.

As I passed Netanya, I spotted a policeman and a military policewoman standing on the shoulder, making hysterical movements with their hands in my direction. The military policewoman informed me that I was way over the legally permitted speed – by about 30 kilometers per hour (20 miles per hour) – and she asked me to give her my drivers' license. I replied that I was in a hurry and couldn't allow myself to be delayed right now, and that if she wanted, she should just copy my plate number. She couldn't believe what I had said and repeated her demand. I said that I had understood her the first time and advised her to quickly copy my plate number, otherwise she wouldn't have this either. She opened her mouth to say something but I was already on my way.

Three weeks later my deputy came into my office and said that a speeding ticket had arrived from the military police. He asked me if I knew who was driving the car at the time, and I replied that I had been behind the wheel. He was slightly surprised and said, "I understand, but who should I write was the driver in the response I am drafting? Thirty kilometers per hour over the speed limit is not a simple matter."

My answer didn't surprise him.

A few weeks later I was summoned to military police HQ to be investigated about the speeding offense. I replied that a battalion commander's schedule is extremely tight and since I had confessed to the offense, there was no need for questioning whatsoever and they should summon me directly to the court hearing.

Two weeks later, I was already on leave and I received another summons for a second round of questioning. I sent them back the same answer I had given the last time.

The third summons arrived when I had already been discharged and my reply remained the same. I received calls from the head of the IDF's Human Resources Directorate at the time, Major General Matan Vilnai, pressing me to appear for the questioning, but by then I was a civilian so I managed to hold up under the pressure and asked once again to be summoned directly to the court hearing.

Two months later, I was perched on a bench in one of the halls of the military court in Tel Aviv. Beside me sat waiting a number of colonels. Judge Nili Peled, famous for her harsh verdicts, heard the cases. I sat patiently and was shocked by what I heard. I was the only guilty person in the hall. Not even one of the officers that were sentenced before me confessed to the charges brought against them. They all claimed that the military policemen, kids who filled out their reports and now were testifying against them, were shameless liars. They each said to the face of those young soldiers, "You are a liar!" Of course the military police soldiers insisted that their reports were genuine, but I sat there slumped in my chair with each officer's denial.

My turn arrived and I stood up. The judge stated my alleged offense: "...33 kilometers over the legal speed... Do you confess or not?"

"I confess," I replied.

The courtroom turned silent. The judge continued and asked me if I had something to say for myself.

I replied that I had nothing to say except that I had known for quite some time that being a religious battalion commander and living in the Galilee was going to cost me, and that I was there to see how much the bill would be.

I got a fine and a suspended sentence, which meant that if I was caught again my license would be revoked. I stepped down from the stand both smiling and ashamed. I was ashamed because of the behavior of those officers I saw in court who denied the charges, but more than that, denied their position – our position – as IDF officers.

Of Shoes and Belts

I once asked the cadets at Bahad 1 my regular question: "Do you know any order that is irrational?"

A cadet stood up and asked me, what was the reason behind the order to buckle your belt from right to left?

I was speechless. I didn't even know that such an order existed. I summoned all my neurons for a consultation and recalled that when I was a teacher and faced a similar dilemma, I had only two options for situations like this one. The first was to tell the cadet I would check into it and return to him later with an answer. The second was to turn the question over to the rest of the cadets. I chose the second road with the hope that one of the cadets would come up with a decent answer. One of the cadets, a paramedic by training, told us that in the paramedics' course they learned the reason behind the order. Apparently, when a paramedic has to give treatment to someone wounded, especially in a dark place, it's important that he be able to unbuckle the wounded person's belt as fast as possible.

I confessed to the cadets that I hadn't had the slightest clue before the cadet answered for me. Then I told them that, assuming the answer is correct, someone unbuckling a belt in an emergency can do it by instinct as a result of the military regulation.

I told the cadets that three hours earlier I had attended a farewell lunch in honor of David and Yitzchak, two civilians who worked at the school mess for more then twenty years. I had two items, a gift and a certificate, to hand to each of the two retiring civilians. In the intimate ceremony we arranged, I turned to David and gave him the certificate, then I turned to Yitzchak and handed him both the certificate and the gift, and finally I turned again to David and gave him the gift.

I asked the cadets why I did it this way. After three wrong answers, a cadet stood up and said: "You did it this way because you didn't want to hurt anyone's pride." That was the right answer. David was the first to receive one gift, but Yitzchak was the first to finish receiving both gifts, so each received the same measure of honor.

I told the cadets that I thought of this tactic through tying my shoes, something I learned from the Talmud. It is written that a man should put on his shoes in the following manner: first the right shoe without tying the laces and then the left shoe with tying the laces. Afterward, he should tie the right shoe. There are several explanations for those detailed instructions but I, as a child, thought that the correct explanation was that one shouldn't prefer one of the shoes over the other. When I handed the certificates and the gifts to David and Yitzchak, I realized that my manners came from my shoes.

I told the cadets that in the Bible, when Moses was ordered to perform the first three plagues against Egypt, he was told to let his brother do all the necessary acts. The other seven plagues Moses was ordered to perform all by himself. The explanation given was that Moses could not perform the first three plagues because he himself was saved by the water of the river, so it wouldn't be "right" if he would now turn the water into blood or fill it with frogs. When Moses killed one of the Egyptian guards as a youngster, the sand covered the dead corpse and saved Moses again, so it would not have been right for him to change the same sand into lice. Such actions would have been a sin against the gratitude he owed the water and sand.

I asked the cadets: Does the sand remember? Does the water have feelings? Naturally they do not. I trust that all those wise scholars didn't believe otherwise. I think that commanding Moses in this way was designed to insert into him and into those who will read the book thousands of years later the immense importance of gratitude. In the same way, my shoes could never feel the insult I avoided, but I became a little more sensitive to insults, and thanks to that I knew how to behave toward David and Yitzchak.

Now I returned to belt buckling. I explained to the cadets that though it might be true that it is faster to unbuckle your belt instinctively, teaching that fact in the paramedic's course is probably designed to emphasize another point – that this is an army that puts human life above all and for that reason everything that is associated with saving lives must be arranged to the last and smallest details. This buckling standardization is also a lesson in discipline. When you are in the army you have to accept orders even when you don't recognize the logic in them. This way a norm of obedience is created and discipline is inserted into the soldiers' lives.

And rules that have their beginning in things such as shoes and belt buckling can be implemented to every field in life – for better and for worse. A commander who abuses his subordinates will end up abusing his friends or children. Somehow, somewhere, abuse was implanted in him. This is a danger faced by every soldier who serves at a checkpoint in the West Bank or has to search Palestinian homes during operations in the dead of the night. Behaving in a disrespectful and humiliating way endangers the soldier's soul and affects the soldier's behavior in other incidents as well.

This is the major lesson I took with me from my term at Bahad 1. I can only hope that my cadets took this with them as well.

Chapter 5

Witnesses in Uniform

The most significant project I initiated when I was commander of Bahad 1 was Witnesses in Uniform, which consisted of sending delegations of IDF officers and soldiers to Nazi concentration and death camps in Poland.

I am the son of Holocaust survivors, and most of our family was annihilated in the Holocaust. I don't need Israeli rock singer Yehuda Poliker to remind me that "a good boy leaves an empty plate." In my house, nothing was thrown away, or to be more accurate, no one was allowed to throw anything away. From my early childhood my mother told me stories about my grandmother who died in the Holocaust at Auschwitz along with four of her six children, and about my grandfather, who jumped from the train and after the war used to go every day to the Jewish information bureau to see if maybe his wife or kids had survived.

Our house existed in the present and the past. Every time someone slammed a door between two and four in the afternoon, the daily siesta, my mother would jump and mentally go back in time to Auschwitz. On the other hand, both my parents wanted with all their hearts to raise us like all Sabras – children born in Israel – free from the trauma they endured. As a result, they allowed me to go to all of the Bnei Akiva events and summer camps. But if I returned home ten minutes late, I knew I would find my mother waiting on the street below. Now, go try and impress a young female Bnei Akiva member with whom you are walking home at 9:30 at night when you see your mother waiting for you outside in her robe.

I call it a "robe" only out of respect for her. Once I invited my parents to hear me lecture to one of the delegations before they left for Poland. I only asked mother that if she had something to say to wait until after I finished the lecture. The delegation consisted of company and battalion commanders. When I told about my worried mother waiting for me on the street in her pajamas, my mother's voice rang out from the front row of the hall: "Not pajamas, Eli, it was a robe!"

Mother and father sat in the front row. In the back of the hall sat one of the members of the delegation – Ilan, my son and their grandson.

HISTORY'S EXPERIENCE

The idea of sending delegations of soldiers to Poland came to me during a private journey I made there with my parents in 1991. Our first stop was Auschwitz. A journey to discover our roots in Auschwitz? Are there any roots in Auschwitz?

"Auschwitz 1" is a well-kept place with a museum that holds several drafts of resolutions passed during the Wannsee Conference in 1942, where the "Final Solution" was approved. In the document, there is an explanation for the Final Solution that goes like this: "Those remaining will have to be given suitable treatment because they unquestionably represent the most resistant segments, and therefore constitute a natural elite that, if allowed to go free, would serve as a nucleus for a renewed Jewish entity."

I came there dressed in civilian cloths, yet the phrase "renewed Jewish entity" moved me because I am a soldier. A strong military force is not only a necessity for, but a symbol of building a national entity. In military courses, we teach how important persistence is in achieving one's goals. But the goals become valid only when they serve a larger purpose. The Nazis' mission was to exterminate every Jew they could put their hands on, but their purpose behind this mission was to prevent forever the possibility of a strong Jewish entity, a purpose that failed completely. I don't want to suggest that we won after we lost six million lives, but I can say very confidently that the Nazis did not win.

From Auschwitz 1, we drove several kilometers and came to Birkenau. My mother always wanted to show me the specific shack in which she slept during the war. I really don't know why.

All those years she used to tell me she was in *Lager* C, Block 21, so I told her I would go with her.

When we got to the gate of *Lager* C, my mother couldn't recognize the place. There were very few blocks still standing, and my mother said with frustration, "Listen, it doesn't look like I remember it. I don't know this place."

I calmed her and said, "Don't worry, Mother. We have a map here, and if it is land navigation that is required, I should be able to bring you to the right place."

I studied the map and we went on our way. We crossed some rail tracks and reached a train's ramp. When we stood on that ramp, my mother told me once again a story I had heard many times before:

My mother had arrived at Birkenau late at night after a journey that took several days. When the train stopped, the cattle car's doors opened and they heard shouts. They wanted only to breathe the fresh air. There were some who didn't make it out of the cattle cars, for they had died during the journey. My mother and grandmother came out, each holding one of my mother's young sisters, who were twins. On the platform stood Josef Mengele, who grabbed the twin my mother held and wanted to also take the other one. My grandmother resisted and fought with him. There were some Jews who stood there and asked my grandmother why she was even bothering. "Why argue," they asked. "It doesn't make a difference anymore."

She didn't understand yet what was this place was, or maybe she didn't want to understand. Maybe those were motherly instincts that made her do what she did. Finally Mengele allowed her to go with the twins. That was the last time my mother saw any of them.

We passed several barbed-wire fences and entered *Lager* C. My mother told me how her aunt Bella threw her a slice of bread over those fences. We passed the latrines, an open shed with thirty holes in the floor and with no separation between them, and my mother described the embarrassment of being there with all of those other women.

Finally, we saw before us the cement floors of the blocks. We counted and found number 21. We looked around. All that was left of Block 21 was the cement floor, a chimney, and a few remains of the heating system. After that we went to the crematoriums. My father said Kaddish for the souls of our family members who perished there. This was the first time in my life that I witnessed my father choke, even if he didn't shed tears.

On our way out we passed the male camp, which still had some standing buildings. We stood at the camp's gate, and my mother asked me if I wanted to see the interior of a block. I said that I did, but my father said he couldn't suffer seeing anymore. "If you want to see the camp," he said, "you will have to go without me." I was shocked. All those years I had always considered my father the stronger one. How did I come to think that? My mother was always the one to talk and complain about the Holocaust, and he never mentioned his experiences. Only later, I learned that silence was not always evidence of strength.

My mother and I entered one of the blocks. Inside we saw a group of German kids led by a Polish tour guide. I stood by the wall, preparing my camera, while my mother entered and approached the group, listening to what the guide was telling them in German about the place. I understood some words he used, because I speak Yiddish, but my mother understood everything. Suddenly I heard her say to the tour guide: "Excuse me, but it wasn't exactly the way you described...."

The guide looked at my mother scornfully and said, "How do you know? Were you here?"

My mother answered him, "I will tell you in a moment, but first look over there," she said, pointing at me. "He is my son. He came with me from Israel and now, let me answer your question. Yes, I was here. I can tell you exactly what happened here, but before I do, there is one more thing you should know. Once I finish the tale, he and I are returning to Israel."

And she went on and told him about life in the block and the camp. When she finished and we left the building, the German youth group followed us out, begging my mother to tell them some more. She told them willingly. Maybe for her, telling them – German kids – provided her some relief, but I wasn't listening anymore. My mind was busy with the Wannsee conference resolutions and my mother's victorious return to the extermination camp. That was the moment when I suddenly realized the potential impact of visits of military delegations dressed in IDF uniforms to these hellish camps.

The Chief of Staff Would Like to Speak with You

I accompanied the first delegation of Witnesses in Uniform on their tour to the extermination camps in Poland. When the chief of staff at the time, Moshe "Bogie" Ya'alon, took one of the delegations, he asked me to join him. I didn't really want to go; the experience was very hard for me, and I always thought that if there was a vacancy, someone who had never been there should go. In the end, though, I accompanied the chief of staff. When we arrived at Birkenau, Ya'alon said to me: "Come on, Stern, let's go to your mother's block, but this time I will navigate" (I had told him the story of my previous visit).

We stood in *Lager* C, Block 21, and I told the officers my personal story from that place. While I spoke, Colonel Alush Noy, one of the few IDF officers to receive the highest medal of honor, stopped me, gave me his cellular telephone, and said to me, "Stern, call your mother."

I called her. My mother asked in a worried voice: "Eli, where are you?"

I said, "Mother, I am at *Lager* C, Block 21."

She was silent for a few seconds and then she said: "I don't believe it...I don't believe it...."

I said, "Mother, hold a second, the IDF chief of staff would like to speak with you."

To be in this hellish place, Auschwitz, *Lager* C, Block 21, the place my mother survived, and from there to let her speak with Israel's chief of staff, was a feeling larger than any words can describe. What did I feel at that moment? Victory? Revenge? I can't say.

A Sandbox and Application Forms

Every lecture of mine before the Witnesses in Uniform groups always began with the same question: "Why do we go there?"

I think there are many answers – maybe as many as the faces I see in front of me when I stand and deliver the lectures. I think that after I finish speaking, each of the delegates finds his or her own personal answer to this question. I tell them that one of the reasons has to do with the fact that when they will return, they will understand why they have to remain in the military. "When you return," I say to them, "and you get off the plane, you will see to your left a stand where you can sign an application to remain in service, and on your right you will see a sandbox. The sandbox is there because you will have a strong urge to kiss the soil of our land with gratitude, and it's practically impossible to find soil in the airport. All is covered with asphalt."

The way memories are blurred with time is one of the luckiest gifts given to humans. Were it not given to us, we would break down after each misfortune and never recuperate. On the other hand, if we look, for example, at the graduation ceremonies at Bahad 1 – when the cadets throw their berets to the sky, every single one of them is convinced that he will be the best officer with the highest set of values. Unfortunately, those sincere desires and wishes also tend to get blurred fairly quickly.

We go all the way to Poland, to understand better what it is that we defend here.

When the president visited the recruiting center in Tel Hashomer, he asked me how I explained the great motivation that the recruits appeared to have for joining elite combat units, and did I thank the ministry of education for that?

I answered, "Yes," took a deep breath and added, "the Palestinian Ministry of Education!"

I also said on the same occasion that since we always pray for peace and – who knows? – maybe one day our prayers will be answered, we should consider very seriously what we will do then. How will we deal with the recruits' motivation when the Palestinian Ministry of Education will stop working for us, when we most probably will still need a strong army even when we will have peace in the Middle East?

There is something upsetting in the fact that in order to increase our motivation, we need an outside intimidating force to come and frighten us. Here in the Middle East we require a strong army to survive. We will always need a strong army. We must be familiar with and proud of our Jewish identities, our tradition, and our culture. Why do we need Palestinian terror to build up our motivation? Why must we travel to Poland to understand that we should give more of ourselves? Why? I certainly don't have the answer! But when the officers return from their journey, the magic works!

Respect Returns

Before I report here how the Witnesses in Uniform delegations became what they are now, I want to say something about my father's silence. As I mentioned earlier, I remember as a child my mother telling her history at length and my father never mentioning the Holocaust. He began to speak about some of his experiences there only when I was already a company commander in the paratroopers. The hundreds of kilometers of the death marches, the dead horse meat they ate, the comrades who collapsed from fatigue and hunger, and the knowledge that there was nothing you could do.

I thought about my proud stories about our hikes in the paratroopers and felt ridiculous.

Delayed speaking is apparently a common phenomenon after such trauma. I sat on a panel of second-generation Holocaust survivors in 1983 with the writer Nava Semel, and we tried to figure out why our parents began to tell their stories after such a long time. I believe that it is partly because they fear that today, when their generation is old and dying, their personal stories will be forgotten and lost. You hear more today about Holocaust denial, and this might also have something to do with this sudden outburst of traumatic memories. Another reason might be the many stimulants one encounters on a daily basis – books, films, the journeys to Poland. Maybe the Holocaust's transformation into a central issue in our culture makes it easier for us to ask questions and for them to tell their stories.

And maybe it is because those silent survivors feel they don't need to defend us any longer. They did all they could to let us grow like normal proud Israelis, and now it is over: we are grownups and they don't need to protect us. They can now tell their stories freely.Their sense of self-esteem has finally been restored.

Writer Lizi Doron wrote about her mother, who used to introduce herself to people with the words: "Martha – a lamb to the slaughter." What must go on inside the head of an intelligent woman to drive her to present herself with such gruesome words?

When Holocaust survivors began to arrive in Israel, the Jews already there looked upon them with ignorant contempt. The old timers presented to the outer world the image of aggressive men who could take care of themselves, while the arriving refugees were those who "let" the Germans do to them all those horrible things without fighting back. Years have passed and the survivors' children became engineers, physicians, officers, educators, and actors – full partners in the economic, social, and technological miracle that the State of Israel became. The survivors' self-esteem healed. They once again began to believe in themselves. They regained their pride and their self-confidence, and now they are ready to tell their stories.

The First Delegation

Soon after my mother and I came out of the building in Birkenau, I received a phone call from Itzik Mordechai, then the commander of the Northern Command, who said to me: "Stern, I just left a nominations debate at the General Staff Headquarters, and we agreed to nominate you brigade commander of the Northern Paratroopers Reserves Brigade. Congratulations."

"But sir," I replied, "I asked to be assigned to an armored brigade."

"Hush, don't let anyone hear you," he silenced me. "This is the last time that you ever mention that."

I continued my journey with my parents. We arrived in the small town where my father grew up. He started to point out places to me and my mother. This was the synagogue, today it is a cardboard factory. This here was the bakery… and then he pointed toward a house and said, "Here, this was our house!"

I asked him to show me inside, but he refused to enter the yard. To my question why, he replied that he didn't want the people that live there now to fear that he had come back to claim his property. We stood on the pavement outside the house and my father was describing to us how it looked in those days and where in the family's soda water plant used to be, when all of a sudden a sixty-year-old man on an old bicycle passed us, stopped less than half a meter from my father, and gazed intensely at him for a few minutes. "Stern?" he finally asked.

I don't really know how he could recognize my father after all those years. Maybe he did recognize his face, or maybe he guessed because we stood in front of the Stern's house. More significant was the fact that if until that moment all the stories and the sights were somewhat abstract to me, suddenly I truly comprehended that it really did happen!

When I returned to Israel a couple of days later, I was already assigned to the Northern Command. Two weeks later, the command organized a commanders' get-together in Kibbutz Lohamei-Hagetaot (Ghetto Fighters' House) to commemorate the approaching Holocaust Memorial Day. I met there with retired General

Amiram Levin and told him I had just come back from a trip to Poland and the camps.

"I want to ask your opinion on a certain issue," I said to him. "Your opinion is very important to me because unlike me you are a son of the kibbutz, with no direct family contact to the Holocaust. Tell me if I'm right or wrong – should we send regular delegations of soldiers in uniform to the death camps?"

"We should," he said. "You are absolutely right!"

I wrote a letter to General Ehud Barak, chief of staff at the time, and explained to him why we should go to the camps dressed in uniform. Barak answered something like: That is a good idea."

I asked myself: "Okay...so what am I supposed to do with this answer?"

I was a commander of a reserve brigade with a barely workable budget, and I served in another position where I was in charge of infantry doctrine, but also there without a significant budget. I could do practically nothing with the "good idea" line.

Time passed. I became commander of Bahad 1 and wrote the same letter to the new chief of staff General Amnon Lipkin-Shahak. He responded with the same, practically worthless, "good idea" response, but now I controlled a substantially larger budget. At last I could see it through.

I decided that for the time being I would send one delegation and see how it went. I knew that it wouldn't be wise to send exclusively cadets from the school, so I turned to all other places that train officers, including the Air Force Pilot School and Navy's Officer School, and together we prepared the list of participants for the first delegation.

I didn't put myself on the list. I demanded to pay out of my own pockets all my expenses down to the last penny, and so I did. I know where I live. I didn't want someone to say that I conducted a correspondence with two consecutive chiefs of staff just to arrange for myself a trip abroad. The officer who handled the logistics, Colonel Shosh, tried to convince me to ignore those people and participate in the delegation like all the others. When she realized I would not change my mind, she told me that in that case I would have to be considered on leave, and could not serve as commander of the delegation. I requested to be allowed to wear uniform, and when that was granted to me, I nominated one of my battalion commanders from Bahad 1 as delegation commander. He accepted the nomination as an honor and a privilege.

The delegation arrived in Poland. Today everything is organized, but this was the first group and nothing was prepared. The Poles didn't permit us to travel all across Poland dressed in uniform. Finally we agreed with them that the touring would be done in regular clothes, and we would change and put on our uniforms for three ceremonies. So, before every ceremony the males would go and change in the buses and when they finished, it would be the females' turn. When the ceremony was finished, they had to go back to the buses and put their civilian clothes back on.

Today, there are over twenty delegations every year that tour all of Poland in uniform and with raised Israel flags.

Four of my five kids finished high school and went with their classes to Poland. Such a trip costs about $1,200. When my eldest daughter went, she declared: "I will not buy anything, not even a soft drink, because I don't want them to have any profit from my visit to the camps." I didn't ask my other kids about it because I didn't want them to think that I expected them to act accordingly. I bought soft drinks from the Poles, so nobody should attribute any hidden intentions to me regarding this issue. In general, I think that our attitude toward the Poles should not ignore the fact that they welcome more then twenty delegations a year, delegations that travel around their state dressed in IDF uniforms and with large Israeli flags, knowing what our message is. I am quite certain the whole issue is quite difficult for them to swallow.

Was Your Grandfather There?

A year after the first delegation returned, we were ready to send the second one. I called General Yiftach Rontal, at the time commander of the 460th Armored Brigade. I told him the second delegation was ready to go and that I was happy he had offered to lead it. I summoned all my battalion commanders and asked them to choose their ten best cadets for the trip.

Two days later, two of them showed up in my office and said: "Sir, we have a problem."

"What's the problem?" I asked.

One of their best cadets was a Druze.

I asked again, "And the problem?"

"The other cadets say that if we are allowed to send only ten men on the delegation, then those who are closest to the issue should go," one of the commanders explained.

I asked, "What do you mean by closest?"

"Cadets whose grandfathers were there..." they mumbled in embarrassment.

"Ah," I said, "you are absolutely right! So get me the best ten but only European. Don't give me Yemenites or Persian or Iraqis. And if you find someone from Morocco or from Libya, find out first if Rommel and his colleagues stopped in his neighborhood."

I was very angry. I asked them why should we prefer to send cadets "whose grandfathers were there"? Wouldn't we be better choosing those who are less acquainted with the issue and whose participation would make them more aware?

And perhaps the purpose of this delegation is not to affect the cadets, feelings about the Holocaust; maybe the purpose is to make a statement by the mere fact that we stand there in our uniforms – "We are here!" meaning "We triumphed!"

And if this is the case, maybe a part of this victory is that we, unlike them, do not recognize any difference between those who came from Poland and those who came from Morocco. We don't see any difference between Jews, Druze, Christians, and Bedouin. This is the way we live and fight here and this is also the way we come over there. This will be the cement that will reinforce our statement: "We are here!"

After the discussion in my office, I made one rule clear: delegations of the Witnesses in Uniform are never all Jewish! There aren't many rules those delegations need to abide by but this is one.

The Druze village of Ussafiya was excited to learn that we had chosen one of their sons for our second delegation to Poland. The village elders asked in return to host the whole battalion. I answered that it wouldn't be practical to travel all the way there but that when the battalion moves to the Golan Heights for maneuvers, we could easily stop on our way in Ussafiya. We set the visit for a Sunday on our way to a week of maneuvers. On the Thursday prior to our visit, I received a phone call from the Military Rabbinate. They wanted to make sure that I had taken all the necessary steps to guarantee that the food served to the battalion would be kosher during the visit to the Druze village. For how could a battalion from Bahad 1 dine without settling this question?!

I said to the caller: "No, I didn't check; and no, I do not intend to check. And what's more, though I didn't plan to come with the battalion to the village, I will join them and eat the food myself!" I knew I would find there food I could eat.

I certainly expect the army mess and food to be kosher. I myself will never eat anything that isn't kosher. But I figured that if someone ate non-kosher food all his life, then here too he would eat non-kosher food. Someone who didn't, I thought, would know how to restrain himself once again. To me, the friendship with the Druze people, paying them the respect and honor they deserve, is far more important than blocking someone from eating non-kosher food.

We arrived as scheduled on Sunday. I wish I knew many Jews who offered hospitality to religious Jews with the same sensitivity as the Druze. There was nothing on the table that wasn't strictly kosher.

We go to Poland to learn that in order to live here together, everyone must learn to make small compromises. If it were not for those compromises, it would be possible that a commander on his way to Lebanon would think not to stop in Haifa or Hadera out of fear that one of his soldiers will eat something not kosher. Such conduct would create animosity and some soldiers would demand to serve under non-religious commanders. The evacuation of the Jewish settlements from the Gaza Strip in 2005 wasn't the first time that someone in our country or in the army was required to compromise his or her values. It happens every day in the army.

Each one of us comes with his or her load of values, and the complexity of our shared life in the military forces us to make compromises. Those compromises are much easier to make after returning from a trip to Poland.

The Most Moral Army in the World

The first delegation we sent to Poland was accompanied by a TV news reporter named Menashe Raz, who shot a documentary while there. He called it "The Generations After."

When the film was ready we were called to approve it. After the screening the IDF chief spokesman objected to only one issue in the film. The film showed a young lieutenant called Erez, the commander of a commando unit, who said that during the visit he couldn't help thinking about us and the Palestinians. The military spokesman said he was not ready to have this scene in the film. We asked him why, when apparently that's what the young lieutenant thinks. The spokesman objected firmly, and the film was screened with a minor change.

This issue came up again in our discussions in preparation for the second delegation's trip. The tour guides met with delegates from the first delegation and told us that there was some talk about the Israeli-Palestinian conflict. They thought that we should somehow explain to the new delegation that it's wrong to think about such things when you are in Poland, in the death camps.

It is common knowledge that the percentage of Jews among Nobel Prize winners (some 22 percent) is much higher than their part in the world population. I have an idea how to win another Nobel Prize. Look for the Jew who will invent something that will enable someone not to think about what they don't want to think about.

I must admit that until now I have failed. There are many things I'd rather not think about, but alas, I do. You can't visit the camps in Poland and block all your thoughts about us and the Palestinians, about what might happen to a nation when it is powerful, and where the boundaries should be drawn. I, at least, couldn't help but think about it.

I believe that we are the most moral army in the world, even if we discover from time to time moral faults, and even if sometimes these are extreme and grave. I think the reason we are so moral is because we have been to Poland's death camps and we remember being in Poland with our collective memory, with our national memory.

I believe that in each generation, a person must view himself as if he had survived one of those camps. To observe ourselves this way means not only when evaluating our statehood and independence but also in the way we treat the poor and the weak. That's why we shouldn't be overly worried if our soldiers think about our relationship with the Palestinians when they visit the camps. Actually, we should be proud of them.

With that said, we shouldn't get hysterical – as some people did – when we read an article about a Palestinian who was stopped at an IDF checkpoint carrying a violin case in his hand and was forced by the soldiers to take the violin out of its case and play it. The army's investigation into the incident proved that he was only forced to show the violin and not to play it, and yet Meir Shalev – a popular columnist – wrote an article in the weekend edition of Israel's largest newspaper, *Yediot Ahronot*, under the headline "The Violin Wins." I appreciate Meir Shalev's writing capabilities, though I appreciate slightly less his political convictions. He writes "The Violin Wins" in order to allude to the harps and violins that the Nazis made the Jews play. This is a low allusion.

Prof. Yehuda Bauer, the famous Holocaust researcher, speaks about how we have acquired a Holocaust terminology. Words like "train" or terms like "barbed wire" will forever hold only one connotation for us. Similarly, there are certain images that bring to mind the Holocaust, like a musician playing his violin in front of a group of soldiers in uniform.

But I think we shouldn't let those images confuse us, because if I were the commander of the checkpoint facing a thirty-year-old Palestinian with a violin in his hands, I would ask him to play his violin – not to satisfy my musical hunger, God forbid, but to make sure it is only a violin. We already witnessed incidents when terrorist groups tried to smuggle explosives on children's bodies and hidden in various tools and instruments with the hope that the soldiers would not search them.

Think about the United States to get some perspective. After the 9/11 attacks, inspections at the airports became extremely meticulous. Everyone who flies in the US knows that he has to take off his shoes and empty his pockets. On one of my flights I beeped even after I removed my belt and my watch. I was in Newark Airport in New Jersey, and I even removed my *kippa* because I thought maybe the pin that holds it to my hair was causing the beeping. But all was to no avail. I had to stand aside and was searched thoroughly with plastic gloves, had a magnetic wand waved across my body, was asked to spread my legs and hands, and all this was done before the observing eyes of the entire line of passengers. One of the passengers who recognized me asked, "Why don't you tell them who you are?"

"Why should my name make any difference?" I asked him. "This is their responsibility!"

On another domestic flight in the US, the security guard at the gate observed my passport and informed me jovially that I had been chosen. Any fantasy I began to nurture about what I was chosen for quickly died out when the guard told me I was going to have to go through a new procedure that includes smothering your hands and other parts of your body with a chemical so that the testing officer can see if you had contact with explosives.

I tell these stories to show that the Americans, after they were attacked, are not embarrassed to do everything it takes to ensure their security, and I guess they have every right to do so. Whoever wants to look upon their procedures as humiliating is welcome to do so, but the great majority understands the necessity of increased security.

But we Israelis, after we had buses explode just fifteen minutes before the checkpoint incident, are expected to be better? The man with the violin case could carry inside the case many more explosives than a passenger could hide inside his shoe or laptop computer, and still, every passenger who wants to carry a laptop with him is requested to operate it before he is allowed to bring it on board. But Meir Shalev thinks that we shouldn't ask the man with the violin case to prove it's an innocent violin. This is a shame.

One of the reasons we go to Poland is to maintain the memory of where we come from and to understand the high level of moral values we are required to keep – and to retain from this memory, more than anything else, the responsibility each of us carries in our life and existence in this part of the globe.

You Haven't Learned the Lesson

The question of the IDF's level of morality took me to some of the strangest places, including the 64th floor of the Metropolitan Tower in New York City.

Zalman Bernstein, a billionaire philanthropist who founded the Avi Chai Foundation (I will tell the history of our special relationship later), called me and asked me to come and say good-bye to him. Zalman was very ill and I was flying home after spending a week with him. I found him playing backgammon with a friend on the 64th floor of the Metropolitan Tower. Zalman introduced me to his friend, Mr. Howard. We shook hands.

"I understand you are a general in Israel," Mr. Howard said.

"No, I'm not a general, I'm just a colonel," I replied. It was 1997.

Howard went on and told me he had many close friends who were generals in Israel, and I said, "Good for you." Ranks never made an impression on me.

"Israel did not learn the lesson of the Holocaust," Mr. Howard suddenly said decisively.

I thought for a second and tried to figure out what on earth he was talking about. "You didn't learn the lesson" must refer to the first Intifada, which proved in his eyes that we were immoral. I responded that there was no army in the world that acted as morally as we did.

He wasn't ready to drop the issue or hear me out. "I'm a survivor from Berlin. I tell you, Israel has not learned the lesson from the Holocaust!"

"Nice to meet you," I said. "I'm a survivor from Auschwitz and Israel has certainly learned its lesson."

"You are not a survivor," he said. "You weren't there. And I'm telling you, Israel has not learned."

So I told him a story:

Before I returned to full service after my discharge, I was a battalion commander in the reserves between 1988 and 1989. On my second reserve service, our battalion was responsible for securing several refugee camps in the Gaza Strip. The first Intifada was raging. On our first day, I assembled the battalion and spoke to my troops. "It is quite possible that someone who shouldn't die will die – an old Palestinian or a child. This might happen, even if we do our best to avoid it. And even if we will not be held responsible, we will carry this load all our lives."

Three days later, I received word over the two-way radio about an incident under way in one of the refugee camps. I rushed to the scene and when I arrived I heard that a sixteen-year-old Palestinian boy had been seriously injured and was evacuated to a hospital in East Jerusalem due to the severity of his injuries.

The man who shot the boy was a sergeant in the unit, a reservist who worked as an El Al security guard. I asked him what had happened, and he said that the boy came at him with a heavy bat in his hand. He wasn't absolutely certain whether the bat could be considered a weapon but he was completely certain that the kid wanted to kill him with it. He shot instinctively and hit the boy's head.

At 4:00 a.m. we were informed that the boy had died in the East Jerusalem hospital. Regulations demanded that we not allow funerals during daytime hours to prevent provocations and violent demonstrations that would immediately lead to new riots. The funeral was scheduled for Friday night.

Obviously, I don't drive a car on Shabbat unless it is for the purpose of saving someone's life. Military procedures demanded that an officer escort and secure every funeral. When my operations assistant came over that Friday afternoon I told him that I would personally escort the funeral. He raised his brow in surprise. Procedure required the presence of an officer, but a platoon commander would do just as well. I had made up my mind – I went to the funeral knowing very well that the whole battalion would be talking about it.

"To save a soul" is an inconsistent concept, and the higher you climb professionally in the army, the more it gets extended. When you are responsible only for yourself and maybe for a handful of soldiers the concept is quite immediate. It speaks then about you, personally, having the opportunity to save a life. As a commander, when you decide to move to attack before your force is attacked, you don't save lives directly, but you prevent definite deaths. I regarded my presence at the funeral, which an officer of the battalion had to attend anyway, as an act of major operational importance and educational significance for our future activities in the refugee camp – a place that crawled with enemies but was the home to many innocent bystanders as well.

"Mr. Howard," I said to him, "if I hadn't learned the lessons of the Holocaust, there wouldn't have been any chance in the world that I would have driven on a Friday night to a Palestinian's funeral."

The story must have left Mr. Howard untouched, for he kept saying to me, "Don't tell me, I am a survivor, you are not a survivor."

I said to him, "You speak about being a survivor and learning the lesson, while I didn't, but there is one major difference between the two of us. In one hour I will board a plane at Kennedy Airport and twenty hours later I will be with my troops somewhere in the Negev, without knowing where I will be next Saturday. You, on the other hand, will still be sitting here, between the East River and the Hudson River, muttering that you have learned your lesson and we haven't. Good-bye, Mr. Howard."

I hugged Zalman and was on my way.

Later, Zalman called me to apologize for bringing me to the meeting. I told him that I didn't mind. I never met Howard again.

SOME MORE HISTORY

As I mentioned, the first and second delegations to Poland were quite small. The entire first delegation could barely fill a bus. I was already the head of the IDF's Education Corps when one day Amir Haskell, head of the IAF's Human Resources Command, asked me why we were satisfied with just one busload per delegation. He suggested that we fill up one of the air force's transport aircraft with soldiers. I liked the idea but I was afraid of the price the air force would demand. Amir promised me the price would be reasonable. We did the math and found out that the cost for each delegate would be about $960.

I went to the head of the Human Resources Directorate, Yudke Segev, and asked him to bring up the issue with the chief of staff, Shaul Mofaz. The chief of staff liked the idea and told me to go to his deputy and look for a budget.

I called Amir Haskell back and asked him how many seats on the plane he would buy for the IAF if I sold them to the different IDF branches. He said he would take 45. I called Yudke and asked him to lend me 600,000 shekels ($150,000). He asked why and I replied that I intended to lease two airplanes. He wanted to know where I was going with those planes and I said: Poland. He asked me how did I expect to pay him back and I explained to him that I planned to sell seats to the different army branches.

To his worried question what would I do if they didn't buy the seats, I said he was welcome to take the money out of the Education Corps's budget. I could hear the smile on his face when he informed me that I had already exhausted that year's budget. I said that in that case he was welcome to take it from next year's budget.

I called the ground forces, military intelligence, the navy, and all the other IDF branches and sold out the seats. We sent two planes, and then we sent four planes, and now we send to Poland twenty-five airplanes each year.

I think it is important that the trips to the death camps do not cost the delegates any money. The entire journey must be regarded as part of the soldiers' training. All expenses are covered by the army except a very small part of the cost donated by the Holocaust Claims Committee, which is mostly used to pay for the delegations' visits to Jewish communities in Europe.

During a meeting of the General Staff that took place on one of the Holocaust Memorial Days several years ago, we heard a lecture from the poet Haim Gouri, who talked about the very offensive welcome that awaited Holocaust survivors when they reached Israel after the war. One of the generals asked him what he thought needed to be done if we wanted to make sure that the Holocaust would not be forgotten in two hundred years.

Gouri had two answers. The first answer focused on the memory agents: museums, films, and books that keep awareness of the issue alive. The second answer, he said, was that we Jews are a remembering people and that we would remember. He gave the Passover holiday as an example.

I would like to ask who really remembers Passover? Who remembers what it's really about? Who remembers the meaning of "You were strangers in the land of Egypt"?

There is a law that prohibits the opening of places of entertainment on Tisha B'Av, the ninth day of the month of Av. But who remembers what actually happened on that day? Those who fast. And Passover will be remembered by those who eat matzah and those who read the Haggadah before dinner is served, or maybe those who discuss the exodus all night long.

I am afraid that two hundred years from now there will be many people who will not read the Haggadah, who will not eat matzah for seven days, but I still want them to remember.

That leaves us with the question: Who will guarantee that the memory of the Holocaust will be kept, and will not end up fading together with the blurred memory of the ninth day of Av, cherished only by a very small part of the people?

We carry on our shoulders the challenge of maintaining this memory. That's another reason we must go to Poland.

Delegations Will Include Bereaved Parents

At a certain point, I decided to include family members of fallen soldiers in the delegations to Poland. As a matter of course, I met the family members separately from the main delegation, and I informed the families that the reason I had decided to include them was my belief that the experience could help them move forward in their endless search for a purpose following their private loss. I said that the widows and bereaved parents and siblings might find some small comfort when they come to Poland and personally experience the reason behind Israel's wars.

I also told them that, though I have passed over bereavement's doorstep hundreds, maybe even thousands of times, I must thank the Lord that it never hit me personally, and I can only imagine how hard it must be to walk among a group of soldiers and see in each one of them something that reminds me of a late brother, son, or husband.

The five-day journey, I explained to them, means being far away from home without anyone to help them process the difficult images they see throughout the day, except the pillows in their hotel rooms at night. This, I told them, would be the hardest part, in my opinion. After saying that, I asked them to think it over before joining the delegations.

The idea was met by wide positive response among the bereaved families. To this day, each bus of delegates carries two representatives of the families. Later I learned that they had several other reasons for joining the trips. Some saw themselves as stand-ins for their killed relative, accomplishing things he or she did not have an opportunity to do. Others went in order to keep their fallen relative's memory alive. Each group of soldiers learns about the fallen soldier, the one whose family member travels with them, and talks about him in Poland. In one of the ceremonies they conduct during the trip, the soldier is officially commemorated.

Officers who participated in those delegations told me that they could not imagine the trips without the presence of the bereaved families. Menachem Granit, father of David Granit, who fought courageously and was killed in Lebanon, called me when he returned from Poland and said: "Stern, there are quite a few things you accomplished as the head of the Education Corps but if all you did were those delegations, I'd say you did all right."

A Torah Scroll Dedicated to Ilan Ramon

Every now and then I give lectures to Jewish communities across the globe. When I was the head of the IDF's Education Corps I spoke one day before a congregation in a very wealthy neighborhood in Englewood, New Jersey.

I returned to Israel and had nearly forgotten about the lecture when I received a phone call from a woman from Englewood named Debra Korman, who told me that when the *Columbia* shuttle crashed, she had been deeply moved by the story of Ilan Ramon, the first Israeli in space. She, and other members of the community, were impressed by the fact that he took with him on his space journey Jewish artifacts, including a painting that had been drawn by a child during the Holocaust.

Being a son and a grandson of Holocaust survivors, Ramon turned to Yad Vashem and asked them to let him take an artifact from their collection. After consultations they decided to give him a painting by Peter Gintz, a 14-year-old child. Ilan thought that by taking the picture with him to space he was helping fulfill Gintz's dream.

The shuttle exploded on Saturday, and the Englewood congregation decided immediately to donate a Torah scroll in Ilan Ramon's memory. But when they turned to the IDF and asked to donate the Torah to the synagogue at Ilan's former base, the army refused to accept their donation. I met with Ilan's wife, Rona, and then looked into the issue a little deeper. I came to understand the IAF's position: due to the ideal of equality among soldiers, the IAF said it could not accept a Torah scroll in the memory of one single soldier – in this case Ramon – when it had turned down similar requests in the past.

I had a different idea and suggested that the Torah accompany the Witnesses in Uniform delegations to Poland. When asked where the scroll would be stored in between delegations, I suggested the synagogue at the Yad Vashem Holocaust Museum. Ever since, all delegations take the scroll with them. Later, a tradition was created and the soldiers take their pictures with the Torah scroll and send them to Rona Ramon. When I came to visit her again in 2009, after her son Assaf – a cadet in the pilot's course – was killed when his F-16 crashed in southern Israel, we were already close due to the Ilan Ramon Torah scroll.

Dreams and Revenge

I received a phone call one day from the deputy head of the IAF, Elazar Shkedy, who told me that the Polish government had invited the air force to send three F-15 fighter jets to participate in a large exhibition they were arranging to commemorate the sixtieth anniversary of the victory over the Nazis. Shkedy, who had led one of the Witnesses in Uniform delegations several years earlier, wanted to know if there was a way we could combine this invitation with the delegations.

Three F-15s crossing the skies over Auschwitz while two hundred IDF officers march on the ground below? Of course I accepted the challenge. A short while later Shkedy returned to me and said that the Poles were refusing to allow us to fly over Auschwitz, claiming that since World War II, Polish law forbade the entry of any active foreign military assets into the area of Auschwitz, either on the ground or in the air.

"Shkedy," I said, "they are right. But go tell them that those F-15s are not instruments of war but are the opposite – instruments of peace!"

"Not a bad idea," the deputy IAF commander responded.

The Poles weren't particularly eager to accept this explanation, but strings were pulled and the airplanes finally received authorization to fly over Auschwitz.

Brigadier General Ido Nehushtan, who after Shkedy became commander of the IAF, was tapped to lead the upcoming Witnesses in Uniform delegation. I met him during the preparations for the journey and asked at what altitude the planes would fly over the Nazi death camp.

He told me that the planes would fly at an altitude of about ten thousand feet.

"What do you mean ten thousand feet?" I asked. "One thousand four hundred feet is the maximum since that is the altitude for parachuting. But 10,000 feet? At that altitude no one will even know that the F-15s passed over."

Nehushtan apologized and said that this was what the Polish government had authorized. I asked what would happen if, when flying over the camp, the planes would suddenly drop and then immediately lift up. I turned to Shkedy, who told me when I entered his room: "I have already given orders to Amir (Brigadier General Amir Eshel, the pilot who was chosen to lead the flyover) to come down as low as he can within safety limits when the planes fly over the camp. We have even prepared the answer he will give – he will say that the last time someone gave us orders in Auschwitz was sixty years ago.... I know it's a bit audacious but that's what we decided he will say."

Until today, the air force keeps the incredible photo from the flyover classified. I have one of those photos hanging in my office, showing three large Israeli F-15 fighter jets and below them 180 Israeli officers, standing in what was once Auschwitz. Under the picture is printed the words Amir Eshel said in his cockpit when he flew above the death camp: "We pilots of the Israeli air force, flying in the skies above the camp of horrors, arose from the ashes of the millions of victims and shoulder their silent cries, salute their courage, and promise to be the shield of the Jewish people and its nation Israel."

I didn't participate in that specific delegation, but I joined them afterwards on Friday morning for a visit to the Jewish community in Kiev. We held a press conference in Babi Yar, where tens of thousands of Jews were slaughtered by the Nazis. An American journalist asked Nehushtan about someone's criticism in Israel about the flyover: that we shouldn't demonstrate our strength in Auschwitz. Nehushtan answered that we hadn't come to demonstrate our strength but rather to remember our victims.

I stood up and asked for permission to speak. "Look," I said to the journalists, "I don't know if our parents, our uncles or grandfathers, who were here sixty years ago, had a dream. I don't know if dreams are a valid term in this place, and I don't know if they had time to dream. I don't know if there exists revenge for what was done to them here. As a rule, we believe that revenge belongs only to God. But if they had a dream, and if revenge exists, then 200 IDF officers on the ground and three Israeli air force F-15s in the air – are both the dream and the revenge."

Years later, I told this story to Holocaust survivor and Nobel Peace Prize Laureate Elie Wiesel during services at the Kotel on the fast day of Tisha B'Av. "You are wrong," he said. "They did have a dream – about a peel of potatoes!"

Chapter 6

America

After nearly three years I finished my term at Bahad 1 in the summer of 1996, the longest I had stayed until then in any one post. Two days later, I was already on my way to Washington, DC, to begin my studies at the National Defense University (NDU). Dorit and our children joined me five weeks later.

Our experiences, some of them rather funny, drove me almost always to self-evaluation and to understand a little better who I was, where I came from, and where I was going.

What Do You Have to Say about Mr. Netanyahu?

The academic year at the NDU was scheduled to start on Wednesday, June 19, 1996. On the following day, Thursday, June 20, I formally finished my assignment at Bahad 1. I failed to persuade university authorities to allow me to arrive two weeks late so I could accompany the class of the school's cadets through their graduation.

It seems that the university authorities had difficulty with the idea that they were about to accept a student who kept kosher and observed Shabbat. They had never had a student like me before, and their schedule included numerous activities and flights on Saturdays. So they did everything they could to discourage my admission. They must have hoped that if they would not allow me to delay my arrival, I would give up, and everyone would be the happier. I did not give up.

I must add that once they accepted me, they did all they could to accommodate my needs. The director of the program arranged kosher food for me everywhere we went, and when the group traveled on Saturdays in an air force passenger jet, they always reserved for me prepaid tickets for commercial flights on Sunday.

Three days after the academic year started, I flew to the US and went straight to the NDU. I searched for the international course and found the group of students assembled in the Eisenhower Building. When I entered the room, I was welcomed by an American air force officer. He said that he understood I was Colonel Stern and introduced himself as Colonel Tom Bishop, the commander of our class.

His first remarks were surprisingly candid. "You must have realized that we did our best to keep you from coming here. Now, since you are here, let's benefit from your arrival and discuss tolerance," he said.

I replied, "Great." In my head, though, I was thinking: "Welcome to the club, colonel...tolerance is my middle name." I had just arrived from Israel, a country that was still in shock following the assassination of Prime Minister Yitzhak Rabin less than six months earlier. A country that at the moment was inflated with tolerance.

On the same day I arrived, another colonel came: Mohammed Abu Hassan. He had a somewhat more impressive resume than mine, being a descendant of the monarchy that ruled his country. We went together to receive a special briefing for the two days we had missed. The briefing took place in the University Officers Club and included lunch.

We were hosted by Colonel Bishop and a certain Professor Groffman from the academic staff. The four of us joined the line along the buffet, each holding a plate in his hand, pondering what to order. I had by far the easiest job since I immediately realized that the only thing I could eat there was the raw vegetables. I looked at Mohammed's plate and was surprised to see that he filled it with all sorts of foods.

We ate and our two hosts filled us in on the material we had missed. After a short briefing, Mohammed turned to me suddenly and asked: "What do you have to say about Mr. Netanyahu?" Mr. Netanyahu had just been elected prime minister for the first time.

I answered that I was always proud of my prime ministers.

Mohammed didn't give up and asked again, "But what is your opinion of him?"

"I am proud of any Israeli prime minister who is democratically elected," I said.

Mohammed wasn't satisfied. He wanted to confirm his prejudice about the political inclination of religious Israelis. "Who did you vote for?"

"Mohammed," I replied, "we are a democratic state, and in democratic states officers refrain from discussing their voting record."

Mohammed, who became a little distracted after I threw at him the term democratic twice in one sentence, thought I had said that officers weren't allowed to vote in Israel.

"You are wrong," I said. "In Israel officers are usually among the first to vote. We just refrain from talking about it."

He said, "Okay, but I know who you voted for."

"Good for you," I replied.

He was silent for some time and then he announced, "You voted for Shas."

I was baffled. First, I was surprised that he knew the name Shas, which is an ultra-Orthodox Sephardic political party. Second, I took pleasure in the very shallow understanding he had of the Israeli political system. I thought I should probably call our intelligence guys and tell them that they could take a long vacation.

After we had broken the ice, I asked him if he didn't have religious restrictions regarding the food he ate. Mohammed said, "You are right. In my country, and especially in the royal family, we are very religious, but when you don't have a choice you say: 'In the name of Allah' and you can eat whatever is available."

"Mohammed," I said, "my religion also has such a rule. My father walked on the death march to Mauthausen, a march of over one thousand kilometers. When those who fell were shot on the spot and the rest had to keep walking, and there were no breaks for eating and drinking, he also had no choice but to eat the carcass of a dead horse. It's only a question of defining what 'no choice' means."

IN PRAISE OF SPONTANEITY

Several weeks after Mohammed asked me for my opinion of Mr. Netanyahu, I had the privilege of seeing the prime minister during his first official visit to Washington. Yoram Yair, the IDF military attaché in Washington, invited me to accompany him to Capitol Hill during the prime minister's speech before the two houses. We sat in the hall, Vice President Al Gore presided over the session, and together with the senators and congressmen we stood up and cheered when Netanyahu entered the plenum, in honor of Israel's prime minister.

When the prime minister reached the podium and was ready to begin his speech we all sat down. Suddenly he stepped down from the podium into the hall, and went to shake hands with one of the senators. It was Ted Kennedy, and the two were not far from falling into each other's arms. The house once again stood on its feet and cheered. We cheered as well.

In the evening, after the prime minister delivered a moving speech in his fluent English, promising that Israel would gradually wean itself off American financial assistance, we continued to a reception at the embassy. I didn't meet Netanyahu that evening, though several of his aides told me he knew who I was and wanted to meet me. Toward the end of the reception some of the prime minister's advisors bumped into me and asked me: "Well, Stern, what did you think of the prime minister's speech?"

"It was a very good speech," I said. "I heard the same opinion from several of my fellow students. They were impressed by what he said and by his spectacular English."

"You wouldn't believe how many hours we worked on the speech," they said. I congratulated them. They then asked me what I thought about the gesture Netanyahu made to Ted Kennedy.

"It was very touching," I said.

"You wouldn't believe how many hours we invested in this as well," they said.

I didn't understand. They patiently explained to me that such a spontaneous reunion had to be carefully arranged ahead of time. They spoke of their purpose in constructing a link between the prime minister and Senator Kennedy. Both were dynamic leaders, both lost brothers in service of their nations, and both came from distinguished families. The prime minister's advisors thought about everything – and I had thought, until that moment, that I knew a thing or two about the way things were done in the world. Apparently, I still had a lot to learn.

A Story about a Beard

Not long after I started at the NDU the month of Av began, and I decided to respect the common religious tradition and refrain from shaving until after the ninth day of the month. I was given a rabbinical permit to shave on those mourning days because I was regarded as a representative of the state of Israel, but exactly for that reason I decided to ignore the permit.

After three or four days my beard started to become noticeable. One day, Khalil, an officer from one of the Gulf States, asked me between lectures: "Alazahr (that was how they pronounced my name), what is that?"

I said, "But Khalil, certainly you must know."

He continued with his questions. "Come on, why aren't you shaving?"

"Don't pretend to be ignorant," I said. "I am sure that you know."

"I swear by the name of Allah that I haven't got a clue," he cried.

I looked around and found Mohammed four rows behind me.

"In that case, Khalil," I said, "go and ask Mohammed. He certainly knows."

Khalil didn't waste a second and asked Mohammed, "Say, why has Alazahr stopped shaving?"

Mohammed shrugged his shoulders to show that he did not have the faintest idea. They exchanged several sentences and the only sentence I understood from their short dialogue was *"Ana aref "* which in Arabic means "I don't know."

Now Mohammed started to interrogate me about why I wasn't shaving. The other students, coming from as many as thirty-three different countries, started to gather around. I smiled and said to Mohammed, "Come on, a man like you who knows what Shas is must certainly know why I am not shaving."

The hall was now silent. Mohammed swore that he didn't know, and I said, "Well, Mohammed, if you must know, it is because of Jerusalem."

One could hear a pin drop in the silence that now filled the hall.

Mohammed raised his voice and demanded, "Why, what happened to Jerusalem?"

"Our enemies destroyed it."

Mohammed was now agitated. He asked me, "When did this happen? I didn't hear anything."

"Two thousand years ago, Mohammed. But you see, since then we mourn for our city's destruction every year."

It took them a very long time until they asked me more questions about my customs.

In my first encounter with Mohammed, I let him know that Israel was a democracy. In our second encounter, he understood thoroughly that we are also a Jewish state. In life, though, the situation is different. We are at the same time a democratic state and a Jewish state and this duality carries with it a price. Sometimes democracy has to succumb to Judaism and sometimes it is Judaism that has to succumb to democracy. This must be the way because this is the only way the Jewish nation will survive.

I don't have to compromise though: my Judaism is democratic and my democracy is Jewish.

WE DON'T HAVE REFUSENIKS

This wasn't the last time I had to discuss the destruction of the Jewish Temple while I was at the NDU. One morning, shortly before the presidential elections, my American classmate Bill, a commander of a squadron of stealth bombers, told me that he had participated the night before in a gathering of Republican activists.

I was surprised. I asked him how he could attend such a gathering when he was a military officer, and he said that he went there dressed in civilian clothes. I asked him what difference that made, when the next day some of his subordinates could learn that he had attended the rally. Now, it was his turn to be surprised. He asked me what the problem would be if that happened. I explained that in the future, a pilot might receive an order, like flying to Vietnam or to Kosovo – a mission he will not like – and in such case he could say that he will not fly for that specific president because he doesn't trust him. "*You* voted for him," he will say, "he's *your* president, so you risk your life for him. You fly!"

Another classmate interrupted our conversation. Her name was Eleanor, and she was a high-ranking official in one of the government offices. She said, "You see, Elazar. Here it's not the same situation as in Israel. We don't have a problem of obedience and disobedience."

I asked her if she remembered the place we had visited two weeks earlier. "Yes," she replied. "We visited Gettysburg."

I reminded her that during the Civil War ten thousand soldiers were killed within twenty-four hours at Gettysburg. I said there were soldiers from the same family who fought on different sides of the battlefield.

"It happened to you 150 years ago," I said. "During that war you lost between seven hundred and nine hundred thousand men, and maybe even more than a million, and you think that the issue of controversy within the military is irrelevant to you. In our army this hasn't happened yet, but we still remember the price we paid two thousand years ago when controversies led to a civil war and destruction at the hands of our enemies. Since then, we are ultra-sensitive about disobedience."

Being a commander, whether in regular service or in the reserves, carries with it a number of prices we are forced to pay – our free time, a normal family life, overall risk, and more. To this list we should add also the need to refrain from political activity. And maybe even more compelling is our duty to carry out orders that serve policies one does not necessarily agree with – be it the evacuation of a settlement or going to war.

The Freedom to Be a Jew

One morning, I walked into the university mail room to check my mail and met Judy, an American classmate of mine. She said she had something personal to ask me, so we walked along the corridor until we found an empty room. Judy closed the door behind us and asked, "Say Elazar, what are the relations between Israel and the Gulf States?" I didn't understand what she wanted.

"I mean, how are the relations between the Israeli officers and the officers from the Gulf States?" she asked, trying to be more specific.

I still didn't understand, so she asked me again, "How is your relationship with Khalil, the officer from the Gulf?"

I replied that we were on very friendly terms and that he even came with a friend to visit my house and have a Shabbat meal with my family.

Judy sighed with relief. I asked her what was on her mind, and she told me that she and Khalil were on very good terms. He shared a seminar with her and they had become good friends, but he didn't know that she was Jewish and she couldn't bring herself to tell him because she thought it would put an end to their relationship.

I told her that I didn't think she should be worried. Khalil himself once told me that among the Arabs, citizens of the Gulf States are nicknamed "The Jews of the Arabs." When I asked why, he said it was because of their success in commerce and finance.

Three weeks later I stood in the corridor with Baher from Egypt and Khalil from the Gulf when Judy passed by. All three of us greeted her. "Do you know her?" Khalil asked me. "She is a very nice lady."

I said that I knew her and added that as far as I knew, she was Jewish.

"Impossible," Khalil said. "I have a very good relationship with her, and she would have told me."

Three weeks passed, and Judy still hadn't found the courage to tell Khalil she was Jewish.

Finding the right moment to declare the fact that you are a Jew – a challenge for many Jews outside of Israel – was completely foreign to me. Being an Israeli, and especially one who wears a *kippa*, I never had to declare my religion. It always preceded me. Sometimes the line from Israel's national anthem, "To be a free people in our land," has a very liberating meaning.

The Ability to Pay Respect

During the weekends the foreign officers at the university were taken on trips so we could become familiar with the United States. Those activities were sponsored by rich groups of Americans, usually army veterans.

On one of those trips we flew to Orange County, California, and went there to a restaurant for a lunch with some of the rich donors. The moment I sat down I noticed a waiter who kept looking at me, and after a few minutes he switched my entire cutlery.

When the group suggested a toast, the waiter approached me with a new, corked bottle of wine and showed me that it was a known brand of kosher wine. He asked me if it was all right and I said that it was perfect. He even knew that he had to leave the uncorking of the bottle and the pouring of the wine to me.

The first dish was grapefruit. We finished eating and the waiters collected everybody's plates and forks except for mine. The second dish was lobster, and I was given chicken. I thanked them but didn't eat.

When the waiter saw that I refrained from eating he went away and returned with the metal tag that had come on the chicken. It said kosher. I said, "Thanks, I really appreciate this," but still didn't touch the food. He approached me again and asked me to follow him. We went to the restaurant's kitchen and there he led me to a corner that was the size of a small room and said: "Here, sir, everything is completely new."

I asked him what he meant, and he told me that all the dishes in that section of the kitchen were brand new and had never been used before. To my question who had instructed them to do so, he told me they had brought in a rabbi from San Diego who showed them what to do. He informed me that when our host saw on the students' list the word kosher, he told him: "I don't know what this means. Find someone who does. I want this Israeli officer to be able to eat with us."

When the evening ended, I asked to meet my generous host. He was the same person who had paid for the entire dinner, and I was told that they were the richest orchard owners in California. I approached him and his wife and told them how much I appreciated their efforts. They looked at each other and said, "Sir, you don't need to thank us. We are the ones who should thank you. Do you know what it means to us to be able to host a Jewish officer, and one who keeps his ancestors' tradition? We should thank you! But we have one request. If you don't mind, please take the cutlery with you, we don't have any further use for it...."

Customer Service and National Pride

On the flight on my way to the NDU in Washington, DC, in July 1997, I purchased a pocket computer English-Hebrew translator made in Israel. During my stopover in New York, I purchased a new Philips shaver.

After four months, the translator stopped working. I checked that it was still under warranty, waited for someone to visit the US from Israel, and sent it back with them to get fixed. A week passed and the shaver also broke. One day on my way home from the NDU, I stopped at the Philips service center and dropped it off. A few days later I returned to the center, and a service representative apologized and said that they couldn't fix the machine and were therefore giving me a new shaver.

Another two weeks went by and a FedEx messenger knocked on my front door with another new shaver. I told him that I had already received the shaver and thanked him for the high-quality service.

Thanksgiving rolled along and we went on a trip to Niagara Falls and to visit family in Toronto. Our relative, Max Gutman, offered me a pair of Rockport shoes that he had bought on a recent trip to New York. I told him that they were not my size – I could not say that they were also clearly not my style – but he insisted and stuck them inside my suitcase.

We returned home, and one night I put the shoes in a bag and went to Nordstrom at the Pentagon Mall. I knew that I had nothing to lose, and I asked if I could switch the shoes for a different pair. The worker asked where I had bought the pair and I retold the story of how my cousin gave them to me in Toronto. I was surprised when she pointed me toward the shoe racks and said that I could select a new pair.

I chose the pair I wanted, went back to the clerk, and watched her scan the code on both pairs of shoes and print me up a receipt – which I didn't have to begin with – with the price 00.00 on it. I was confused and she explained that this way it would be easier for me to return the new pair in the future.

Easier than this? I envied the Americans and their high-level of customer service.

A few weeks went by and I finally received my answer from Top Technologies, the manufacturer of the pocket computer translator. The company said that it had inspected the machine and found that I had probably not operated it correctly and that moisture had gotten inside; it was therefore not covered by the warranty. My immediate reaction was to be angry but then I was overcome with embarrassment. As a proud Israeli, I knew that we had a lot to learn.

As a last resort, I wrote a letter to the CEO of the company. I related the shoe and shaver story and told him that at the NDU we discussed issues of national security and national pride. Customer service, I explained, created a strong sense of pride and, as a result, a high level of security.

Here is one more story: It was a few weeks before the end of the school year and we began planning our return home. I knew that we would have some space in the shipping container, and we decided to use it to buy new mattresses which were significantly cheaper in the US. I did a quick market survey and discovered that the best place to buy the mattresses was the PX store, something of a civilian department store but just for military personnel.

I walked into the store on the NDU campus and bought four mattresses from the catalog that cost a total of $675. I made sure that they would be delivered to the store by the end of the week when we were supposed to close up the container and then leave for a two-week road trip through New Hampshire and Maine. I offered to pay for at least part of the purchase, but the clerk refused and said that I should pay upon delivery.

The Friday rolled along and I came back to the store to pick up the mattresses but to my surprise I was told that they had not yet arrived. I reminded the clerk that I had told him in advance that I needed the mattresses today since I was shipping them back to Israel. The clerk asked me if I could wait one hour while he looked into the matter and to see if he could get them from a different store. He couldn't find anything and after an hour he asked if I could wait three hours for him to widen the search. I had no choice and said yes, but I wouldn't be able to wait longer because of Shabbat.

The clerk suggested that if that was the case then I should go to a nearby mattress store and buy the mattresses there. I explained to him that I could have done that weeks ago but I went to the PX store because they had the best deal. He said that since the mess-up was their responsibility, they would cover the difference between the mattresses. I said that there was a possibility that I would not find exactly the same mattress, and he said no problem. So I went to a nearby store and bought four similar mattresses for $970.

Before leaving for our trip, I sent the receipt to the PX with a copy of the original order. When we came back after two weeks, there was a note on the door asking me to go to the post office, where I found an envelope with a check for $295 and a note: "Sorry for the inconvenience, have a safe trip home."

I hadn't paid a single cent when I first ordered the mattresses at the PX, and the sales clerk knew that I was returning to Israel and would never come back to his store. It must be that for Americans customer service is something inherent in their culture.

Several years have passed since then. Customer service has come a long way in Israel, but there is still a long way to go.

Of Jews and Eggs

During my stay in the US we frequently invited classmates of mine to eat with us on Friday night. Those dinner invitations led to weird situations, like the time when Khalil, the officer from the Gulf, explained at length to another officer the significance of Kiddush, the blessing on the wine, and challah and the blessing on the bread.

One day I met Baher, the Egyptian colonel who had already visited our house with his wife Amana and their children. I asked him how he was doing, and he told me that his wife and two of their children had returned to Cairo and he had stayed back with the older son. I asked him how he managed, and he said that it wasn't particularly easy. He told me that in the middle of the week he tried to cook and shop but on the weekends they either went out for dinner or ate at friends' houses. I told him to come to my house. The Passover holiday, I said, was in a few weeks. "Why don't you come over," I said. "After all, we were once slaves in your country and the first person to define us as a nation was Pharaoh, your king of Egypt."

Baher looked at me and said, "Yes, and when you left you took all our gold with you...."

"True," I said, "but you didn't pay us for our work!" I had found this explanation in an ancient textbook dealing with the days of Alexander the Great.

When I came home and told my wife, Dorit, that I had invited Baher for the Seder, the ritual dinner on the first night of Passover, Dorit looked at me and said, "I don't believe you; this time you are really insane."

Our daughter Adi, then nine years old, said to her, "Mommy, I know Dad – in a couple of weeks we are going to have an Egyptian for the Seder, then he'll invite a German for Holocaust Memorial Day. We are very lucky that on Hanukah we will already be back home...."

Baher came to our Seder and meticulously followed all the songs we read with a translated Haggadah we arranged for him (an uncensored version that included lines like "Pour Your wrath on all of the gentiles who refuse to worship You..."), and he gladly stayed later after the formal dinner was over.

A month later, we traveled to the Grand Canyon. Baher was there dressed like a tourist, in elegant shoes that weren't suitable for hiking. Even more ironic was the fact that he, of all people, came unprepared for the desert conditions and heat. He was very thirsty and I gladly shared my water with him. After that we strolled together toward the Indian village. On the way, we met – like in a corny joke – an Englishman and a Dutchman.

An Englishman, a Dutchman, an Egyptian, and an Israeli meet in the Grand Canyon. The Englishman and the Dutchman ask: "Where do you come from?" We answer that we are from Israel and Egypt. The Englishman and the Dutchman said they didn't believe us.

We explained to them our special relationship, and the two were even more surprised. I didn't understand why, but at that point

I suddenly recalled what Baher had said about the gold that the Israelites had taken when they left Egypt. After they left, I asked him how he had heard that story.

He told me that he was a battalion commander in the 1973 Yom Kippur War. "I was convinced that we were going to win that war," he said. "After we didn't win, I decided you must have some special virtues, and I decided to learn all I could about you. I was absolutely certain that I knew everything about your people – until Passover night at your place. Then I learned something new."

I asked him what it was and hoped that it wasn't the "pour out Your wrath" bit that appears in the Haggadah. He said my wife's father taught him why we ate a hard-boiled egg during the Seder, and he said, "You do know, don't you?"

I was worried that I might lose Baher's trust by not knowing which of the explanations grandfather Shlomo chose. It was a delicate moment both for me and for the Jewish nation's credibility.

With fine diplomatic style I returned the question to him, and he said, "Your wife's father explained that you Jews are like eggs. The more an egg is boiled, the harder it becomes. And the same is true with you Israelis: the more someone tries to 'boil' you, the harder you become. And what's more, just as the yolk and the white of the egg do not mix, so you never mix."

I understood that he meant we don't mix with them, the Arabs, but I thought about us, having such a difficulty mixing among ourselves – secular and religious, right-wing and left-wing, veterans and new immigrants. Maybe that is why I have always preferred a plate of egg salad over a hard-boiled egg.

Nabi Musa and Texas

One day we were taken to the Marines officers' academy to observe a graduation ceremony. As I had just concluded my term at Bahad 1, I had many questions for the officer who escorted us. He must have gotten tired of my endless questions and told me that an Israeli soldier had participated in the last course and that I should meet him.

Soon afterward, a tall soldier with a helmet on his head showed up, saluted, and said: "Colonel Stern." I asked him if we knew each other, and he replied that his name was Josh and while I didn't know him, he knew me. He said he had served in the IDF's Paratroopers Brigade while I was a battalion commander. I asked him where he served and found out that he had been stationed in southern Lebanon on the eastern Lebanese border, and underwent training at Nabi Musa in the Judean Desert.

"So what are you doing at this officers' school?" I asked.

"I'm American," he answered.

"Okay," I said, "but why are you here, in the army?"

"I was promised I will become a pilot in the Marines!" he answered.

"What do you mean you were promised?"

"They tested me and said, you were a paratrooper in Israel so you'll be a pilot in America. They didn't tell me on what aircraft, but they promised me I would fly."

I invited him to visit us on a weekend, and three weeks later he called and told me that his parents were coming to visit his brothers in Annapolis and suggested that I bring my wife and children and join them on their yacht on Sunday. I tried to convince him to bring his family to my house, but at last I gave in and agreed to go to him.

On the way to the marina, I thought that it was very strange for American parents who own a yacht to send their son to serve in the army in Israel and when the boy returns home to again send him to serve in the American military. It seemed like they just couldn't afford for him to stay at home. What kind of a yacht would they have, I thought? Probably a small rowing boat.

Josh was waiting on the pier when we arrived and took us on a guided tour around his family's huge and elegant yacht. We realized that people with such a yacht could easily afford to raise a few dozens kids. We released the anchor, turned on the engine, and the boat took to sea. Then, the engine was killed and the sails were raised. Blue seas, calm, and then Dorit asked Josh: "Say, why on earth did you come to serve in the IDF?"

"Yes, ask him," chimed in Josh's mother, smiling. "I would like to know myself."

I interrupted the conversation and said to Josh's mother, "It's your fault!"

Josh looked at the two women and said, "He is right, Mother. I knew all through high school that I would pay back the United States for all that it gave me. I even knew I wanted to enlist in the Marines. But then, when I graduated, you took me on a trip to Israel, and on our way back we stopped in Poland. There, in Poland, I realized that I want to repay my country, but first I have to serve my people. So I went to serve eighteen months in Israel and now I serve here."

After that sail, Josh visited us on Saturdays and on holidays. After two years, when I was already in Israel, I received a note from the commander of the American navy stating that Josh had finished his training and serves now as an F-14 pilot. Last time I checked, he served in Japan and his wife and two daughters lived in Texas.

Ever since I met Josh I always tell his story in the lectures I give to Witnesses in Uniform delegations. I say to the soldiers: "Josh, in order to serve both his country and his people, had to serve both in Texas and in Nabi Musa. You get to serve both with an 'all-included' voucher."

Jokes and Jewish Complexity

Before my relationship with the Hesder yeshivot turned sour I was asked by the leadership of Bnei Akiva in Israel to travel to the United States and to represent it at a number of functions as a graduate of the movement. However, I felt that it was inappropriate for an IDF officer to travel on behalf of Bnei Akiva, which in recent years has, unfortunately, become a political movement. Rabbi Haim Druckman argued that the yeshivot were apolitical and that my visit would be strictly education oriented. They submitted an official request to the IDF Spokesman's Office and it was approved. Due to my rank, the chief of staff and the defense minister also had to approve the request.

A number of days before the trip, the Hesder yeshiva affair erupted and I came under attack. I called Rabbi Druckman and told him that since I was now considered an enemy, I thought it would be best if they canceled my trip. He asked me to reconsider and said that I was not an enemy by any means at all.

Of course, every place I went on the trip I was asked why I was against the Hesder yeshivot, and I answered by explaining that Bnei Akiva had ordered and paid for my ticket.

On Shabbat I was in New York and went to pray the morning service at the Orthodox synagogue Congregation Kehilath Jeshurun, on the Upper East Side of Manhattan. After the service, a young rabbi named Meir Soloveitchik, the nephew of the late famous Rabbi Yosef Dov Soloveitchik from Yeshiva University, rose to give the sermon. I understood that the young Soloveitchik was a rising star, a lecturer at Princeton University as well as other places. His sermon focused on the importance of Jewish-Christian relations. The young rabbi mentioned that a group of cardinals had visited the synagogue the previous week, including the chief cardinal of Paris, a Jew who had converted to Catholicism. The rabbi finished the sermon with a joke:

"Two engineers and two accountants are standing in line to buy train tickets. The engineers buy two tickets but notice that the accountants buy only one. They are intrigued. After everyone boards the train, the engineers notice that the two accountants enter the bathroom together and close the door. A few minutes later, when the ticket collector passes through the car, he knocks on the door of the bathroom and asks for the ticket. A hand reaches out and hands him the ticket, which he takes and carries on.

"On their way back, the two engineers decide to try the same trick. They stand in line and buy one ticket. While they are collecting the change they notice that the accountants didn't even buy one ticket this time. They are again intrigued.

"The engineers quickly board the train, enter the bathroom and shut the door. After them, the accountants board the train and enter the bathroom stall across from them. When the train starts moving, one of the accountants comes out and knocks on the bathroom door across the aisle. A hand emerges with a ticket. The accountant takes it and reenters the other stall."

Even now, I am not sure if I missed the connection between the joke and the sermon because of my English or if it was just meant to add humor.

After the sermon, I was invited for lunch to the home of Rabbi Haskel Lookstein, the senior rabbi at the synagogue and a known community leader. There were other guests at the meal as well, some of them also known community figures. During the meal, I asked how many other synagogues in the neighborhood would have invited Rabbi Soloveitchik to deliver a sermon about the importance of the connection between Judaism and Christianity.

The people around the table admitted that it was a tough question and after some thought agreed that not a single synagogue in Brooklyn or New Jersey would have allowed such a sermon. Maybe, they said, another synagogue in Manhattan would have allowed this.

And then I asked what would have happened had the rabbi preached about the importance in Orthodoxy of maintaining a relationship with the Reform and Conservative movements. How many synagogues would be open to that, I asked. This time, no one hesitated and everyone immediately answered: "Not a single one."

Unfortunately, I said, I had a different joke about a train.

A Jew enters a train car and meets someone he knows.

"Where are you going?" the Jew asks.

"To Berdichev," the acquaintance answers.

The Jew gets upset and says, "You say you are traveling to Berdichev so I will think that you are going to Zitomer, but you are really traveling to Berdichev so why lie?"

That is how we are, I told the other people around the lunch table. Everyone first looks to see how the other person is taking advantage of him.

When the military conversion issue first broke into the headlines, I was asked to come speak to some donors affiliated with the Edgar Bronfman Fund. I flew into the US before Shabbat and decided to try a different synagogue this time, called Bnei Yeshurun, a synagogue that I was interested in seeing after reading an article about it in an Israeli magazine.

When the synagogue was undergoing renovations, the administration rented a nearby church, covered the Christian symbols, and held services there. The place was extremely popular so that even after the renovation was completed, the synagogue continued to use it for services, particularly since the newly renovated synagogue was not large enough to hold the crowd that came for services. So they extended their lease on the church and held two services on Friday night.

The services I attended were led by two female cantors who used microphones. I enjoyed the service as well as watching how involved the crowd was, but I could not bring myself to join the prayers. Later, the crowd joined hands and began dancing. I do not think this is wrong but just strange. Due to the complex experience, I decided to go to a corner and pray on my own.

After the services ended, my hosts offered to take me to the converted church to see the other service. I asked how it was still going on since it was already late, and my hosts explained that the service in the converted church started later so that people who worked late on Friday could participate, even those who worked after Shabbat had begun. My hosts claimed that in the 1940s Orthodox rabbis had also permitted this.

The service ended with a massive dinner, which I was told was the main singles' event in New York City.

After the lecture at Edgar Bronfman's house I was asked to give a talk at Yeshiva University. I agreed, and after I finished one of the rabbis came up to me and said that his student mentioned that he had seen me three weeks earlier in the Chassidic neighborhood Meah Shearim in Jerusalem.

"That is true," I said. "But tell him that last Shabbat I prayed at Bnei Jeshurun."

The rabbi smiled and said, "You did well."

The answer that the rabbi gave me demonstrated the complexity of the issue. Not every synagogue – even for the Orthodox – is immediately considered off limits, even though not everyone agrees with this.

On another trip of mine, heads of the Orthodox Union in the US bragged to me that the Conservative and Reform movements were moving closer to Orthodoxy, since "they know that our way is the right way." I asked them how many Jews lived in the US in 1948 and they said 6 million. I asked how many Jews live there now, and they said 5.2 million. "Good that you think your way has won," I said. I wanted to say to him: What good is being right if ultimately the Jewish population declines? Another such victory and we are lost!

Obviously the Reform and Conservative movements are to a large extent to blame for the declining Jewish population in the United States. I also blame this decline on the fact of Orthodoxy distancing itself from the Reform and Conservative movements. Maybe the Orthodox succeeded better in staying Orthodox and Jewish, but the price in terms of numbers is too high.

In Israel, we are living a similar story. If we stick to a radical stream of Judaism we may survive, but how many will we lose on the way? How many will want to say in the end that they are proud to be observant Jews and how many will simply prefer to say that they are Jewish?

Chapter 7

Education

When my year at the National Defense University ended, we returned to our home in Hoshaya. I was temporarily appointed an operations officer in charge of IDF exercises.

After several months I was appointed deputy commander of Division 36, stationed in the Golan Heights. I stepped into the shoes of Erez Gerstein, who had been appointed commander of the Southern Lebanese Front, where, a year later, he was killed in an ambush. Deputy commander of Division 36 was one of my last combat assignments before turning full-time to education.

After a year as deputy commander, I became commander of an armored reserve division. A few weeks before I was scheduled to start the new assignment, I was informed that my main mission there would be to dismantle and shut down the division. People who tried to console me said that shutting down a division is much more complicated than establishing one from scratch. In addition to worrying about the future of the division's soldiers and staff and ensuring that the best use would be made of the unit's tanks, armored vehicles, ammunition, and equipment, I also had to preserve the division's history and the memory of its fallen.

Toward the end of my assignment in the division, I started hearing rumors about the possibility that I would be appointed head of the Education Corps. I hoped the rumors were false but I soon learned that they were true. I had always believed that field commanders were the most important educators of soldiers.

When the chief of staff at the time, Shaul Mofaz, and Major General Moshe Ya'alon summoned me and informed me of their intentions, I told them that I had already filled the role of educator as commander of Bahad 1. I knew that traditionally the assignment of head of the Education Corps was a career graveyard.

At Adi and Daniel's wedding, 2007. From right to left: Shimon, Liron, grandfather Shlomo, Dorit, Adi, Elazar, Amichai, grandfather Lipo Stern, Ilan, Hodaya. Sitting: grandmother Irene Mannes (right) and grandmother Sara Stern.

Ilan's graduation from the officers' course at Bahad 1, the Officers' Training School. Adi was already a one-day-old officer, and Liron was an officer in miluim.

We captured Har Dov for good! Prime Minister Yitzhak Rabin's visit to Har Dov, together with Chief of Staff Motta Gur, winter, 1976.

Chief of Staff Moshe Levi visits the Sanur training base as part of his campaign to become battalion commander.

Shaking hands with Chief of Staff Ehud Barak upon receiving the rank of colonel.

Chief of Staff Shaul Mofaz and Dorit bestow the rank of brigadier general.

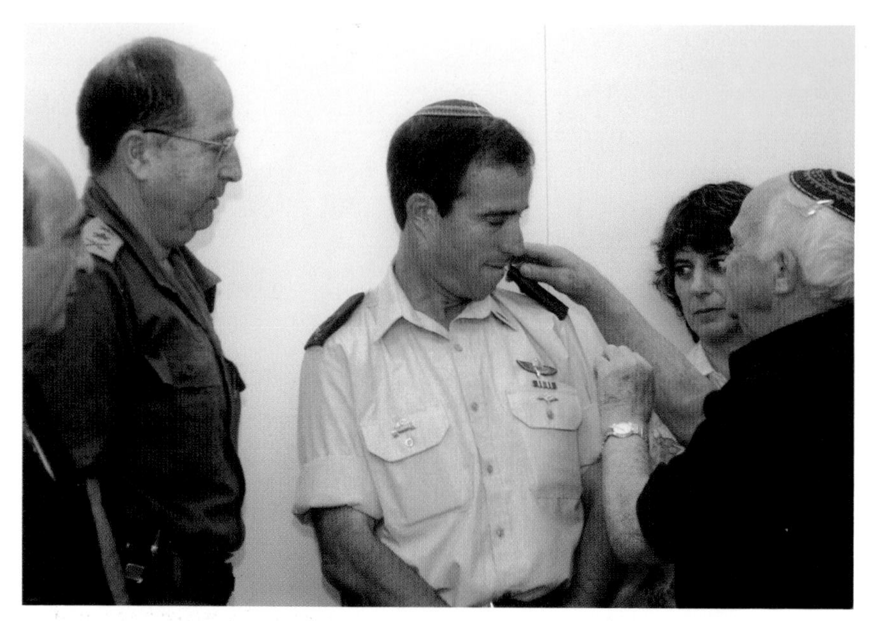

My father and Chief of Staff Bogie Ya'alon bestow the rank of major general (Dorit gave up her place for my father). Left: Defense Minister Shaul Mofaz.

Accepting the position of commander of Bahad 1, the Officers' Training School of the IDF, alongside Emanuel Sakel, the commander of GOC Army Headquarters, and the legendary Yitzhak Taito, chief warrant officer of the Officers' Training School.

Prime Minister Yitzhak Rabin at Bahad 1 on the day that the peace treaty with Jordan was agreed upon. My office certified the flying of King Hussein's plane in Israeli skies.

With my paratrooper son Ilan, dropping in from a very high altitude…though it was only 1200 feet.

With General Shalikashvili, chairman of the Joint Chiefs of Staff of the American army.

The first delegation to Poland, at the gates of Maidanek.

The General Staff Forum gathered in Yad Vashem on Holocaust Memorial Day.

Another encounter with Prime Minister Yitzhak Rabin. Left: Chief of Staff Amnon Lipkin-Shahak.

The graduation of the officers' course.

The prime minister's sukkah, Sukkot, 2006. From right to left: Defense Minister Ehud Barak; Prime Minister Ehud Olmert; Zeev Bielski, chairman of the Jewish Agency; and Elazar Stern, head of the Human Resources Directorate.

The fulfillment of another dream: the inauguration of the Druze military academy. From right to left: Akram Hassoun, mayor of Carmel City, and former Knesset member Amal Nasser el-Din.

The graduation of the first class of bagrut 2000, the fighters' bagrut. With Education Minister Yossi Sarid, and Brigadier General On Ragunis, the spirit behind the project.

President Weizman visits Bahad 1, following the meeting in Caesarea.

With Prime Minister Ariel Sharon.

The General Staff Forum in the Kotel tunnels.

With President Shimon Peres.

Speaking with Knesset member Shaul Mofaz at a retired paratroopers' convention, Kfar Maccabiah Hotel, Ramat Gan.

Honor guard marking the appointment of Amir Peretz as defense minister.

With Major General Eliezer Shkedi, commander of the Israeli Air Force.

Inspecting an exercise. From right to left: Brigadier General (Res.) Pinchas Buchris, director general of the Ministry of Defense; and Major General Dan Harel, deputy chief of the General Staff.

Colleagues on the General Staff. From right to left: Major General Gantz, Major General Marom, and Major General Shamni.

The chief rabbis visit the Israel Defense Forces.

With Rabbi Yitzhak Grossman.

With Prime Minister Ehud Barak at the Bible Contest, 2000. Right: Sali Meridor, chairman of the Jewish Agency.

Rallying against draft evasion, together with Chief Education Officer, Brigadier General Eli Schermeister.

Commander and friend, Chief of Staff Gabi Ashkenazi.

Nobody ever advanced from this post to higher positions. But this did not trouble me too much, since I never considered myself to be destined from birth to be a member of the general staff.

As a part of their pressure on me, the two generals explained that I might have an opportunity to be a "different" type of commander in the Education Corps.

I began my assignment in the summer of 1999, though I hadn't yet left my post as head of the reserves division. I was now the chief commanding officer of the Education Corps and I had never regretted it. Not even when it became clear that this assignment turned me away from the central avenue toward the IDF's high command. I knew by then that if I were to become a combat general, I could probably do a better job than some present generals, but then, there are many – I'm glad to admit – who can also do a better job than I. On the other hand, I knew that as the commander of the Education Corps, I would be doing something completely different than anyone else would have done.

I was the commander of the Education Corps for almost five years, from the summer of 1999 until the spring of 2004. I do not regret even one of those days, and I hope that I succeeded in performing my job as a "different" type of commander. I feel that my mission had a direct impact on the battlefield as well as on Israeli society as a whole. I always looked for where we made mistakes and tried to fix things to the best of my ability. I felt that we were making a difference.

RETURN, HEBREW SONG

When I was a student at the Netiv Meir Yeshiva High School during the 1970s, the boy who sat to my right, Yishai, knew the entire Bible by heart. Avshi, who sat to my left, knew all of the Gashash episodes – a famous Israeli comedy trio at the time – by heart. I sat between them, and I knew all the Hebrew music by heart. In our senior year I even had a notebook into which I copied all the songs I could find.

I always believed that music was a major cultural vehicle for the Jewish and Israeli people. When I became commander of Bahad 1, I insisted on distributing songbooks to the cadet dormitory rooms. I regarded this as something as important as reading war history, which was obligatory in the school, because for soldiers Israeli music could be an important bridge to their country's scents, people, and landscapes.

When you sing "If you go to the market…," the market is right here. When you sing "You took my hand and said: let's go to the park…," every one connects to a special hand and a special park.

Once I visited one of the cadets' rooms and saw a cassette player on the table. When I pushed the play button, a strange noise filled the room. I asked them if that was what they called "Technics."

"You probably meant Techno," they answered. "But no, this is a different type of music."

I said to them that they were more than welcome to listen to any type of music they wished. Then I asked if they could pass me the songbook that had been placed in their room. I opened it randomly to a song by Didi Menusi, which opens with the words "someone painted the Gilboa Mountain red." I told them the song was written in honor of Kibbutz Geva's sixtieth anniversary. I didn't waste time asking them where Kibbutz Geva was but instead asked them where Mt. Gilboa was. The room was silent, and the cadets stared at one another with despairing hope. Finally one of them raised his hand. Out of eight cadets, only one knew the answer.

That was the instant when I learned that the Palestinian Intifada had its advantages. The cadet knew the answer because he had to drive from his base to training grounds via a bypass road, and he remembered that on his way were road signs to the Gilboa Regional Council and to the community of Ma'ale Gilboa.

I turned a few pages to the song "Dudu." I asked them if they knew who Dudu was and about the battle that was mentioned in the song. They didn't have the faintest idea. Since they were part of an infantry officers' course, and since the infantry soldiers spent most of their time those days on Israel's northern border, I gave them a hint that a junction they were familiar with up north was related to the song. I couldn't give them a clearer hint. Finally I told them that the song was written in memory of Lieutenant David Tcherkesky, who died in the battle of Nabi Yesha Fortress, near the Koach Junction, which is on the road leading to Lebanon.

From that day, everybody knew that Bahad 1 had a crazy commander who compelled cadets to answer questions about songbooks.

When I began my term as head of the IDF's Education Corps I organized a workshop to set the corps' goals for the coming year. It was 1999, and among the goals I put on the list was one I defined with the sentence: "Return, Hebrew music. Don't be shy."

Several of the officers, including the director of the workshop, said that this was not the way goals were phrased – but I said that being that I was the one who signed the orders, I didn't see anything wrong with this phrasing. I also said it would add a melodious input to the corps' additional objectives. I met with several of Israel's major poets and singers and arranged a budget for Hebrew sing-along evenings in army bases. The response I got was positive.

When the project was launched I mourned the total indifference of today's youth toward poetry and language. Who writes today like the poets Itamar Pratt and Rachel Shapira? Do youth still recognize the Friday night Kiddush that hides in the lines of some of these poems?

Today, after all the years I spent promoting Hebrew songs among soldiers, and after having taken part in dozens of song nights, I am a little more optimistic. Not very long ago, I was invited to a private farm in the Negev Desert for a song night, during which the participants sang from the book of Isaiah. This wouldn't have been possible ten years ago. After the evening was over the professional singer who directed the event confessed to me that ever since I inserted the restoration of Hebrew music in the IDF as one of the corps' objectives, he and his colleagues were getting a lot more work.

PROTECTING HEBREW CULTURE

The struggle to raise Hebrew music's status didn't end with producing songbooks. I was surprised to find that many of the shows put on by the IDF choir included songs in English. You can find me at times singing to myself songs and melodies that weren't necessarily created here, but I think there should be a line between private use and the abuse of national and military resources.

A military band is a recognized icon of Israeli culture; it is a group that was created to present that culture and should not support the implantation of foreign cultural elements into Israeli society. I considered this to be a manifestation of the decline in our national self-esteem.

Many years later, toward the end of my term as head of the IDF's Human Resources Directorate, I learned that foreign music had made its way into the IDF's band. I reissued instructions that forbade singing foreign songs unless the performance was in front of foreign visitors or took place overseas. I also banned singing in foreign languages during tryouts for the military choirs.

I don't think that singing in a foreign language is wrong in and of itself. It even carries some advantages like learning new languages and getting a more thorough understanding of another culture. Still, when it replaces our culture – and especially in the army – one must vigorously defend one's roots.

CONDUCTING A HARP

One day, when I was still in charge of the Education Corps, I read in a newspaper that a young and talented Israeli musician was invited to conduct the Irish Symphony Orchestra. The article mentioned that the young man, whose name was Yaniv Dinur, was still a soldier in active service. I checked and found that he was serving in my headquarters, and I summoned him to my office.

He arrived looking a little bewildered. I congratulated him for his outstanding achievement and the honor he brought to Israel. I said that I invited him to my office because of the contribution his achievement carried for our army and because I wanted to ask him something.

I told him that when I was commander of Bahad 1, I frequently compared the role of a commander in the field to the role of the conductor in a concert hall. I made this comparison even though I had never met a real conductor. I said to the young musician, "Now, when I have the opportunity, please tell me if I am right or wrong."

I could see that he didn't understand what I was talking about so I gave him an example. Suppose I'm a platoon commander or a company commander and I need to instruct a squad commander to remain in a secured area and cover the advancing troops while shooting according my instructions. I will then order another squad commander to outflank the target via a small ravine and be ready to storm the enemy on my command. In addition I have mortars and artillery fire, which I will expect to act in rhythm with everyone else. Add to this the attack helicopter that received my instructions regarding the specific moment when we will require their assistance.

"That's exactly the role of a conductor," Yaniv said.

"How do you control all the instruments?" I asked.

Yaniv said he had a notebook, with a separate line for each instrument, and two lines for the piano, which he relied on when conducting.

I asked him to tell me how he communicated with the different musicians during the concert. "I do it with my hands and eyes," he replied, giving a few demonstrations of the way he moves when standing on the conductor's stand.

"How do you know the precise moment you want an instrument to join in?" I asked.

"According to my ears. I hear the separate instruments."

"How many separate instruments can you hear at the same time?"

"Approximately fifty," he answered.

"In that case, you will remain a conductor and I will remain a commander."

The following day, I was giving a lecture to air force cadets about leadership. I explained the role of a ground commander by recalling my encounter with Yaniv. I could see in their eyes, however, that they didn't grasp my intention. I didn't give up. A new idea came to mind: "I don't need to teach you about orchestras. If we are talking about music then your instrument is the harp."

The cadets' eyes said plainly: "What harp, and what has this got to do with us?"

"After all, each of you is a different string on the harp," I continued.

They looked even more confused, and I admit that at this stage I felt a slight panic rising inside me. I tried to solve the unpleasant situation by explaining that if one of the strings ripped, the rest had to continue working.

Out of the forty cadets in the room I could see four or five that began to look a little more at ease and seemed to understand the metaphor. I asked the cadets if they were familiar with the name Benny Peled. Many were. I asked them who knew the line from the song "This melody can't be stopped, got to keep on playing." Five of them knew the song even though they didn't know it was connected to Benny Peled.

I don't know many songs like that one, which accurately describe the atmosphere of a company or air force squadron at war.

I told the cadets that the lyrics from Benny Peled's song were taken from a speech delivered by a commander of the air force and they tell the story of a squadron during the Yom Kippur War. The song relates how some of the aircraft did not return and how despite the losses, it was necessary to "keep on playing; keep on playing; because this melody can never be stopped...."

As I said, only five cadets knew the song. It pained me, because they were the future of the air force in the last stages of their training. These cadets were probably the elite of our youth – over thirty years have passed since the Yom Kippur War and almost all is already forgotten.

When I came out of this meeting I went directly to my friend, Brigadier General Rani Falk, commander of the flight school.

"This can't be," I told Rani. I wanted him to assure me that this was an extraordinary incident and that most of the cadets in his courses were familiar with the song by the time they graduated.

Rani agreed that this specific song might have value for motivating the cadets but he admitted that most of the cadets have probably never heard of the song. "Yes Elazar," he nodded, "it certainly isn't uncommon."

I pondered once again the advantages of Hebrew music and whether we did enough to instill within our youth a love for their heritage and traditions. Beyond providing our clever and talented pilots with the necessary technical skills, do we also develop their spirit?

My words didn't fall on deaf ears. The gaps were recognized by the flight school command even before my visit. Today the time and effort invested in the course on issues like tradition, values, and Jewish identity, is ten times more than it used to be.

FOUR LINES

My ideas on education were not created the day I was appointed head of the IDF's Education Corps. They were developed much earlier, throughout my military service, and especially during my different command posts.

One day when I was commander of Bahad 1, I was inspecting the cadets' dormitory. I came into one of the rooms and naturally focused on the cadets' equipment. Since I knew, however, that the cadets were already subject to a number of daily inspections, I used the encounter to interview them. There were four cadets in the room who were in a very advanced stage of the course.

The cadets were already accustomed to my questions about details from the songs that were printed in the songbook they had in each room. I knew they prepared themselves carefully for my questions, so I decided to use a new strategy.

I asked one of them where he came from. He replied that he was from Balfouria. I then asked his neighbor where he came from. This one was from Nechalim.

"Please tell us where Balfouria is," I asked the second soldier. And then I turned and said to the first soldier, "And you tell us where Nechalim is."

The room was silent. I told them that I found it strange that roommates who leave each other every Friday and say to each other "See you on Sunday, brother" don't really know where each of them is on Saturday or how long it takes for their friend to get home. I wondered also if they weren't interested where each of them was coming from on Sunday mornings. Maybe if they knew that their friend had to travel to somewhere far away they could invite that friend to stay at their house Saturday.

By the time the inspection was over I had developed a plan. I assembled my accompanying staff members to the hall on the first floor of the barracks and told them that I intended to publish a new order. From now on, in every course that will open, each cadet will be obliged to write four lines about the places where each of his classmates comes from.

Members of the staff objected to the idea and said, "Sir, this isn't the way to educate someone." This was a typical response that I often heard when issuing new orders that were inconvenient. This time, the staff said that education comes by explaining and discussing and guidance and not through orders.

I replied that maybe they were right and this was not the way to educate, but at least the cadets would learn a bit about their country and maybe this will increase their love for the land; and at the same time, when those cadets become platoon commanders and lead their first conversations with their subordinates, the information that they'll learn here might help them.

I explained that if the subordinate tells his commander that he comes from a village in the south, and the commander stubbornly requires the name of the village, and then when he hears that his soldier is from Patish, he is able to say, "Oh, you mean when you pass the turn to Ofakim and then a few kilometers later the turn to Maslul, you come to a junction and there is a right turn to Patish" – such a dialogue will mean a lot to the soldier being questioned.

First, he will feel proud and confident about his hometown. And what's more, he will see that the army cares about him. And later on, when the soldier is about to go on leave, the officer could summon him and tell him that he is allowed to go a few hours earlier than his friends, because he lives in Patish, which is farther away. It's almost impossible to explain how such a gesture would be appreciated by the soldier.

"You think that caring for your soldiers means ensuring they sleep six hours at night? This is plain obedience of regular army orders. Caring about details like these is something that lies beyond army orders, and if you like, it is also leadership. But above anything else, it is education."

Somewhat to my satisfaction, one of the staff members stuck stubbornly to his opinion. He said again, "But sir, this is not the right way to educate someone."

I answered him, "Yes it is." I then calmly walked away.

Years later, during the ride I gave Yoaz Hendel, the navy commando team leader who I mentioned earlier in my story, Yoaz told me that he remembered during his days at Bahad 1 writing the four lines about his friends, and that he adopted the custom and instructed his own soldiers to do the same. I was glad to find that to some it appeared to be a fine way to educate.

The Definition of Leadership

The next story also occurred when I was commander of Bahad 1.

I accompanied the first delegation of the Witnesses in Uniform project to Poland, and our guide, Dr. Aharon Weiss, told the delegates about the ghetto children who secretly sang Hebrew songs at night. Listening to him, I tormented myself for not bringing our songbooks along for the delegates. I didn't give up; I called my deputy, Arie Itach, and asked him to send fifty songbooks to Krakow. Arie's son, Tzachi, was killed later in Lebanon and was the last casualty before the withdrawal in 2000. When we lived in Mitzpe Ramon, Arie and Tzachi – a teenager then – used to come to our house on Friday afternoons each carrying a musical instrument and would put on a pre-Shabbat performance. Due to his talents, Tzachi could easily have found a job in one of the IDF's bands but he chose to join a combat unit.

Arie heard me out, was silent for a few seconds, and then asked me: "Sir, aren't you a little confused? Do you remember where you are and where we are? If the songbooks are here with me on Tuesday evening in Mitzpe Ramon, how do you expect them to arrive in Krakow by Friday?"

"I arranged everything," I told him. "The IDF Orchestra is accompanying Prime Minister Yitzhak Rabin to Moscow tomorrow morning. All you have to do is deliver the songbooks at the airport at 4:00 a.m. to a representative of the orchestra and I will find a way to get them from Moscow to Krakow."

And so it was. On the tables of the Friday night dinner in Krakow, each delegate found a personal songbook next to their plate. During the meal, I asked the delegation commander to tell the soldiers to sing. The commander knocked on the table with his spoon and said: "Guys, your attention. Please open your songbooks and sing."

The group sang two or three soldiers' songs they knew by heart, and finally did me a favor and sang three more songs from the songbooks, which we had brought from thousands of miles away. After that they closed the books and adjourned to their rooms. I complained to the delegation commander that, though I understood that they were tired – we gave them the evening off – why did they have to leave so soon? Couldn't they stay longer and sing?

"Stern," he said, "you don't know today's youth."

I replied that maybe I didn't know the youth so well, but a year and a half ago my driver promised he would show me what a discotheque looked like and though we hadn't yet found the right opportunity, with God's help we'd find the time. What's more, I said, I think I actually know today's youth quite well; and lastly, why should I know the youth? Let the youth know me!

Several months later, I finally visited a discotheque. It was 11:30 at night and I had left Beersheba on my way to Mitzpe Ramon. When we approached the open road, I said to my driver, "Turn right!" and we came to a nearby nightclub. I went in.

Someone said to me, "Good evening, can we help you?"

"Yes, I have come to the discotheque."

"Please wait, you have come too early."

Since I was already in the place I asked them to start up the lights and the noise, so I would be able to check off a discotheque visit on my to-do list. The owners decided to play along and did what I asked. I stayed a few minutes more, made a check in my pad, and was back on my way to Mitzpe Ramon.

Later, in the school, I told the story to a group of cadets who had assembled to hear details about the upcoming delegation to Poland. I told the cadets that the commander on the last delegation had said that I don't know the young generation today, while I said that I did and that even if I didn't, the young generation should get to know me.

I said that I should learn about the young generation with the same methods that I learn about the enemy. They smiled but they knew that I meant something different. What I meant was that I should use the same methods, even though not for the same purpose: to know their strong and weak points so that I will know how to reach them and lead them to the destinations I think they need to get to.

"I failed in my life more times than any of you who sit in this hall," I said to them. "But, at the same time, I also have to my account more successful enterprises than anyone else here. What am I to do with all my failures and successes? Should I throw them to the wind? Would you rather have me come here and ask you what you would want me to teach you today?

"This is the fundamental question for any leader," I continued. "There are commanders and leaders who check where their subordinates want to go and do their best to lead them there. And then there are those, and I hope you will be among them, who face their subordinates and know where they need to be taken even when the crowd doesn't show any desire to go there. My definition of leadership is the ability to take people to places they wouldn't reach without you, whether because they need your lead to find the place, or because if it wasn't for you, they wouldn't want to go there."

A Nation Builds an Army; an Army Builds a Nation

I created this slogan and am happy to see that it still is relevant and in daily use. We had it appended to the badge of the Education Corps. Short slogans provide a significant benefit when you intend to convey a clear message.

When I was commander of Bahad 1 I created the slogan "An officer at all times" – always, anywhere, in uniform or in jeans, in the army or in the reserves. Immediately after it was published, this phrase became a platform for several nationwide debates on the status of the officer in Israeli society and what can be expected from him.

Later, when I was assigned to the Education Corps, I tried to find a slogan that would serve us in a similar way. I searched for something that would be communicative, that would fire up imaginations and aid us in achieving our goals as soldiers and commanders.

I wanted the slogan to represent my personal philosophy on the educational responsibility that we all share, in the army in particular and as a nation at large. I came up with the following:

"A nation builds an army" – everything we all do while preparing our youth for their military service.

"An army builds a nation" – everything the army contributes to its soldiers, both in education and in training, helps build a nation. The best examples of this are the female soldiers who serve as teachers in IDF units, the incredible contribution the army makes to the absorption of new immigrants, and of course, the military support of weak and deprived fragments of society. But it means even more: during their service the soldiers pass through a melting pot, and when they come out they are more tightly linked to the state, they have better manners, and they are more resourceful and imaginative.

I hope that David Ben-Gurion, Israel's first prime minister, who spoke of Israel as a melting pot, had in his mind a low, not high flame. We don't really want to "melt" anyone, and force them to give up their identity and forget their distinctiveness so that they will become a "new" Israeli person. We look for the opposite. By the direct encounters of all spheres of Israeli society and the camaraderie that evolves during military service, we want our youth to enjoy the richness of different cultures without attributing a priority to any particular one.

Not everyone agrees with this philosophy. Many think that the army steps into fields that are not its concern. From their point of view they ask: Who wants the army to build us a nation? This is the role of the Ministry of Education or the Ministry of Housing or perhaps the Ministry of Science. But one should inquire whether those who say this are truly sincere.

In principle, we would be foolish to ignore the potential contribution that the army provides by putting people together for two or three years, with all the encounters we experience there and all the educational work that the army does. There is no doubt in my mind that this benefits us as a nation and a society, and we should raise awareness of this point. If our commanders were more aware that they are helping to build a nation, it would drive them to try harder and to do a better job.

We know that many mothers say, "I sent a child to the army and I got back a completely different boy. Much more mature, responsible, one who talks about things he never did before and brings new friends home." And then you hear other mothers who say the opposite – they are fewer but nevertheless you hear them. They say, "I sent a flower to the army and the army sent me home a son who is brutal, aggressive, and has zero self-confidence."

The decision to use the slogan – "A nation builds an army which builds a nation" – was a conscious decision. It is an incontestable fact that the army builds the character of the nation. The question is: what is the right way to do that? How can we ensure that the building is done well? I believe that if we will do it decently, we will have an excellent army and eventually an excellent nation.

A nation builds an army, which builds a nation, which builds an army, which builds a nation, and so on.... This is a condensed description of our reality here in the decades since we established Israel, and it will describe us probably for many years to come.

I was surprised to learn how well the slogan was accepted by people. One day when I sat in a lecture given by an officer to a crowd of high school students, the officer said to the kids: "A very old, wise, and important man once said: 'A nation builds an army which builds a nation!' Now let us talk about it..."

I am certain he didn't have any idea who coined this phrase, and I don't even know what it was that I felt when I heard this imaginary description of me. This was nothing, though, compared to once when I heard someone say that Ben-Gurion himself invented the slogan.

Soldiers at the City of David

A British joke tells of a man who enters an antiques shop and asks, "What's new?" This is the feeling that descends upon anyone who visits the City of David in Jerusalem several times. Each time you go there, you find something new, though of course this something is usually older than the oldest things you saw the last time you were there. A new excavation, a new theory that explains the old findings, or a new finding that requires an even newer theory.

On one of our recent wedding anniversaries, I met with David Be'eri, founder of the Ir David foundation, in the City of David (Dorit says that only *our* anniversaries can begin at the Yad Vashem Holocaust Museum and finish at the City of David). Davidele, as he is called, said to me, "You were absolutely right!" I asked him what he was talking about, and he said that three days earlier he had met a secular employee of the Shin Bet Israel Security Agency who had been on an organized tour of the excavations recently, and since then he reads the Bible every day.

I had good Bible teachers both in elementary school and in the yeshiva. But the most important lessons on the Bible I received weren't taught to me by any one of them. The lessons from others made me understand just how much we belong to the Bible and how much the Bible belongs to us.

The first lesson was taught me by a secular Jew, Ilan Zaharoni, who lives not far from ancient Megiddo. A group of us were standing on a hill called Saul's Shoulder, on the Gilboa Mountain, and there he described the final days of King Saul and his son, Jonathon. I felt that I could literally see King Saul's horse tied outside the house of the sorceress of Ein Dor (a kibbutz in our days) and the Philistine forces gathering in Shunem (Sulam in the vicinity of today's Merchavia), and then Saul and his son climbing the Gilboa Mountain on their horses. He brought the Bible to life.

The second lesson I received was from the religiously observant Davidele. I went on one of his guided tours of the City of David with a group of rich donors, whom I invited in order to demonstrate to them how important it would be to bring soldiers on those tours. I thought that each soldier – with a *kippa* or without – should share this experience of being part of the Bible, or at least realize that he is a link in a chain that starts in biblical times and continues until today. I knew quite a lot about the City of David before the tour since this was one of the subjects I studied in university, but visiting the place with Davidele left a tremendous impression on me. During his lecture I once again felt that I could see the men he spoke about come to life. I followed the Israelites of Hezekiah's days on their way to bring water and sneaked back with them into the besieged city.

This tour ended with the creation of "Project Moriah" – the name of the mountain upon which the Jewish Temple used to rest. The project enables us to bring soldiers to tour Jerusalem and the City of David. We launched the project after we became aware of an alarming statistic – half of the soldiers in the IDF had never visited Jerusalem. Since the beginning of the project, tens of thousands of soldiers have made their first tours to the ancient sites. When those soldiers later became commanders, they escorted their own soldiers to Jerusalem. During their civilian hours, they bring their families and their friends.

There were several projects that brought soldiers to Jerusalem before we launched Moriah; the novelty of our project is that the soldiers now come to Jerusalem not to achieve a specific purpose and then return to their bases; they come to see the city and its main attractions. Now all commanders who want to take their soldiers to the City of David and to other parts of Jerusalem can receive all the necessary funds and assistance they require.

The central purpose of those visits is to emphasize the Jewish people's bond to Jerusalem, though it is indisputably a sacred city to all three monotheistic religions.

News of the project made its way fairly quickly to the press. The *Haaretz* newspaper criticized the initiative, and claimed that the army was organizing the project with the right-wing Elad Association and that the project was financed by right-wing philanthropist Irwin Moskowitz. I responded that I don't regard either Elad or Irwin Moskowitz to be improper in any way, and we don't check how our donors earned their money and what they do with it. I said this because the question itself infuriated me, but the truth was that we never received any money from Moskowitz or Elad.

When soldiers began arriving in larger numbers for the tours, I called Davidele and asked him to purchase two hundred Bibles. I wanted every soldier on the tour to carry a Bible while walking through the narrow alleys and passageways. We had a loud dispute over it. Davidele didn't see any reason to give Bibles to the soldiers when anyway during the tour their guides read the chapters out loud to them.

I argued that if soldiers hold a Bible in their hands, when the guide says Jeremiah, chapter 5, the soldier might browse through the book and notice by accident that there's also a book called Genesis or Samuel. And when the guide reads a certain verse, the soldier's interest might peak, and he or she might want to know a little more about the background of what they had just heard. And then the soldier will read a couple more verses and might be curious about what happened afterward and read a few more. What's more, I thought, in our days mere walking with a Bible in one's hand was itself a virtue.

Davidele said to this: "But certainly you know…?"

I asked him, "What?"

And he repeated, "You know!"

"What do I know?" I demanded. "That people will claim we are giving out Bibles because we are religious and that it is religious coercion?"

Davidele confirmed his fear and said that distributing Bibles might lead to the abolishment of the project because people will say that the religious are forcing the secular to read the Bible.

"Perhaps," I said, "but there will be people on the other side who will be furious and ask who allowed the soldiers to carry the Bibles without a *kippa* on their heads."

I knew from experience that when both sides are not satisfied, there is no reason to worry and that all will work out. Davidele remained unconvinced, and I had to threaten that if I saw a group walking without Bibles in their hands, I would stop the project immediately. He finally conceded, and until this day, all soldiers who tour the City of David do so with a Bible in their hands.

At one of our subsequent meetings, after more than thirty thousand soldiers had visited the City of David – after he told me the story about the Shin Bet employee who now reads the Bible and said I was right – I felt a slight exhilarating sensation, as if he had said to me: "You won." You should understand that Davidele lives and breathes the City of David. I came there as a guest only for a brief visit, and yet I was fortunate to be able to contribute something of myself.

Zalman

It is because of Zalman Bernstein that the Avi Chai Foundation, which works to unite the secular and religious, exists.

When I had just come to Bahad 1, I thought that we needed to add some classes on Jewish topics to the school curriculum. Being new, however, I was worried people would say, "Look how this new commander immediately begins with religious coercion...." So I went to the commander of the Education Corps at the time and represented my idea.

His response came in the form of a question: "Do you know Elazar Shtrum?"

"Yes," I said, "I believe he is with Peace Now, or another organization called Roots."

The commander continued, "He just received a large amount of money from a billionaire by the name Bernstein. Do you know him?"

I said I didn't and added, "I am not going after money. I'm looking for content."

And so, to promote content, the commander of the Education Corps organized several meetings with rabbis and secular leaders like Elazar Shtrum, and some others whose expertise was Jewish identity, and together we created a Jewish studies curriculum that could fit everybody – religious and not religious.

Shtrum arranged for the necessary funds from his donor. When I was asked when I expected to launch the program, I answered that I could do it immediately, meaning during the next officers' course that was about to begin in three weeks.

A couple of months later Elazar Shtrum called me and said that the donor wanted to visit Bahad 1 and see how his money was being spent. Naturally I agreed, and Shtrum gave me two potential dates to choose from. One was impossible and the other, once I checked it against the Jewish calendar, proved to fall exactly on Holocaust Memorial Day. I asked that the donor come the evening before. We had just returned then with the first Witnesses in Uniform delegation from Poland.

Zalman Bernstein arrived in a private plane with an entourage that included his wife, Mem, Elazar Shtrum, another woman, and two female translators. They left their luggage at a nearby hotel in Mitzpe Ramon and came at 7:00 p.m. When he entered my office, he said, "Hello, I'm Zalman. I came to see what you do here with my money."

"That's perfectly fine," I replied, "but right now we have something else we are doing. It is Holocaust Memorial Day, and we have a ceremony to attend. You can come with us if you want."

We went to the ceremony, which was impressive and moving. When the ceremony was over, I said to him, "Now please return to your hotel." He asked when he should come back, and I said eight in the morning.

The next morning, he showed up in my office promptly at eight and said, "Hello, I came to see what you do here with my money."

"All right," I said, "but first you must understand what 'here' means. There are three jeeps outside. There is a maneuver in the field. If you want, you're welcome to join me."

We climbed into the jeeps and toured the fields for several hours. We observed a live-fire exercise performed by the cadets, during which the Holocaust Memorial Day air siren went off. All the soldiers stopped where they were. The machine guns and the mortars became silent, maneuvers came to a standstill. Everyone froze in his place and stood with his head lowered. A megaphone in the battalion commander's vehicle transferred the siren screech from his car radio to all the surrounding soldiers. This was Zalman's way to learn about the complexity of our life here.

We returned to base. It was already noon. He came again to my office and said: "Hello, I want to remind you that I came to see what you do here with my money."

"Our chief instructor officer is waiting outside for you with our education officer," I said. "He will show you what we do with your money."

Thus began my long friendship with Zalman. He must have appreciated the fact that I wasn't impressed by his billions of dollars. Later we became real friends. He was a unique person, as the following story will demonstrate.

One day, Zalman came to Israel determined to buy himself a burial plot on the Mount of Olives. Rabbi Shlomo Riskin from Efrat set up a meeting for him with someone from the burial society. Since Rabbi Riskin is a *kohen* and cannot enter a cemetery, he remained waiting at the Seven Arches Hotel chanting chapters of Psalms while Zalman, accompanied by a man from the burial society, walked down to the cemetery. All of a sudden, wild screams were heard and Zalman appeared at the gate, entered his car, and took off. After he left, the man from the burial society showed up, pale and shaking.

"What happened?" asked Rabbi Riskin.

"The man is a complete lunatic! I showed him a nice plot and he says to me, 'I don't want this one,' and he points to a plot next to the holy Rabbi Kook's grave. And if that's not bad enough, it is in a section of the cemetery that is saved for observant Jews only. How can I let him be buried there? He is married to a non-Jew!"

The man told Riskin that when he told Zalman he couldn't buy a lot in that section, Zalman said, "How do you know I can't? How much will it cost?"

So the man said, "But you can't! You simply can't!" and Zalman kept shouting, "But how much?"

Afterwards, Rabbi Riskin tried to explain to Zalman that he couldn't demand to be buried so close to the grave of Rabbi Kook. He said that he didn't consider even himself to be worthy enough to be buried there. Zalman replied that he knew that after he died either he won't see anything at all, or he will see everything, and therefore he insisted on this specific plot....

After the incident on the Mount of Olives, Zalman wrote me a letter, trying to explain his stubbornness: "I didn't do so well with my children's Jewish education. But after I pass away, if they visit my grave and see the most sacred place for the Jewish nation, from the most beautiful point, maybe this will move something in them."

Rabbi Riskin met Zalman frequently in New York and they used to study together. They even started learning the book of Genesis. Zalman would order kosher food for Rabbi Riskin and a cheeseburger for himself. He was a kind of straightforward, no-nonsense man. Several months later, Rabbi Riskin called the man from the burial society and said to him, "Listen, I take full responsibility. Before the day he will require your services, this man will become an observant Jew. Give him the burial plot he requested." The man agreed to give the plot to Zalman, and another appointment was fixed.

They once again drove to the Mount of Olives. Rabbi Riskin again stayed outside the gates and Zalman went down with the burial society man, and once again Riskin heard loud shouts. Once again Zalman came up, jumped into his car, and drove off.

"What went wrong this time?" asked Riskin.

"The man is insane. We agreed on everything, but when I showed him the plot I hadn't even finished my sentence when he threw himself on the ground and started yelling: Don't you see I won't fit in here?"

Zalman is buried there today. He died of cancer. During the hard days of the treatment he called me and said: "Stern, remember you once said that if I ever need you, you'll come over?"

I said I did.

"If you could come this week, when I receive radiation treatment, I'd be very grateful," he said.

I bought a ticket on the cheapest airline in those days, called Tower Air. I truly believe that I was Tower Air's only passenger who had a limousine waiting for him upon landing.

I spent the entire week with Zalman. In a previous chapter I wrote about the last time I saw him on the 64th floor of the Metropolitan Tower in New York City just before I returned to Israel. Zalman left all his fortune to the Avi Chai Foundation he had founded, in order that it may continue to open people's hearts to Judaism and to unite the religious and secular.

Birthright Meets the IDF

When I became head of the IDF's Education Corps, Birthright was already an ongoing project, highly popular and appreciated. Birthright, *Taglit* in Hebrew, organized intensive tours to Israel for Jewish youth from all over the world, and was intended to build a connection between these kids and the country and turn them into Israel's goodwill ambassadors. The tours included a visit to an army base for a couple of hours.

One day, Dr. Shimshon Shoshani, head of Birthright, came to my office with my friend and neighbor Binny Shalev, to ask me to arrange that the responsibility for the brief visits to the army bases be transferred from the IDF Spokesman's Unit to the Education Corps. I refused, saying that I didn't see any advantage that could be gained through such a change and that the Spokesman's Unit was just as good as I would be in coordinating visits to IDF bases. I added that the Education Corps did have certain advantages in other fields and I would be happy to talk about how we could integrate them into Birthright.

I also told Shoshani that I would be ready to accept the kind of responsibility he was asking for if he allowed me to put several soldiers on each of the Birthright buses for the duration of the trip. Shoshani asked me what the purpose would be, and I said that bringing soldiers together with Jews from overseas, who do not know much and will ask the soldier questions about Israel and Judaism, will force the soldier to think about his or her own

Jewish identity. Our soldiers, in short, will be forced to cope with the challenge.

I assumed that in cases where the soldier did not have a developed Jewish identity, the encounter could quickly turn embarrassing, and I hoped that the embarrassment would inspire soldiers to learn more and to search for answers. The next group of Birthright participants will then find the soldiers more competent.

The program in its new mode started, and because of its importance and the resentment I was afraid it might raise, I assigned Yael Wolf, my assistant, to coordinate our side of things. From Birthright's side the program was directed by Ofira Bino. Dr. Shoshani and I closely followed the program, which was later called by Birthright "Mifgashim" – Hebrew for "encounters."

Tens of thousands of youth from all over the world and additional thousands of soldiers and officers have participated in these encounters. Following a number of trips, a survey that the Birthright board of directors ordered from Brandeis University, revealed that for the Diaspora participants, the best part of the trip was meeting the IDF soldiers.

This excellent education workshop was supplied to the army at no cost and ended up providing the military with a sense of camaraderie with our Diaspora brothers and sisters, demonstrating the common challenges we all face as Israelis, soldiers, and Jews. It also gave a nice twist to the definition of the IDF – the military for the entire Jewish people.

Minerals and Jewish Identity

Toward the end of my military service, I had some free time one day and used the opportunity to get a haircut at a barber in the Kirya Military Headquarters in Tel Aviv. While he cut my hair, the barber informed me that Yulia, one of the assistant barbers, had just finished her conversion. I was thrilled to hear that.

Several months earlier, while getting my haircut, Yulia sat on one of the chairs in the barbershop and I interviewed her. Since I couldn't simply ask her if she was Jewish, I asked if she had heard about the IDF's Nativ Program, a course I had established as head of the Education Corps for soldiers seeking conversion.

She said yes, but that as the sole provider for herself and her grandmother, she couldn't attend the course. Yulia told me that she had a special permit allowing her to work a few hours in the mornings or in the evenings for a private cafeteria inside the military base. I asked her if she would succeed in saving enough money to attend the course, if I arranged for her to work an entire month – from the morning until the evening – in the cafeteria.

An hour later, Yulia was sitting in my office with the base commander. He confirmed that he knew the civilian who ran the cafeteria but hesitated whether to authorize special leave from the army for Yulia for an entire month. Finally, I had to remind him who was the officer with the final say. Yulia left to participate in Nativ, and now I was being informed that she had converted to Judaism.

I sat enjoying the happy news when suddenly I heard someone behind me say, "Sir, allow me to salute you."

I looked at the mirror and saw an air force lieutenant-colonel standing there. "Thanks to you," he went on, "the village I live in, Kfar Yona, added a special class in Jewish studies at the local elementary school."

I didn't understand how I was connected to this, and the officer explained. "I am a graduate of the second graduating class of the Mehtzavim Program. I joined the project without great hopes and without my commanders' support. I only came because you ordered me to. When we finished the program, we all agreed that we needed to do something to ensure that the next generation will not be as ignorant as we were before the project about our Jewish identity. I took upon myself to lobby the education committee in my hometown, and today, two years later, our school has adopted a new Jewish studies program."

Mehtzavim – Hebrew for "minerals" – was a program I had started toward the end of my career in the IDF with the aim of reinforcing Jewish identity among high-ranking officers

– lieutenant-colonels and higher ranks. I believe that being a good combat soldier is not enough but that our soldiers and commanders also need to understand what they are fighting for, what it means to be Jewish, and what it means to live in the Land of Israel, the homeland for the only Jewish and democratic state in the world.

In addition to meaning "minerals," the word Mehtzavim is also a Hebrew acronym for "IDF Leadership Education in Jerusalem." The program lasts a week and, as its name gives away, takes place in Jerusalem. During the week, the officers tour the city, meet representatives of different streams of Judaism, and, mainly, discover themselves. The project met a lot of resistance when it first began, and as the air force officer mentioned with his personal story in the barbershop, the first participants attended only after being directly ordered. Today the list of attendance is prepared a year in advanced because of the large number of officers who sign up.

Ya'akov Castel, the coordinator of the project on behalf of the Jerusalem-based Hartman Institute, likes to quote the commander of one of the IDF's largest training bases, who said after graduating the program, "You have given me back Judaism."

Castel says that the project's success makes him sad and happy at the same time. Happy, because he gets to see the great thirst for something a little more spiritual, ethical, positive, humane, fresh, and authentic, and how people yearn for more knowledge about our past, our traditions, and our people. On the other hand, he is sad because of the great tragedy of Israel's education system, which has estranged young and intelligent people from their Jewish past.

It's a pity we need such a seminar to peel off the armor of alienation, but I'm glad that the seminar exists.

I was already getting ready for retirement when Dorit and I came one Friday night for Shabbat services to the Kotel in Jerusalem. The plaza opposite the holy prayer site was crowded with people, including a large group of soldiers. Rabbi Moshe Hager, the head of the pre-military academy at Yatir, was there. He said,

"I just told them that Elazar Stern is responsible for bringing the IDF back to Jerusalem and nobody can take that away from him."

I then told him that as Dorit and I walked into the plaza, I had said to her that maybe we shouldn't have come to the Kotel on Friday night.

"The last time I was here on a Friday night I made money since the rabbi who heckled and attacked me was ordered by court to compensate me and my family," I told Rabbi Hager. "And, as you know, a Jew is not supposed to earn money on Shabbat."

KNOWLEDGE EQUALS STRENGTH?

A few days before I was scheduled to start my assignment as head of the Education Corps, I decided that I wanted to learn a little about Havat Hashomer – the Shomer Farm – a base under the Corps' command in the north for disadvantaged youth who come from difficult backgrounds and often have criminal pasts. It is frequently their last chance for a future in society.

I informed the base's staff that I would be coming but ordered them to treat me like any other soldier. I took off my ranks and came there dressed in a work uniform, with a small kitbag and a rifle.

I arrived at the base in the early evening so I could have a chance to meet the soldiers before they went to sleep. The base commander sent me to one of the companies and from there I was directed to one of the platoons. I approached the platoon commander and said to her, "Hi, good evening."

She replied, "At ease, Elazar."

I said, "Okay."

She quickly turned around with a serious look on her face and said, "Elazar, that isn't an answer. To you, I am 'Yes, Ma'am.' If you don't get it right by tomorrow morning, you will start to get punished. Is that clear?"

"Yes," I said.

"Elazar, it's 'yes ma'am.' From tomorrow morning this is a violation, clear?"

"Yes, ma'am."

Then she walked around me and noted that my fingers were not lined up straight over my rifle and that this too would be punishable starting the next day. And, so it went on and on, with me saying, yes, and her correcting me, yes ma'am, again and again. I started to think that I would be late to meet the soldiers but luckily enough the deputy base commander passed on the sidewalk, and I approached him and asked him to convince the young platoon commander to let me go and meet the soldiers. He took her aside and after a brief conversation he convinced her to let me go, and even directed me to my designated quarters. She simply took my request to be treated like the other soldiers a bit too seriously.

The soldiers had just finished their evening roll-call when I entered their barracks. I asked where I could put my things and was directed to one of the top bunks. I decided to use my kitbag as a pillow. I must admit that being at Havat Hashomer, I was quite certain that I would wake up in the morning with my bag empty – a prejudiced, distorted image which I must humbly apologize for.

I sat in the room and tried to join the conversation with the other soldiers – Eran, Moshe, and Ido. When I opened my mouth, Ido said to the others, "No one speaks with this guy. He is here to rat on us."

They began a conversation about girlfriends, and I hardly managed to say a few words. They then started discussing me. They thought I had come to replace their sergeant. My red boots – standard for paratroopers – looked very suspicious. Toward the end of the evening, they started to warm up to me a bit.

Next morning started with loud shouts of "Platoon 3, good morning," and then personal calls: "Eran get up, there is a new figure in the company today; you're going to be surprised! Moshe, come down, you'll meet a new person today. Ido, I told you before, why are you still in bed? There's a new person in the company!"

I was certain they were going to expose my true identity. I didn't understand why they were doing that. And the shouts went on and on, promising the sleepy soldiers a great day and a new person.

Unlike in the paratroopers, where one squad commander tells one of the soldiers to wake up the rest of the soldiers, here the entire staff does the waking up. I say this with great admiration for the hard work they do.

After a few minutes of shouting, the staff finally succeeded in getting all of the soldiers out of bed. They then announced that the new member of the company the soldiers were going to meet was their new training officer. I relaxed.

Hours later, I asked the platoon staff to explain to me the reason for the morning shouting. "Why wake up people in such a way?" I asked. They explained that their soldiers needed a good reason to get up every day. Otherwise, they would just stay in bed.

I needed to pray in the morning so a squad commander was summoned to accompany me to the synagogue. The synagogue was two hundred meters from the barracks where we slept. The squad commander told me: "From here to the black pillar is thirty meters. You have ten seconds to be there. Move!" She came after me and continued: "From here to the corner over there. You have twenty seconds. Move!" And she went on like this until we reached the synagogue. I said the morning prayers while the commander waited for me outside, and the road back was done the same way. Later I asked why they didn't simply say, "You have two hundred meters, move," instead of dividing the distance into short segments. The staff asked me if I wanted to see what would happen if they didn't break up the rout into segments. They let the entire platoon out on the road and asked everyone to run the entire distance to the training fields. Each soldier ran in a different direction.

Later, two hundred of us sat in the hall sweating and waiting as patiently as we could for the new training officer to come. We waited for twenty minutes, and in front of us stood all the commanders and watched over us. "Hey, you," they would yell out at some random soldier, "why are you smiling?" No one was smiling, of course, except for me, since as usual I could not erase my smile.

Finally the new training officer arrived. The company commander saluted her, despite the fact that he was a first lieutenant and she a second lieutenant. When I asked him later why he saluted her and not the other way around as rank demanded, he explained that he wanted to teach the soldiers a lesson that teachers needed to be respected.

The officer introduced herself and started a PowerPoint show. One of the slides showed the words "Knowledge equals power." She turned to the soldiers and asked, "Who would like to explain this sentence?"

I looked around. Maybe five soldiers raised their hands. After three of the soldiers answered, she got the answer she was looking for. Itzik, one of the soldiers said: "Ma'am, 'knowledge equals power' means that the more knowledge I possess, the stronger I become."

The officer said, "That's a good answer. The rest of you, please put your hands down." But Ido, who sat behind me, kept his hand raised. She turned and said, "I asked you to put your hands down."

Ido said, "Ma'am, I have another answer."

The officer said he should keep his answer for the next question, which of course was a degrading response. Why should he keep his answer for the next question when it's an answer for this question? Ido said, "But Ma'am, I don't agree with the answer."

The words "I don't agree" at Havat Hashomer warmed my heart. I was now beginning to have a good time.

The officer asked Ido why he didn't agree. "Look, Ma'am, if knowledge equals power, it is true that when I have more knowledge, I have more strength, but it also means that if I have more strength I have more knowledge, and I don't agree. It isn't true."

The training officer stood there speechless. I thought to myself, who knows how many training officers stood there before her, using the same lesson's outline and reading the same stupid equation from the same slide show. And here, stands up a soldier from Havat Hashomer, and says: "I disagree with you." And then he adds a sentence that is 100 percent logical, mathematical, and correct and she is unable to cope with it.

I learned a lot from my day at Havat Hashomer. The tests we do in the army, what do they really predict? How much do they predict? You encounter time and again, in the army and outside the army, people who do extremely well with no correlation to their education or to our standard measuring methods.

When I was commander of Bahad 1, people used to say that with me in charge it was difficult for them to expel a cadet who was Ethiopian, Bedouin, Druze, or a new immigrant. The staff was very upset about it.

When I was asked about it, I explained that these people hadn't had the same starting point as other cadets and that I would like to see the staff members who want to expel the cadets come to Bahad 1 speaking a brand new language. No one graduates the school with a perfect score. The important question is whether you have the qualities, the capabilities, and the right values to be an officer and whether you show progress in the right direction.

This cadet might graduate from the school and have lower grades than other cadets, since the starting point of a Bedouin, a Druze, or a new immigrant is lower. But then, three months after his graduation, he will continue to climb and might overtake the other cadets with his leadership skills. People also need to bear in mind that it is important for those weaker sectors of society to have representation at the graduation ceremony as long as a minimal standard is maintained.

Many times the staff got annoyed mostly out of ignorance. One day, an Ethiopian cadet stood before me; the staff claimed he lacked the necessary amount of self-confidence. I asked the staff how they could tell, and they referred to his refusal to look his commanders in the eyes. I summoned the cadet and asked him about this, and he said to me, "I don't look straight into my father's eyes either. It is one of the ways we show respect in our community: we don't look directly into the eyes of people we respect."

The two examples – the soldier at Havat Hashomer and the Ethiopian cadet – led me to doubt our true ability to assess people who are different. How accurate are the assessments we make of soldiers and whether they will be good commanders? Can someone really test another soldier's capabilities without disengaging from his or her own personal set of standards? I think there is a lot more we can do. Is it possible to judge who is a Jew and who is not? Is a *kippa* or the observance of a certain commandment proof of being a Jew? What should we say about a person who lives in the secular Kfar Shmaryahu or a person who lives in the religious and right-wing settlement of Yitzhar? We are quick to pass judgment, and I spoke earlier about how fast we label people, put them into a drawer, and throw away the key, without ever intending to open those drawers again.

When I was the head of the Human Resources Directorate, I led a number of discussions on the issue of promoting special sectors in society. Following one discussion about Ethiopians, I decided to establish the Amir Course, designed to bridge the gap between Ethiopian youth, their unique cultural symbols, and Israeli culture and language. It is a course that prepares Ethiopian youngsters to meet the standards and requirements of the army, a sort of adapter between their cultural world and the cultural world of the people who write the tests.

Brigadier General Nissim Barda, a senior officer in the directorate, took responsibility for the project. The achievements of the graduates and the careers they developed in the IDF surprised even us, the people who believed in them to begin with. A good example was an experiment we did once on the way soldiers are selected for flight school. We borrowed for our experiment several selectors from the air force, and I spoke with one of them, an Ethiopian girl. She was a graduate of the Amir Course. She told me that she had asked to be released from her work because she felt she wasn't good enough. I turned to her commanders and was informed that she was by far their best selector.

A graduate of Amir – selecting air force pilots!

IMMIGRANTS AND THE PARATROOPERS

I was invited to visit the paratroopers training base in Sanur to speak with the staff commanders ahead of the arrival of the upcoming draft.

I enjoyed returning to the place where I had spent a large part of my military service and even more the encounter with the young commanders, nervously awaiting the arrival of a new group of soldiers. As usual, the stage of the lecture that I like most – the Q&A – arrived. I was asked by a young platoon commander: "Sir, how do you define volunteering today and how should we educate our soldiers to volunteer?"

Facing a question like this, to which I didn't prepare an answer beforehand, I turned to my old response and said, "Wait with your question and I'll get back to it later." The conversation rolled on, and I asked the audience if any of them were new immigrants. No one raised his hand, and I thought that maybe they weren't familiar with my definition of a new immigrant, so I added, "Anyone who came to the country in the last three years or less, please raise your hand." No one moved. "Four? Five?" I began to feel disheartened. At seven, I stopped. A hand finally went up. I asked the sergeant who raised his hand where he came from.

"New Jersey, sir." I was now truly disheartened.

I now remembered a piece of information that had been brought to my attention. Though all the other infantry units had among their recruits large numbers of new immigrants from the former USSR, the paratroopers had hardly any. Now I returned to the platoon commander and said to him, "Let me tell you now what volunteering is in our days. If volunteering means doing something that you don't have to do, for you today it means treating new immigrants like everyone else. The next time I come here, in a little more than a year from today, and have a similar conversation with the staff, and I repeat this question, at least three hands will be raised, belonging to sergeants and to platoon commanders – all of them soldiers whom you personally trained."

The platoon commander stared at me and said, "But they will not want to cooperate." I said he is probably right but he has to persuade them in such a way that they will in the end. This also is a sort of volunteering.

He continued to ask, "But how will I succeed?" I told him that a few days after he receives his recruits, he has to mark among them two or three soldiers whom he will direct toward command.

"But how? What method should I use?"

I gave him an example: "Some of the new immigrants do not feel comfortable speaking Hebrew. Select one and give him an assignment – to give a lecture before the unit about how it feels to be a new immigrant in the country. The second one can talk about his experience being a new immigrant in high school, and the third can tell about his experience as a new immigrant in the platoon."

On the one hand, I said, this will build up the immigrant's self-confidence and on the other it will benefit the rest of the soldiers in the unit.

The officer, so it seemed, liked my idea, but repeated: "They will not play along..." I said again that he was probably right, but that's why he should take one of the top soldiers in the unit and make him sit with each of the new immigrants for half-an-hour a day to help him prepare the lecture. I could see in the officer's eyes that he got it. "Thanks, sir!"

On my way out, I was escorted by the base commandeer, Colonel Itay Virov, and even before we stepped out of the hall he hurriedly asked me, "What do you want from the poor commander? He doesn't know what I already know."

"What do you know?" I asked him.

"That there won't be even one immigrant in the company he will start training on Sunday," Virov said.

We spoke some more and I left.

This was before I became head of the Human Resources Directorate; nevertheless I went to the head of the directorate at the time, Major General Yudke Segev, and asked him to transfer responsibility for immigrants' absorption in the IDF to the Education Corps. It wasn't a simple matter since other military branches claimed ownership over the issue. In the end we reached a compromise and the Education Corps received responsibility for "leading immigrant absorption in the IDF."

One of the first things I did was set up a meeting to discuss the draft of new immigrants into the Paratroopers Brigade. I invited representatives of the Human Resources Directorate, the Ground Forces Command, and the brigade.

During the discussion, everyone agreed that there was a problem. Immigrants didn't make it to the paratroopers, and it didn't really mater if it was because they didn't pass the tryouts, or simply didn't volunteer. Maybe they lost any hope in advance. The brigade officials were frustrated by this, because they felt they were missing the many fine qualities of those immigrants. We agreed that the brigade would make a special effort to persuade new immigrants to try out for the paratroopers. Everyone agreed but they added that the fruits of such efforts would not be visible until next summer, because kids who were scheduled to enlist in the coming months were no longer in school and could not be easily reached.

Next year seemed too far away for me. I told them that if it could wait until next summer, we wouldn't have assembled a meeting in such a hurry, and I added that in one of the Education Corps bases there were one hundred new immigrants preparing for service in a combat unit.

I suggested we start with those kids. Since the paratroopers had already completed their recruiting quotas for the upcoming draft, and enlistment information had already been sent to those who passed their tests, I agreed that each immigrant kid they managed to recruit would be counted above their quota. Yudke Segev, to my satisfaction, approved this, though because of human resources planning he limited the total additional number of paratroopers in the coming draft to twenty.

Weeks passed, and one day I was invited to visit and have a conversation with no less then eighty immigrants who had signed up for the paratrooper tryouts. I met them in the evening at the Tel Hashomer Induction Center, and the only issue I had to tackle was a petition by six of the soldiers who the doctors had rejected on medical grounds.

The next phase was the actual physical tryouts scheduled to start at 3:00 a.m. in the fields around Tel Hashomer. I went back to my office and called Yudke, told him what I had seen, and invited him to accompany me later that night and see the kids during the *gibbush*, Hebrew for "tryouts." Yudke quickly accepted my suggestion.

When we arrived at the *gibbush*, Yudke and I had an opportunity to learn several Russian curses that we were not familiar with. The bottom line was that out of the group, the paratroopers received even more than twenty new immigrant soldiers.

In the next draft, the paratroopers approached me with a request to do the process the same way, that is, to receive immigrants as a surplus addition to their quota. I said that they would receive an equal number of immigrants, but only half of them would be counted above their quota. They didn't like my decision so I calmly explained that starting with the third draft, all new immigrants recruited would be considered part of their regular quotas. The paratroopers threatened that in such a case they would have to reconsider recruiting new immigrants altogether. I laughed in their faces and said, "Go ahead, try me. After your experience with these new soldiers, you will beg me for more of them." Needless to say, I was right.

Not very long afterward, the Paratroopers Brigade became the leading combat unit in recruiting new immigrants.

Two months later, I visited another brigade in the West Bank, and knowing about my special feelings for new immigrants and my past service in the 202nd Battalion, the commander, Colonel Roni Numa, took me to visit one of the companies stationed in Ramallah, where Yasser Arafat lived at the time. We put bulletproof vests and helmets on and ran into the building that was being used as the company's headquarters. I had a wonderful time interviewing the soldiers and especially the immigrants among them. Alex was a graduate of the first *gibbush*, the one Yudke and I had visited in the dead of the night. He informed me that now he was on his way to a Nativ seminar. Another victory.

Soon after he was appointed commander of the Paratroopers Brigade, Aviv Kochavi called me and said: "Sir, we succeeded with new immigrants and I am looking for new challenges. I would like the paratroopers to try to assimilate youth from Havat Hashomer into our ranks."

I was pleased and enjoyed working with Aviv and witnessing how excellent officers like him are able to understand what is truly important in what we are doing in the IDF.

There's No One Else to Help Kids Like Yossi

Of course, not all the efforts to integrate weaker sectors into the IDF succeeded. I believe with all my heart that the IDF is the army of all the people. I believe Ben-Gurion's "melting pot" can serve as a banner we should raise high above our heads, just as relevant today as it was when he first declared it.

What makes the IDF exceptional compared to other militaries around the world is its diversity. It consists of a mix of people who in normal circumstances would never consider befriending one another – and here they are willing to give their lives for one another. If it wasn't for the IDF, chances are that they would never even have met, and now that they have met, it isn't only the army that benefits from this friendship, it is the entire nation.

And being the army of the people, it welcomes different types of soldiers, some who naturally will take away much more than they could ever give. The investment in these soldiers is the IDF's gift to civilian society. A soldier who learned a profession, finished his matriculation exams, or even went through a conversion in the army, enters the civilian world a prouder citizen, both in himself and in his state, with greater potential to make a contribution to his community.

Not everyone in the IDF thinks this way. There are those who believe that the army should be more practical, invest the resources it has in the soldiers' professional capabilities, and remove all those who require special efforts. Major General Gil Regev believed in this practical approach, and we had quite a few disputes on the subject.

The conflicts between us began as soon as Regev was appointed head of the Human Resources Directorate. As head of the Education Corps, I was then promoting the delegations to Poland. He was more interested in tailoring costumes for the entire high command, for a big party he was planning based on the theme of Swan Lake. The party was later cancelled after news about it was leaked to the media.

Gil Regev laid out his objectives for the Human Resources Directorate in a speech he gave during a strategic workshop in November 2002. To avoid any doubt, Regev spoke before cameras and even said during his lecture: "You can write down my words, and it is recorded on film so that anyone who wishes will be able to go back later and quote me."

Regev spoke about the shift from "an army of the people" to "a professional army." He presented a new concept for managing human resources that would support an efficient utilization of human resources – "not in the quantitative aspect but in the qualitative one." He also said that to save us a long afternoon of discussions and efforts, he would spell out his intentions. "I do not intend to recruit weaker sectors into the IDF. It is expensive, ineffective, and I do not have the money for this. Maybe, if circumstances were different, values would take precedent over economics. We are not in such a position, and therefore we will not be doing that anymore."

I asked, and to my regret I was the only one who did, what does he mean when he says weaker sectors? The head of the Human Resources Directorate said he meant communities that "we have to nurse a large part of the time, instead of them doing their job."

I said I still didn't understand, and the head of the Human Resources Directorate instructed me to think about the definition he had just provided. I insisted that it wasn't a definition at all. I felt that his words were opposite to the position of the Chief of Staff at the time, Moshe "Bogie" Ya'alon. Meanwhile those words found their way to the media (I had nothing to do with leaking the news to the press, though I wasn't sorry about it), and Gil Regev hurriedly sent an officer from his headquarters to collect all the recordings of his speech that could be found and destroy them.

After the article came out, I received a letter from the commander of Havat Hashomer in which he described the important work they were doing there as well as the investment in soldiers who had "lost their faith in everything that comes from the authorities, the establishment, and the social system." He gave an example of fifteen soldiers who had just graduated and were recruited by the Paratroopers Brigade, getting another chance to reach the Israeli mainstream.

He attached to his letter a note he had received from one of his corporals, who was outraged by what Regev said. The young commander – Liron was her name – wrote how she had read Regev's comments after returning from an exhausting day of work with soldiers like Yossi, who has to support his entire family because of his mother's disability.

"I don't know if it is the IDF's responsibility to help kids like Yossi, but I do know that what we do here has to be done and there's no one else who will do it. Our work here is hard, paved with failures and small successes, but we do it with profound faith. And this is exactly what I would expect from my superiors – to have faith in me."

There are times when a corporal expresses herself better than a general.

CHAPTER 8

THE SPIRIT OF THE IDF

When work began on composing the IDF's ethical code I was still commander of Bahad 1. The initiative was launched by head of the Human Resources Directorate at the time Major General Yoram Yair together with Israeli Prize laureate and Tel Aviv University Professor Asa Kasher. The professor presented us a nearly finished code in a meeting that took place at the Kirya Military Headquarters in Tel Aviv. I was surprised to learn that the word "Jew" did not appear in the entire document. I did not keep my opinion to myself, and Major General Yom-Tov Samia joined me. Afterward, the word was inserted into the document.

Later, the final draft of the code was presented to a high-ranking forum headed by the chief of staff at the time Ehud Barak and I was once again invited. I sat in one of the last rows and when Professor Kasher finished his presentation I raised my hand and asked why the document did not mention the concept of "love for the land" in it. The document was named "The Spirit of the IDF," and I couldn't understand how there could be a spirit within the IDF without a love for the land. Professor Kasher replied that "love for the land" belongs to only one sector in society.

I was shocked. Being a guest, I expected one of the members of the General Staff to ask some questions, and when this didn't happen I decided to speak up: "Which sector do you mean?"

Professor Kasher didn't reply. I then asked why the IDF could not use a term just because some people in society used it for political purposes. I went on and said that I had noticed a certain political party was using the Israeli flag in its logo. If that was the case, maybe the IDF should also refrain from using the flag. I didn't let go, and asked specifically which sector of the society Professor Kasher was referring to when speaking about love for the land.

I played stupid, even though I knew perfectly well that he was referring to a certain political group called Gush Emunim, which was led by right-wing political activists who believed in settling all of the occupied territories. But even if they use the idea of love for the land for political purposes do we from now on have to present an alternative position? If someone will say that he loves his land, will he be thus declaring his alliance with a specific political group and its ideology? And the main question is, what does all of this have to do with the army?

The presentation took place on one of Ehud Barak's last days as chief of staff. Later I learned that several generals were discontented because the words "love of the land" were omitted from the document and the chief of staff himself demanded to know how this had happened But all those questions unfortunately remained behind closed doors, and Kasher's code remained unchanged.

I decided to write a letter to the new chief of staff, Amnon Lipkin-Shahak, under the headline "The Neutral, Universal, and International Code." I used this headline to express that this was how I regarded the code and to emphasize that the entire document had a foreign feel to it and lacked a connection to the country and the nation that the army is supposed to secure and defend.

At Bahad 1, I found a way to bypass the document and received permission to issue my own code of ethics called "The Values of an Officer"; there I included love for the land and patriotism. My action led to several arguments with people who claimed that this wasn't "The Spirit of the IDF," but I replied that there was a special spirit for officers within the IDF. I also gave the document to the staff that was responsible for training cadets after they graduated from the school and told them that this was what we taught at Bahad 1, and they should stick to it. Some accepted it and others thought the document contradicted Kasher's code.

The new chief of staff, Amnon Lipkin-Shahak, didn't mention "The Spirit of the IDF" in his first public speech. I asked him how the code could ignore the subject of love for the land and why he hadn't mentioned the code altogether. He replied, "Leave it alone."

As far as he was concerned, it wasn't important. I absolutely agreed with him. I thought that the way the code looked, it would be much better to ignore it, since it wasn't our code. Apart from what I have already mentioned, the code was written in academic language and not in military language. Officers and plain soldiers didn't respond to it. Maybe it was also that no one in the army was pushing it forward, as Professor Kasher claimed. As commander of the Education Corps, I met reservists who were supposed to promote the code in different units throughout the military, but I kept on hearing the same criticism: that the document was not suitable for soldiers.

After some time, when I was appointed head of the Education Corps, I decided that it was time to bring the code up again. Chief of Staff Barak had announced at the meeting when the code was approved that after five years it would be up for consideration again. When the five years had passed, I was commander of the Education Corps and jumped at the opportunity to adjust the code like a blessing from heaven.

I decided to try and work together with Professor Kasher and was very careful not to show him any disrespect. As for Yoram Yair, I was determined to make sure that it would not look at any point as if I was undermining his work. I always respected Yair for his singular qualities as a commander and as an educator, and I still do.

What upset me the most was the lack of any reminder of patriotism, love for the land, and the connection to the Jewish nation within the code. The first step was to insert these concepts. The next step, I believed, was the need to simplify some of the texts and make the code easier for regular soldiers to comprehend. I suggested we replace the term "integrity" that appeared in the code with the term "honesty." Integrity, as far as I understood the term, is something that depends on others who observe you. Honesty on the other hand is something more personal; it is about you opposite the mirror. It's sharper and deeper.

I called Professor Kasher and explained to him the corrections I had in mind. I wasn't looking for a fight. He replied that he would think it over but never called me back. A few weeks later I heard that he had called the chief of staff, who was Shaul Mofaz at the time, and asked to be nominated to do the corrections alone, according to his discretion. I informed the chief of staff that I did not intend to fall into the trap of issuing exclusive nominations, since once that happens people will start counting how many left-wingers there are and how many right-wingers, how many religious and how many secular, and that as a result any chance of producing a commonly accepted code would go down the drain. I didn't want the IDF's ethical code to be attributed to any one group, and certainly I didn't want it to be attributed to one man, as was the first draft.

Authorized by the chief of staff, I assembled a committee of experts to check the original code and to come up with changes. The committee was composed of high-ranking officers and acclaimed academics. Professor Kasher also attended the meetings.

After three meetings, the majority of the committee voted in favor of recommending to the chief of staff to alter the first draft of the code. Professor Kasher was among the minority who opined that the code did not require modifications, except maybe minor corrections in its introduction. When his opinion was rejected he chose to leave, slamming the door behind him.

Can "Love" Be Commanded?

Asa Kasher and other philosophers tried to explain to me that we couldn't insert the term "love" into the code since love is not something that can be commanded. Of course they immediately connected this with the Biblical law to "love the Lord," a sentence that always triggered discussions of whether love can be forced out of someone. I told them that the golden rule appears in Leviticus, chapter 19, to love one's fellow man like one loves himself. It appears in verse nineteen, after eighteen verses that deal with various practical commandments.

I guess this is the Bible's way of saying that love can be forced – maybe not directly, but we can and should try to help shape the way man will treat his neighbor or friend. Someone who behaves decently toward his fellow man, who learns to listen to his hardships and sufferings, and who is considerate toward him, can reach the feeling of love. This is another expression of our saying that "hearts are drawn after deeds." So too, love is something that can be nourished and developed.

The lesson is obvious. If we put in the code the words "love of the land," then the road toward such love will start with touring the land, learning about it and its history, feeling compassion toward its people, supporting them and their progress. Only after that, one will develop love for the land, or love for the people and the land. And if one never reaches the love phase, at least he or she has fulfilled everything that's on the way to this love. The ethical code of the army should be the basis. That is why I had no doubt that the term should enter the code. Patriotism is first of all about loyalty and devotion to our land – and love will develop, if it does, from those two.

Correcting the Code

After we finished preliminary discussions, I selected a team to carry out the rephrasing of the code, which included a number of academics.

The process of composing the new code was accompanied by intensive consultations with professionals from the IDF and the academic world. We sat in numerous meetings, many of which started in the early evening and adjourned at sunrise. Every time we added another small piece. After that, we sent the revised paper to different focus groups in the army, from simple combat troops to cadets at Bahad 1 and generals at the highest IDF levels. Soldiers and officers made their remarks; from these we chose the ones that seemed appropriate for the soldiers in the field and commenced a new session of marathon discussions.

Altogether, it took us a year and a half. After that, we presented the new code to the General Staff. Out of appreciation for the effort that was invested in the first code, we invited Professor Kasher and Major General Yair to voice their opinions before the forum. After a few meetings, the General Staff approved the new code.

Nowadays, every recruit receives the printed code when he or she joins the IDF, and the great majority of the soldiers are familiar with its contents. The success of this paper can be measured by the fact that today it is accepted as a basic document, and is reflected upon during discussions at the highest military levels. It was even referred to by the commissions of inquiry set up after the Second Lebanon War in 2006 as the document which spells out the basic rules of conduct expected from commanders.

* * *

The new "Spirit of the IDF" code's four parts:

The introduction defines the IDF's purpose and basic missions regarding the role it plays within a Jewish and democratic state. There are non-Jewish soldiers who serve in the army, and we made it our duty to ensure that they feel that the army is theirs in the same way it belongs to a Jewish soldier. We kept this rule throughout the code through consultations with Druze and Bedouin thinkers.

In the second chapter, alongside "Jewish and IDF Traditions," which served as the basis for the original document, we added another source of inspiration: "universal morals of human dignity," aimed at ensuring that every soldier receives basic rights no matter what his or her religion, race, or gender might be.

The third chapter, which wasn't included in the first code, lists the fundamental values we expect soldiers to hold – defending the country and its citizens, love and loyalty to the homeland, and protecting basic human rights. We chose the word "homeland" and not "land" to avoid political controversy, specifically due to the presence of non-Jewish soldiers in the IDF who also need to feel committed to protecting the State of Israel in a time of war.

The fourth chapter, safeguarding basic human rights, was one of the major changes we made when writing the second code. This is a crucial value, particularly in a military environment where there is potential for soldiers to abuse their authority not just toward other soldiers but also toward people with whom they come into contact during their military service.

From this value, derives an important rule called "Purity of Arms," according to which, "The soldier shall make use of his weaponry and power only for the fulfillment of the mission and solely to the extent required; he will maintain his humanity even in combat. The soldier shall not employ his weaponry and power in order to harm non-combatants or prisoners of war, and shall do all he can to avoid harming their lives, body, honor, and property."

Such a cautious phrasing was needed to provide a framework for asymmetric conflicts like the war against Palestinian terrorism that raged in Israel for most of the past decade. Purity of Arms stresses the requirement to differentiate between terrorists and non-combatants and to make sure that even when facing a terrorist, soldiers should understand that the terrorist is still a human being and that IDF soldiers are required to maintain their humanity even in the most difficult of circumstances.

Comparing the texts of the two codes, it is easy to see how much sharper and precise the new version is. The old code said: "The soldier will use his weapons and his strength to subdue his enemies and will then restrain himself to avoid unnecessary damage to human life, body, dignity, and possessions."

This phrasing permits certain damage to human lives, and even to non-combatants, as long as such damage is considered "necessary." I believe the authors of the earlier code intended to refer to damage only to combatants but it is not particularly clear.

Having served as both a combat soldier and an educator, I am proud that when the IDF launched Operation Cast Lead in the Gaza Strip in December 2008 we were already in possession of the new and clearer code. It prevented our soldiers from making tragic mistakes. Even when there were civilian casualties, I have no doubt that those were not intentional.

The values in "The Spirit of the IDF" are not listed according to a certain order apart from the demand for persistence to complete a mission and the imperative to strive for victory. In our world, where values tend to collide and intertwine, we found it wiser to leave the final responsibility to the commanders and soldiers in the field for setting the order of the values.

Here is one difficult example: Salah Shehada, a top Hamas commander responsible for dozens of suicide bombings against Israel, was killed in an Israeli Air Force bombing together with fourteen civilians. I have always been pained by collateral damage and particularly harm to innocent civilians. Such damage would – on the surface – appear to contradict the value of Purity of Arms as it appears in the code.

The IAF command decided to launch the bomb at Shehada under the assumption that he had not surrounded himself with so many civilians. Proof of this is the fact that several months earlier, after Shehada had already launched several suicide attacks and was planning more, we had the opportunity to assassinate him but decided twice to call off the operation at the last moment because he was, at the time, surrounded by civilians. Each cancellation occurred in real time and was in accordance with the Purity of Arms value as dictated in "The Spirit of the IDF."

As a result, until Shehada was finally killed, several dozen more Israelis were killed directly because of him and because of the discretion that was exercised in the first aborted raids.

In hindsight, maybe in this case we should have preferred other values like "persistence" and "defending the state," even at the expense of slightly harming the Purity of Arms value. We cannot, however, condemn the pilots who saw civilians around the target and decided to abort the mission.

Every commander has to ask himself when the safety of our soldiers surpasses the need to avoid endangering innocent lives on the other side. There are not many answers but, rather, only two cruel choices. He must consider the question of proportionality and then choose one or the other. In the Shehada incident, when the aircraft dropped the bomb on his hideout, it was clear that though innocent bystanders were put in danger, he could not be left alive since Israelis would definitely die. The IDF made the decision and I absolutely agree with it, with all the remorse we feel for the innocent lives that were lost.

Part of the price we pay as commanders, beside the banal need to give our lives for our country, is very often the need to confront some of the most complicated moral dilemmas that exist.

Some time after the end of the Second Lebanon War in 2006, I said to reporters that in the war we had exaggerated the priority we gave to soldiers' lives over the lives of our citizens. Instead of striving to complete their missions at any price, some commanders decided to minimize the risk to their soldiers.

It seemed to me that in order to protect the lives of our soldiers, commanders restricted themselves in ways that impacted the missile fire on the civilian home front. I was immediately attacked for saying this from all sides of the political spectrum in the Knesset. Several months later, I was vindicated when the Winograd Committee, which was tasked by the government to probe the war, used my remark as one of their final conclusions.

Chapter 9

Human Resources

When I had completed a term of four years as head of the Education Corps, chief of staff at the time Moshe "Bogie" Ya'alon decided to promote me to the rank of Major General and to make me the head of the Human Resources Directorate. The ranks for such senior positions are usually placed on one of the officer's shoulders by the chief of staff and on the second shoulder by his or her spouse. Dorit gave my father an opportunity to fulfill another dream by placing the ranks on my shoulders together with the chief of staff.

Toward the end of three years in the post, the standard duration of the position, I informed the chief of staff at the time, Dan Halutz, that I intended to step down, but Halutz asked me to remain in my post. After Halutz resigned following the Second Lebanon War and Gabi Ashkenazi was appointed chief of staff in his place, I was summoned to meet him shortly before he took up the post.

Our discussion covered two main points. The first filled me with joy. Ashkenazi asked me to do all I could to strengthen the Nativ seminars and to convert as many soldiers as possible. The second point was mine. I informed Ashkenazi that though I had accepted Halutz's request to remain in the post, I didn't consider this to be binding now that he was taking over and therefore, since the three nominal years were almost over, I was prepared to present my resignation. Ashkenazi asked me to take back my resignation and stay in my post. I accepted his request and was very happy to receive an opportunity to head the Human Resources Directorate for four full years.

Shortly after leaving the post, I received a phone call from the IDF's Retirement Department asking where I would prefer to complete the retirement process – my home in the Galilee or my

Tel Aviv office. I was told that this personal service was part of the process for retiring generals. I said to the soldier who called that I wanted to go through the process the same way every soldier does – at the Tel Hashomer Induction Center. They called again to coordinate a time and a date, so that the department's commanders could welcome me. Once again I explained that I wanted to undergo the process exactly the same way every regular soldier does it.

I was then told of a specific day every month, when retiring officers assembled in a hall near Tel Hashomer and passed one station after the other on their road toward civilian life. I was asked to show up at 8:30 in the morning. I asked when the rest of the officers were supposed to arrive, and was told that they come at 9 o'clock. I asked why I was being told to come earlier and was told that the commanders wanted to be able to give me special treatment. Once again I stressed, hoping for it to be the last time: "I was drafted like everyone else and I will be discharged like everyone else. All the ranks I was given along the way were only tools I used to perform the jobs I was assigned."

My service as head of the Human Resources Directorate entailed a number of diverse challenges that dealt with some of the most critical issues at the core of Israeli society, from education to economics to reservists, retirees, and career officers. During my term, the IDF carried out the disengagement from the Gaza Strip. The question of military service for ultra-Orthodox Jews was dealt with almost daily, and if that wasn't enough, I decided to launch a war against draft dodgers. I also did everything possible to institute reform in the structure of Hesder yeshivot and the benefits received by IDF personnel with disabilities, many of which were unnecessary in my opinion. I wanted to make sure that we took better care of the real IDF disabled and at the same time saved the state billions of shekels.

All of these issues were neglected for years for the simple reason that they were extremely controversial and everyone before me was afraid to play with fire. I wasn't naive, and while I expected some opposition I felt that those issues could no longer be ignored. Still, I must admit I was surprised by the responses and sometimes ferocious criticism.

There was one issue that made me especially grateful for the privilege of serving in the post: the conversion of non-Jewish soldiers in the IDF.

CONVERSION IN THE IDF

On the wall of my office at the Human Resources Directorate there was a cartoon showing a military funeral. On the ground there was a soldier's coffin wrapped in the national flag with a sign reading "non-Jewish." Standing next to the coffin was an honor guard of four soldiers shooting upwards and my figure, with the title Commander of Education Corps, shooting at the coffin.

This is one of the most horrible cartoons ever drawn against me, and it wasn't published in the Nazi *Der Sturmer* but in the Israeli newspaper *Ma'ariv*. I instructed my office staff to hang under the framed cartoon stats of the number of soldiers who underwent the conversion process with the army's assistance and to update it every few days.

The combination of this cartoon on the one hand and the conversion information on the other accurately represented the way I regarded media criticism. Behind the numbers were real soldiers who wanted to convert to Judaism while in the military, where they would receive more assistance and support than had they done the conversion outside the army. Rabbi Haim Druckman, a leading national religious authority who was involved in the conversions, said that through my work with these young converts I have earned a place in heaven. I am not sure about that, but I certainly feel that I was privileged to be in a position that allowed me to relieve some of the converts' hardships and to assist them in becoming an integral part of the Israeli people and state.

I also believed that what I was doing was extremely basic and was part of my duty as a Jew – showing those soldiers the sympathetic face of Judaism and not just the distorted one that is shown by those who claim to speak for God.

My sensitivity for new immigrants was not a secret, and everyone who worked with me knew that I would do everything in my power to help them. I must confess, though, that the idea of initiating a conversion project for soldiers was not the first thing on my mind when I was appointed head of the Human Resources Directorate.

The idea didn't occur to me until one day, during a routine discussion on how to improve immigrant absorption in the IDF, one of my colleagues, Colonel Michal El-Al, mentioned that each year we hand out around 600 New Testaments to soldiers during their swearing-in ceremony instead of the Bible. When I asked why, she said that the soldiers ask for them.

I never realized that those were the numbers of non-Jewish immigrants within the IDF. I figured that some of the soldiers must be devoted Christians, but I thought that they were a tiny minority. Most of them, I regretfully thought, must be asking for a New Testament as an act of defiance against us for treating them as gentiles and foreigners. Many of those immigrants considered themselves Jews and were defined as such in the places where they came from, but when they arrived in Israel they found out that by our religious standards they technically didn't qualify to be called Jewish.

I didn't have then – and I don't have now – any problem with supplying the New Testament to soldiers. There were people who thought that the army should stop distributing the books, and I reminded them that the IDF is the army of a democratic state, and as a result if a soldier asks for the New Testament, we are obligated to provide it. Our challenge should be to create for the soldiers an environment in which only a few – only those who are devoted Christians – will want to ask for it.

Several days after this meeting, I assembled the staff of one of our main immigrant training bases. I explained that I considered the large number of soldiers who requested New Testaments a challenge we should deal with. Hands went waving and I heard several shouts claiming that "it wasn't the army's business."

I tried to explain myself: In my opinion we needed to present those soldiers with a broader and more liberal side of Judaism, so more of them will want to join it. If we are successful and soldiers will show an interest, we will then need to produce for them a friendlier conversion process than the one currently in existence.

To the question whether this was "the army's business" or not, I had several answers.

First, those soldiers will be better soldiers after they learn what they are fighting for. They will learn about Judaism and Jewish history, and about Israel and its traditions. If some of them will decide during their studies to become Jews, we will enable this.

Second, the state needs a reserve force. Chances are much better that soldiers who convert will remain in Israel after their military service. Also it is common knowledge that life here is easier for Jews, and this is true also for their children. If their children grow up as Jews, they stand a much better chance to be drafted into the IDF when the time comes. In my mind this second answer is less important, but it seemed a sound response for antagonists who will claim that the issue should not interest the army.

Always looming in the background was the issue of burial for soldiers who weren't recognized as Jews. I believe that a soldier who dies here, who is killed while giving his or her life for the country, should be buried just like any other soldier.

The injustice is even more obvious when we see the efforts that Judaism has made in recent years to allow people who commit suicide to be buried in a Jewish cemetery with everyone else and not, as tradition requires, outside the fence or in a separate lot. With considerable sensitivity and wisdom, the rabbis decided that in the split second between the pulling of the trigger and death, it is quite probable that the person regretted committing suicide and therefore it should not be regarded a suicide from the religious point of view. I tried to convince representatives of the Military

Rabbinate to demonstrate an equal amount of creativity and grace toward immigrant soldiers killed in the line of duty. Who knows, perhaps the immigrant soldier declared in his last moments his wish to become a Jew? I told them that I couldn't think of any conversion process that was more thorough than this. Isn't such a death the ultimate conversion?

The Military Rabbinate was not particularly enthusiastic about my initiative to set up an in-house military conversion process. This obstacle led me to meet the Sephardic chief rabbi of the city of Tel-Aviv, Shlomo Amar, who later was appointed the Sephardic chief rabbi for the State of Israel. Our meeting left a strong impression on me, and our relationship is very special to this day. His great knowledge of the scriptures and his efforts to help made him a giant in my eyes.

I had great pleasure later when Rabbi Amar agreed to officiate at the wedding of our daughter Liron and her husband Shimon Abuhatzeira. When our second daughter, Adi, married her husband, Daniel, Rabbi Amar again came to the wedding even though he wasn't officiating. He simply wanted to join in our celebration. The rabbi even surprised me and spoke at my farewell party from the IDF.

After I spoke with Rabbi Amar, I met with other rabbis from the various streams of Judaism and often cited the ancient rabbinic ruling that non-Jews can sometimes be buried next to Jews to "maintain peace." The rabbis told me this was only true for the Diaspora, and that it was not relevant in Israel. In my opinion, what was relevant for the Diaspora is even more relevant in Israel. Is the need to maintain peace relevant only between Jews and gentiles, and not between Jews and Jews?

I am sorry to say that my position on the burial question was not accepted, and since then we have made only limited progress. The immigrants whose Jewishness is in doubt are still buried in separate lots, but not like they used to be – outside the regular military cemeteries' walls. The burial issue is still a problem for many families of deceased soldiers. I am careful not to revisit this issue too often since the solution is in the hands of the Military Rabbinate, and I don't want to add pain to the bereaved parents more than they are already suffering.

As a soldier it was easy for me to explain the logic behind my decisions. I have always believed that the IDF was far more than just a military and also plays an important educational role in Israeli society. I realize that taking responsibility for conversions is getting near the boundary of what we should not deal with in the army, but it does not cross the line. If the IDF invests in preparing soldiers for their matriculation exams, something that does not directly support the army (especially since it is done as the soldiers near their discharge), why can't the army provide Judaism and conversion classes that will benefit civilian society and might even guarantee that these soldiers will remain citizens of the state after their discharge?

Not every commander at the staff meeting at the main immigrant training base agreed with me. Some even suspected that I had a hidden agenda of religious coercion because of the *kippa* on my head. Less than forty-eight hours after the meeting I saw headlines in the newspapers quoting the head of the Education Corps as saying that "non-Jewish soldiers are not as good as Jewish soldiers." All the efforts of the military spokesman to correct this false quote didn't help. Yuli Tamir, the Immigrant Absorption Minister at the time, who has usually viewed our work favorably, called Ehud Barak, then the prime minister, and asked that he fire me. Articles against me appeared almost daily in the newspapers and I was called a bigot and compared to the Nazis.

I was denounced by both the religious and the secular. The secular people claimed that the army should not be responsible for conversion, while the religious people demanded to know what I meant when I suggested a "friendlier" conversion process. Did I mean that their conversion wasn't friendly? The Military Rabbinate refused to cooperate with my initiative. They were most probably afraid to step on the toes of civilian rabbinical authorities.

The IDF high command weren't very happy either. The head of the Human Resources Department at the time, Yudke Segev, summoned me to his office after reading some of the articles and getting a number of phone calls from the rabbinate. He asked me what it was all about. I explained, and I think he understood me and even approved of my idea, but he still wondered how I could expect to launch such a program without the Military Rabbinate's support. I told him that just as no one can obligate a soldier to be married by a military rabbi, the same applies to conversion. A soldier could ask for a military rabbi to do the conversion or for a civilian rabbi, as long as the conversions are acknowledged by the State of Israel.

I decided to meet with Rabbi Zefania Drori, Rabbi Druckman, Rabbi Avraham Almaliach, and Rabbi Yosef Avior – national-religious rabbis involved in civilian conversions – and they all agreed that my idea was appropriate. Some of them thought that the conversion process should last a full year. I told them that if they insisted on this demand, and if they would also check whether the convert's mother or girlfriend turns on lights in the house on Shabbat, then the initiative would never succeed. And in fifty years we will no longer have a Jewish state, not just because of the immigrants who are labeled as non-Jewish, but because of their friends who serve with them in the army. A day might come when they will say to us: "If our friends are not Jewish enough for you, then we also don't want to be Jewish!"

Either Convert or Enlist

We all know that there are many difficulties faced by a person who wants to convert to Judaism. I am ashamed to say it, but I learned that girls who want to convert face one more difficulty – enlistment in the army.

Shevah Mofet is an established high school in Tel Aviv famous for the large percentage of immigrants among its student body. The studies there, and especially the sciences, are on a high level, and as a result students from outside Tel Aviv are also attracted to the school. It received some publicity when many of its students were among the casualties in the tragic Dolphinarium discothèque suicide bombing in 2001, which killed twenty-one people.

I visited the high school and met with the young students. We came to the issue of conversion, and I told the students what we, the IDF, had to offer. I had to be very careful discussing such a sensitive subject in such a large forum. When the meeting was over and I was on my way out accompanied by the school's principal, a young girl approached me and said she had a question about conversion. I asked her if she wanted to convert during her military service, and she told me she had already started the process. I asked her if she wanted to complete the process during her service and she said that she would finish it before her enlistment, but that she has a different problem.

"My problem," she said, "is that I can't enlist in the army." I asked her why, and she told me that when she started the conversion process, she was forced to sign a declaration that she would not enlist in the army.

I wasn't particularly surprised but I was deeply disturbed. I couldn't believe that the Israeli Chief Rabbinate would actively or even passively support a clause inside the "conversion agreement" that forces the converted, if she wants to become a Jew, to denounce enlisting in the army! In other words, you have to make a choice whether you want to be a Jew or you want to enlist in the Israel Defense Forces!

The girl wasn't alone, and I discovered later that girls from other schools who wanted to start the conversion processes as early as the age of sixteen or seventeen, so that they could finish it as early as possible, were not allowed to do so by the Chief Rabbinate. I asked why and was told that one of the Chief Rabbinate's conditions was that the girl agree not to enlist in the army, and if the process started very early the rabbinate would not be able to confirm that she kept to the agreement. This revelation drove me later to initiate the beginning of the conversion process in high school, and in some cases even once the girls began their pre-military training.

I investigated this outrage and regretfully learned that it was well-known and even tolerated by many public leaders. I also learned that in several rabbinical courts, even male conversion was conditioned on the converted agreeing to serving only in specific units and with other religious youth and not in regular army units where they are in danger of meeting, God-forbid, gentiles like me.

Tears in the Rabbinic Court

In face of the wave of opposition to my project and the total lack of support from within the military and outside, I realized I needed to act quickly to succeed. I contacted Professor Benny Ish-Shalom, who heads the Beit Morasha Institute in Jerusalem. This body was established following the recommendations of a government-appointed committee several years earlier, which determined that it was important to start to connect all of the three major streams of Judaism in order to simplify and homogenize conversions. I knew the institute's policies were constructive, and tended to achieve compromise and unity. The institute is an official state organization, and I hoped this would somewhat protect me from my opponents' criticism.

We launched the program in the spring of 2001 – a first conversion course with only thirty-seven soldiers. Half of them were registered Jews who simply wanted to broaden their knowledge of Judaism, but I accepted them since I wanted to get the first course going with as many participants as possible, for I feared that the opposition would succeed in torpedoing the initiative. The course was operated by Beit Morasha, the Jewish Agency, and the Ministry of Immigrant Absorption. A major part of the funding was received from the Genesis Philanthropy Group. We soon reached several courses a year, and in every course we had more then four hundred soldiers.

The soldiers learn for seven weeks about Judaism, Jewish history, and the IDF. Every week they are taken on a tour to another

Israeli site. When this part is over, soldiers who declare that they are interested in conversion are summoned for two more segments – two weeks each – after which they come before a rabbinic court, to complete their conversions.

After the nomination of Rabbi Avihai Ronsky as the IDF's chief rabbi, Rabbi Ronsky and I went together to one of those rabbinic courts to watch the conversion process. We saw the rabbinic court secretary; on his one side were the three judges and on his other side the converting soldier. A minute after he said, "We accept you to the Jewish people. Say *Shema Yisrael*," he needed to give out tissues to the soldier's family. I also needed tissues, as did Rabbi Ronsky.

What helped in changing the Military Rabbinate's hostility toward the conversions was the undisputed and affectionate support we received from Prime Minister Ariel Sharon. I know that Sharon summoned the chief IDF rabbi to his office and explained to him the significance of the project. In addition, Rabbi Druckman's prestige in the Torah world also helped immensely. The generals who didn't fall for the project at first all changed their minds after meeting the soldiers who attended the courses. I don't remember even one of those tough generals who visited the course and didn't walk away crying.

By the beginning of 2010, more than four thousand soldiers had completed the conversion course; 75 percent were female soldiers. When I'm asked about this percentage I say, "One, it is more important because religion is determined by the mother. Two, it is less painful," a reference to the circumcision males need to undergo.

I met one of the first soldiers who graduated from the course in the chief of staff's sukkah one year. She came there pushing a baby stroller. Ashkenazi turned to me and said, "Stern, this baby is Jewish thanks to you."

I replied, "Sir, don't think about this baby. Think about the baby's grandchildren, and then do the multiplication and you will realize the strategic importance of these conversions to our future in this part of the world."

Making It Difficult

Dana was a young Jewish woman in her twenties. Dana was born in Kazakhstan, educated in Berlin, and spent a number of years in Israel working for the Rothschild Foundation. I met her at a Keneski, a Jewish convention in northern Italy in 2011. The week-long convention brings together young Jews from around the world to ski and to find a spouse on the slopes. In the winter of 2011, I was invited with Dorit to speak at the convention. It was quite fascinating and we were extremely impressed with the high quality of youth that we met there. Dorit invited Dana to join us for Shabbat the next time she visited Israel.

It didn't take long, and in June 2011, Dana arrived in Israel to attend the President's Conference in Jerusalem. Public transportation does not reach all the way to our home in Hoshaya, so as she got closer Dana called to arrange a meeting place for us to pick her up. She was visiting a friend in Haifa whom she knew from her days in Berlin. She said that her friend could bring her but that she didn't know exactly where Hoshaya was. "She knows how to get as far as Shfaram since she has family there," Dana told me.

Now, I was intrigued. There are no Jews in Shfaram, and I began to wonder about this friend. I asked to speak with her. She said her name was Debora and that she would be happy to take Dana to the nearby junction but that she didn't know how to drive all the way to Hoshaya. I explained to her how to get here and promised coffee and a great view if she made the ride. She agreed.

It turned out that Debora was Christian. As I made the coffee, I asked her a few questions and understood that she had arrived in Israel two years earlier, after completing her medical studies in Berlin where she had met her husband, an Arab Christian from Haifa. She was now working as an intern at Hillel Yaffe Hospital in Hadera, and her husband was working as a surgical intern at Rambam Hospital in Haifa.

I told her that I was extremely impressed with her proficiency in Hebrew. After the conversation ended and I began making my final preparations for Shabbat, I invited Debora to stay with us for Friday night dinner. She declined politely. I asked her if she had ever had the opportunity to join a Jewish family for a Shabbat meal. She said yes and that she would have loved to stay, but she needed to return to Haifa since it was her last chance to sit down and eat dinner with her husband before they each went off to their hospital shifts.

I went for my pre-Shabbat jog, and as I returned, I found Debora leaving the house, saying good-bye to Dana. I again pleaded with her to stay for dinner, and when she again declined, I bid her farewell and extended an open invitation to her to return in the future. As I walked back into the house, Dana whispered to me that Debora had wanted to stay for dinner and had called her husband, who vetoed the idea. I was surprised...but this was only the beginning.

Dana then told me that Debora had been born in the former Soviet Union to a Jewish father and a non-Jewish mother. In her first years in Berlin, she met a Jewish boy from Morocco and they had thought about getting married. She then spent two years taking conversion courses alongside her medical studies since her boyfriend insisted on only marrying a Jew. The conversion process failed after the so-called converters – or in this case the "non-converters" – said that Debora's boyfriend was not an observant Jew and therefore she could not be converted. The wedding was called off.

In the end, there was a different wedding and Debora – who could have been Devora – is a doctor, is married to a doctor, and has family in Shfaram.

We, on the other hand, are proud Jews who so easily give up on Debora and other people like her, their children, their grandchildren, and their generations to come. We are a people in constant fluctuation – one day we are growing, another day we are shrinking. But what difference does it make if we are constantly making it more difficult to be a proud Jew?

A Conversation with the President

A few months after I retired from the IDF, President Shimon Peres invited me to his official residence. We spoke about a wide range of issues and when we got to the issue of conversion, Peres asked if there really were 300,000 people that were affected by the state's conversion policies. I said that it was not 300,000 – but rather 3 million.

The number 300,000, I explained, includes just the new immigrants from the former Soviet Union who arrived in Israel since 1990 and are eligible for Israeli citizenship under the Law of Return. The immediate and strategic challenge, I said, includes millions of Jews around the world – in the US, France, South America, and other places – who have a father or grandmother who is Jewish, and maybe even survived the Holocaust, and want their children to also be Jewish. They are joined by the hundreds of thousands of former Israelis who live around the world and also want their children, born in the Diaspora, to be Jewish.

If we don't act now to bring these children into the Jewish people – some by conversion, some by welcoming them into Jewish life – we might lose them forever. In another generation or two these children, who have many opportunities to marry non-Jews, will not want to be Jewish.

Chapter 10

Disengagement

Soon after the Jewish settlers were evacuated from the Gaza Strip, while tensions were still high, some of those who had opposed the evacuation would chant in our faces the infamous Nazi defense, "we only obeyed orders," comparing us to war criminals.

The truth is that during the evacuation, IDF soldiers and commanders, myself included, were not simply obeying orders. Immediately after the decision was made by the political echelon, the army was invited to participate in the intricate and delicate planning of the operation. We were given a chance to help reduce tension levels in order to prevent the outbreak of a civil war.

Since I never spoke in public about the Israeli government's decision to evacuate the Gaza Strip, nobody really knew what my personal opinion was on this matter. I was happy to hide behind my uniform, which restricted me from making any political declarations, especially on issues as controversial as the evacuation. The duty to keep your opinions to yourself can be a heavy price for an officer to pay for a military career. I must admit though, that more than once, it definitely saved me from having to rationalize and formulate a personal opinion about seemingly irrational government resolutions.

I believe that we should do everything in our power to ensure that if there is another resolution to evacuate settlements in the future, the task will not be given to the army. I knew from the start the high price the army would pay, as well as the time and preparation that would be involved in planning the operation. But I also knew that if the army were ordered to carry out the evacuation it would use all of its resources to minimize costs. Naturally, we had to send our best commanders to deal with the threat the evacuation posed to our national unity.

The slogan we composed for the benefit of the soldiers who were sent to fulfill this mission was: "Courage and determination on one hand, and exceptional sensitivity on the other." The courage required was not the sort of courage one shows when facing bullets, but more of a civil valor. I am honored to have been able to contribute personally to the flawless execution of such a complex and sensitive undertaking. The IDF received many compliments from the US and from Europe for the smoothness of the operation. A Swiss official was quoted as saying: "We always knew you were an efficient army with rifles; now we learned that you are just as good without any weapons."

This is why I am not dismayed when attacked for my part in the evacuation. I am proud to have contributed my share and have no regrets. I'm not ashamed, but I am sad – sad for us all.

When I was personally attacked, before the evacuation began and while it was in progress, I was asked by many how I managed to restrain myself amidst all of the profanities, pushing, and damage to property, as well as attempts to physically harm my family and myself. Assaults on me and on my family still occur to this day, though to a lesser degree. I still receive letters fraught with profanities, as well as threats to my own life and those of my children.

To those who asked me then how I managed to control myself, I replied that we demand that our soldiers demonstrate restraint – even when suffering humiliation – and that they never let situations deteriorate into violence, which can easily turn into bloodshed. If I demand this from my soldiers, I certainly must require it of myself. There are many silent voices in Israel who appreciate the patience with which we completed our mission. They admire the fact that this bitter dispute, which still tears our society apart, did not involve any bloodshed or insubordination.

But a dark cloud looms over the successful role the army played in the process, and that is the handling of the evacuated families after the operation by the civilian authorities. The authorities mishandled the evacuees from early on and to this day have failed in their treatment of the families. Although this issue does not fall within the army's responsibilities, after being active in the process of removing these innocent people from their homes, I cannot help but feel responsible for their welfare, and I have publicly expressed my opinions on this matter on more than one occasion.

Insubordination to the Right; Insubordination to the Left

Even before the evacuation of the settlers from the Gaza Strip, I considered instances of left-wing refusal to serve in the occupied territories as a mirror image of right-wing insubordination regarding evacuation of settlements. Conceptually there is no difference whatsoever between the two. I referred to this issue already in my first major interview, when I was commander of Battalion 202, just before my discharge. The year was 1986, and in answering one of the reporter's questions, I said that whoever refused an order to evacuate Yamit should not condemn those who refuse an order to serve in occupied Lebanese territory.

Insubordinates from all sides of the political map and their supporters usually claim that the other side has crossed the line and caused harm to our democracy, or crushed the values of the Israeli state. In my humble opinion, both commit a similar crime against democracy. Each bases its claim on some sort of ideology. One argues that he is directed by values of human dignity, while the other will cite the biblical commandment to inherit and settle the land. Both are convinced that what they say comes directly from the mouth of God, and sometimes they believe they must even sacrifice their lives for their cause. But the bottom line remains that insubordination is illegitimate, both from a military standpoint, as well as from a democratic one.

My perception of Judaism is democratic in nature, and the democracy I accept as true is Jewish. My Jewish philosophy and my religious outlook regarding government resolutions are based on the words of the great Rabbi Joseph B. Soloveitchik. When asked shortly after the 1967 war whether Israel should remain in the occupied territories or withdraw its forces, he replied, "This is not a question for rabbis; it's a question for politicians."

I also follow what my Netiv Meir *rosh yeshiva*, Rabbi Aryeh Bina, used to say, "Every time rabbis intervene in matters that they do not fully understand, or in matters for which they are not responsible, great blasphemy occurs!" I am sorry to say that I witnessed with my own eyes just how true and relevant Rabbi Bina's words were on many occasions.

I was commander of the officers' academy when the first rabbinical decree calling for insubordination was published. The rabbis ruled that any evacuation of houses and military bases in the West Bank was forbidden. I was asked by the media to comment on this and I said that I hoped the rabbis were not referring to me because I could not believe that a rabbi who lives in Israel and understands the complex reality in which we live would think that I should refuse to obey an order given to me by a superior, and this applies to any other soldier. I added that I hoped the ruling was issued as a political act to intimidate politicians from reaching certain conclusions, and I explained why there is no way I would refuse to obey an order.

The reporter persisted: "But it's a rabbinical decree!" I answered that I am not bound by just any trio or quintet of rabbis that congregate in a room in Jerusalem and purport to issue a halachic ruling.

Several weeks later, at a meeting in Kfar Blum in northern Israel, a high-ranking religious officer challenged me in front of a large group of officers and accused me of defying the rulings of Torah scholars. He added that I was no doubt guaranteed a nice promotion by the chief of staff for committing this "infidelity." I despised him and did not hide it. Years later he approached me and asked why I always ignored him despite the many things we had in common. I reminded him of the incident at Kfar Blum. He claimed not to remember it and apologized. I think that the ideology he represented later, especially after his discharge from the army, rejected the legitimacy of any insubordination.

My approach to the matter has been the same for many years: we must always try to understand the other side. In November 1994, when I was commander of the academy, a reserve paratroopers unit was posted to defend the area of the settlement Netzarim in the northern Gaza Strip. Even though I wasn't the commander of this unit I could safely say that around 50 percent of the soldiers believed that Netzarim was the defensive line protecting Ashkelon from being targeted by enemy artillery, while the remaining 50 percent believed to the same degree that because of our presence in Netzarim, artillery shells would eventually start falling on Ashkelon. Both opinions can be logically defended, and as a soldier I certainly have no intention of judging between the two. The main thing is that proponents of both opinions had come to do their duty without protest.

On Friday some of the unit's soldiers went home for a short leave. On their way they were approached by a suicide bomber, who blew himself up, killing three of the fighters. The 50 percent who believed that Netzarim should be evacuated could have stood up at this point and said that they didn't believe in defending Netzarim and that if the battalion commander – a settler himself – and others in the unit thought the place deserved to be defended, they were welcome to stay there while the others went home.

Of course, the soldiers didn't act this way; they said and did nothing of the sort. But if they had thought for one second that the other 50 percent – those who thought differently from them – might in the future refuse orders to evacuate Netzarim, they would certainly have left. When the government resolved to evacuate the settlements in Gaza, I recalled this incident and what I had thought then.

In the many conversations I have had over the years on the subject of insubordination – usually opposition to serving in occupied Palestinian territories, guarding roadblocks, and participating in night arrests in Palestinian villages – I have always pointed out that a day may arrive when insubordination will come from the other side, when the orders will be favorable to those who refuse orders now. I don't see any other method of sustaining our army except the method by which part of the time some soldiers identify with the orders while others comply unhappily but without complaint, and at other times the balance shifts in the opposite direction.

I always knew that the support I received over the years in synagogues and in religious congregations – as a religious officer promoting the army's involvement in Jewish issues and speaking out against insubordination by left-wing activists – would not go on forever. I knew very well that such support was not unconditional.

But even when criticism against me began, there were always those who came forward and supported me. After the incident of the rabbinical ruling in 1996, the first rabbinical decree calling for insubordination, I received a strange envelope with my name on it, written over an older erased address. I examined it and found that it had come from Rabbi Shlomo Aviner. This is how I learnt that Rabbi Aviner recycles envelopes, which only added to my prior admiration of this wise man. The support he gave me in his letter was a true comfort.

Worst-Case Scenario

The fear that a line might be crossed, that an incident might occur that could lead to the outbreak of a civil war, even on a small scale, kept myself and other army commanders on our toes at all times. The army was determined to avoid bloodshed at all costs and simultaneously sincerely desired to be considerate toward settlers about to lose their homes. Therefore, it needed to prepare for the worst-case scenario.

I came with the chief of staff one day to observe the preparations being conducted in the south. When I saw the simulations it seemed that the settlers were being unfairly demonized. The forces were trying to prepare for any possible scenario and, the soldiers simulating settlers in the drill did everything possible apart from gunfire, including physical confrontations, spitting, and using profane language.

Although at times we did encounter such behavior during the evacuation, in most cases the simulations were far more brutal than the operation itself. I don't think many Israelis would have shown such restraint if they were evacuated from their homes. Here I am referring to the settlers and not to the thousands of extremist youth who came to show their support for the struggle, and certainly not the hoodlums who assembled in the Gaza Strip from all around the country with the clear intention of getting rowdy when the moment came.

We Lost a Generation

In one of the numerous meetings that took place before the Gaza evacuation began, the Officer in Charge of the Southern Command, Major General Dan Harel, said, "We just lost a generation." I replied that not only did we not lose a generation but in the future we are going to look back and say, if only we could have another generation like that. Harel's words upset me so much that I left the meeting shortly after I spoke. I truly do not think we lost a generation. I believe we should look at the larger picture, at these wonderful people that will contribute greatly to our country in the future.

During December 2005, I learned that young religious recruits were being interviewed before their enlistment and asked about their thoughts and opinions of the evacuation of the Gaza Strip. They were asked what they did during the evacuation, what their opinions were, and if they would follow their rabbis or commanders were such a question to arise again. I immediately issued instructions to those who oversaw the enlistment of new recruits forbidding such questions. The IDF should be left outside all political issues and the views of recruits on the evacuation of the Gaza Strip are none of the army's business. As far as whom a soldier will follow, the soldiers had already proved themselves, as the phenomenon of soldiers' insubordination during the evacuations was scarce and insignificant.

After the evacuation, I issued an order that children from the evacuated settlements who requested to enlist in certain military units upon their recruitment gain priority over other recruits. This was done in order to simplify their enlistment and restore their trust in the army. Five years after the evacuation I met Amatsya Yechieli, who used to be the youth coordinator in the Gaza settlements and a settler himself. Amatsya told me that the youth proved their unwavering loyalty and that 80 to 90 percent of them enlisted – thanks largely to my order. He said they realized that the army that forced them out of their houses is also the army that takes care of their needs now.

The IDF is the people's army, and as such, its soldiers hold diverse political opinions, including some that sometimes do not correspond well with the army's missions. And yet, the soldiers understand their job and remain loyal. The basic approach of the army must be complete trust in those who are about to become its soldiers, regardless of their political views. One of the more emotional examples of this is the story of Lieutenant Amichai Merhavia, who was killed in the battle in Bint Jbeil in Lebanon on July 27, 2006.

Prior to the evacuation from Gaza, Lieutenant Merhavia wrote a letter to the chief of staff in which he described the pain he suffered from the evacuation. Merhavia wrote that he was going through "a crisis of trust regarding the essence of the justice and morals meant to be reflected in the army's orders." He wrote that the harsh images of the evicted will forever be a stain on the army's uniform and that he is ashamed of the army and disappointed in its commanders. Following this letter, Lieutenant Merhavia, who prior to this incident had been considered a promising young officer, was punished for his statements and suspended from all commanding responsibilities.

Merhavia wrote his letter just before the evacuation and sent it through the army's computerized network, but due to some unfortunate technical problem, the letter was not sent. Several months later, the computer problem was fixed and the letter was automatically dispatched to its original address, the offices of the chief of staff. If the letter had been received when it was originally sent, it would probably have been read with a larger degree of tolerance toward the sender; but when the chief of staff received it, three months after the evacuation, the public atmosphere was already much calmer and the letter's style stood out sharply. The chief of staff immediately directed Merhavia's commander to release the lieutenant from his command post. At the time, Merhavia was busy commanding a platoon of fresh recruits. I heard about this for the first time when the chief of staff read the letter at a meeting of the General Staff and used it as an example of the type of statements that should not be tolerated.

Shortly afterward I again heard about this letter from at least two of my friends. Both told me about the unintentional time lapse that had occurred and their opinion that the time factor made a big difference. When I asked the lieutenant's brigade commander for his opinion, he also thought that the time lapse should be taken into consideration in the soldier's favor. He also told me that Merhavia was an outstanding officer.

I approached the chief of staff, explained to him all the different aspects of the case, and beseeched him to reconsider his decision and reinstate the young officer. He promised me he would think it over. Several weeks later, I visited the training base from which Merhavia had been suspended, and I asked the base commander what he thought about Amichai Merhavia. He replied that his best officer was being wasted because of the suspension!

Five months after he wrote his first letter to the chief of staff, Merhavia wrote a second one. This time he apologized for the harsh words he used in his first letter and claimed that they were written in "the middle of a stormy period and while he was going through a personal crisis that had left him very conflicted." He went on and told the chief of staff how hurt he was by the decision to withdraw and how, after serious thought, he had decided he must remain loyal to army orders and avoid acting against the government's resolution. He did not sign proclamations, nor did he publish anything outside the army. He wrote the first letter to the chief of staff, he explained, as a legitimate piece of dialogue – for it was done within the army and not outside it. I must say I understood his point of view.

After I spoke with the base commander I returned to my office and once again contacted the chief of staff. The chief of staff, Dan Halutz, who by then had Merhavia's second letter in front of him, was finally appeased and agreed to let him return to his command post.

The tragic end is well known. During the Second Lebanon War, Merhavia, who fought with exceptional bravery, was killed. "I will not be lying if I said that building and defending our country are to me the most important issues," wrote Merhavia in his second letter to the chief of staff. In my eyes, if that's how things are, this generation has many virtues. We certainly have not lost a generation.

★ ★ ★

I did not go to funerals during the Second Lebanon War, but preferred to pay visits to the bereaved families in their homes. I was sitting in my car facing east on my way to Mitzpe Shalem to visit the Cohen family, whose son Nimrod was killed on the first day of the war. Suddenly I decided that due to my personal involvement and the complexity of his circumstances, I should go to Amichai Merhavia's funeral that was set to begin in thirty minutes. I informed my office about my new destination, and they informed the unit responsible for guarding my personal safety. The security unit replied that they couldn't possibly come on time to the funeral, which was expected to include extremist opponents of mine, and prohibited me from going there. I informed them that I was going there anyway and that all they could do was inform the police officers stationed at the cemetery that I intended to be there.

I arrived minutes before the coffin arrived and made my way toward Amichai's father, Moshe. I reached him amid whispers from all directions, people wondering – in the best case – what I was doing there. Moshe, who knew very well my indirect connection to his son's tragic death, hugged me warmly. He even asked me to have a seat in the line of dignitaries and rabbis that were sitting by the grave. The majority of the mourners were standing, and I too remained standing; sitting was an honor I did not deserve.

I Accuse (1)

I accuse certain rabbis of the Religious-Zionist movement of misleading their congregations and, I might say, even deceiving their followers. Following the withdrawal, they caused the rift in the religious community, and among settlers from the Gaza Strip, to grow larger than necessary. They created confusion among the youth, causing them to lose faith in their religion and lose trust in their state. All this could have been mitigated, and in many cases even avoided, had the rabbis chosen a different approach to the issue.

The rabbis are the leaders of their congregations and all eyes turn to them. They are the ones who should have taken responsibility and looked after their congregants' peace of mind. In my opinion, those rabbis actually neglected their followers by instilling in them a false hope that "the evil will not come about." These rabbis put themselves in God's shoes, sometimes explaining His intentions, sometimes telling God what they expected of Him (they actually got a little mixed up, thinking that He worked for them). They did not consider the weight their words carried with some of the members of their congregations.

The irrevocable statement "This will never happen" jeopardized the faith of a large number of people. It also caused confusion about the term "rabbinical ruling" and falsely elevated the status of the rabbis who made such statements. The statement "This will never happen" was put to the test within a few weeks, and for some, it shook their faith in their rabbi's words. Most of all, it lead to tragic results for those people who had complete faith in their rabbis and did not prepare for the evacuation.

If some of those rabbis were truly concerned about the well-being of their followers, they would have prepared them for the inevitable – and I am not implying that they should have asked their followers to collaborate with the evacuating forces. They could have mentally prepared them for the tragic eviction from their homes and thus strengthened their faith in a positive future of growth and production, and maybe even a future that included a return to Gaza. That would have made a difference; their followers would not have been taken by surprise, and the harm done to them would have been diminished.

We will suffer the consequences of the behavior of those rabbis for months, maybe even years to come. The young generation of Religious Zionists, many of whom live in two worlds – the religious world and the modern world – will respond to the disappointment and leave the fold in massive waves. Many of them might say to themselves: if Judaism revolves solely around the dilemma of where the borders of the Jewish State shall pass, if its relationship with the "other" can either be one of complete love or utter repulsion with nothing in between, if the road must always be one of extreme measures, then I do not want to belong to this religion anymore.

It should be stressed, however, that there were others who contributed to the Religious-Zionist communities' sentiment just as much as those rabbis, and I will mention them as well.

Just as You Do Not Prepare for Cancer

On the last Independence Day before the withdrawal, I went with my wife, Dorit, and our son Amichai to the Gaza Strip. I wanted to observe, to learn a little about the local settlers, and be with friends during their toughest hours. Dorit wanted personally to part with the settlements. Our daughter had volunteered during the second Intifada and joined one of the settlements, assisting the settlers. Our son Ilan signed up for the yeshiva in Atzmona on the same day that five of its students were murdered, and he studied there for a year and a half. We had many memories from the Strip.

First, we drove to the house of Guy Yeshua. Guy, who was born in Tivon, was my friend during my early days in the paratroopers.

He was a great friend and at the same time the best soldier in our platoon – innocent and kind. After he was discharged, he moved to a tiny village in the Arava Desert. Over the years he became religious and moved to one of the settlements in the Gaza Strip, continuing to practice agriculture.

We sat in his yard and talked. Children came and went. Normal household activities were taking place. My wife Dorit asked Guy's wife, Michal, if they were preparing their children psychologically for the forthcoming evacuation. Michal answered that she had tried to arrange a communal preparation but the other settlers wouldn't hear of it and that she was doing what she could to prepare her children on her own.

From there we went to the house of Rabbi Rafi Peretz, who later became the IDF chief rabbi in Atzmona. We sat on the balcony and Dorit repeated her question, about preparing the children for the evacuation. "What evacuation?" asked Michal Peretz, the rabbi's wife. "This will not happen! Do you know anyone who prepares himself for cancer? Just like no one prepares for cancer, we won't prepare for the evacuation."

When we left, I told Dorit that she had just witnessed the two opposing approaches taken by settlers in the Gaza Strip. I knew that on the day of the evacuation both families would act in a similar manner. There would not be any violence in either of the two houses, and yet those differences meant something. Michal Peretz, whose house I visited on the day of the evacuation, symbolized for me the naive trust in God's will and in the rabbis' rulings.

I recalled my father's tale of how, just before the Holocaust, when the voices of Nazism were already being heard throughout Europe, his rabbi in Slovakia prohibited his congregation from walking on a street where there was a school that taught the Hebrew language in preparation for life in Palestine. This rabbi probably also trusted that some miracle would occur. His prohibition of Hebrew learning served to prevent potential immigration to Palestine, and we all know how that ended.

"Let It Come Apart"

Prior to the evacuation, one of the settler leaders, Adi Mintz, and I arranged several meetings between the army commanders and the settler leadership. We searched together for ways to better understand the local problems and thus to minimize the potential danger of violence.

In one of these meetings something was said that frightened us very badly and drove us almost to despair.

When one of the officers explained to Rabbi Elyakim Levanon the dangers that massive insubordination could pose and how it could lead to the collapse of the army and of the state, the rabbi said, "So let it come apart. Maybe this is a necessary step toward redemption."

I shared with my colleagues the notion that by saying those words, the rabbi crossed a dangerous line. The other rabbis did not say a word, even though I knew they did not agree with Rabbi Levanon. We discussed between ourselves whether we should continue the discussion with Rabbi Levanon after what he had said, and decided that since he was chosen by the settlers we would respect their choice and continue the debate with him.

Those meetings began during the era of Chief of Staff Moshe Ya'alon. When Dan Halutz was nominated as chief of staff, I informed him of the meetings, and he asked to participate. Halutz joined the final meeting, which took place in the offices of the Human Resources Directorate. Rabbi Levanon reiterated his opinions, and Dan Halutz said that if he had known that the rabbi was going to speak like that, he would not have sat with him at the same table.

Dancing in My Office

Aside from those high-ranking meetings with generals on one side and the elected leadership of the settlers on the other side, I conducted meetings in my office with rabbis, heads of Hesder yeshivot, heads of pre-military academies, and field commanders who were supposed to oversee the actual evacuation.

In one of those meetings a rabbi said that for him, the evacuation of a settlement is comparable to the desecration of the Shabbat for the officers. Nimrod, a commander in the paratroopers, responded, saying, "I want you to understand that for me, to evacuate a girl from her home in Nablus in the middle of the night is the same as a Shabbat desecration for you. As long as you won't realize this, you will not understand me."

It is human nature to add humor to tragic circumstances. One morning while I was in the middle of one of those meetings, Rabbi Yitzhak Grossman from Migdal Haemek called to say that he was in the neighborhood and asked if he could pay me a friendly visit. I said that, unfortunately, I was in the middle of a meeting, but if he came at two thirty I would be free and more than happy to see him. The rabbi came at two thirty, but because the meeting was still going on, out of courtesy, I asked him to join us. Later on, I realized I should have invited him from the beginning – not only out of respect, but also because of the significance of his attendance and his status. But I was reluctant to mix Rabbi Grossman, who is loved and respected by everyone, in issues as controversial as the evacuation.

The rabbi was deeply impressed. He had not imagined that such meetings take place, and when the meeting was finally ready to adjourn, I asked him to say the final words instead of me. Rabbi Grossman, as he usually does, spoke about love for the Israeli people.

At three o'clock I already had my next meeting scheduled, with the rock singer Rami Kleinstein, about Hebrew songs in the army. This meeting was also delayed, and Rami waited in the entrance, trying to attract as little attention as possible by wearing a hat on his head. I invited both of them to my office, and we put three chairs in a circle and sat down.

Rabbi Grossman told Rami that he envied him for his ability to compose and sing and said that he had once tried to write a melody to a song. Rami asked him to sing the melody, and the rabbi started to sing the Bible verse, "Guardian of Israel, guard the remnants of Israel" with his own melody, while keeping the rhythm with his foot.

Rami put the hat back on his head, and within a couple of minutes the two began to dance in my room. All I could do was join them. If someone would have entered the general's chambers at that moment and witnessed a secular rock musician dancing and singing with a bearded Orthodox rabbi and the general, he would better understand why, ultimately, we can overcome anything.

The Art of Shady Business

During preparations for the evacuation I was informed that Rabbi Shmuel Tal, of Neveh Dekalim, was one of the most militant opponents of the evacuation. Therefore, during one of my visits, I accepted an invitation to visit his yeshiva, known to be the stronghold of the extremist wing of the settlers. Visiting this yeshiva was like visiting a lion's lair; there were several cases of violence already attributed to its students. Nevertheless, I figured I should go and see the rabbi. I wanted to have a few words with him in order to map out the lines that might save us all from bloodshed.

When I entered the yeshiva I saw people walking around with their prayer shawls and phylacteries in the middle of the day. Every observant Jew knows that this indicates a time of fasting and lamentation. The secretary, who recognized me, asked me who I wanted to see. I told her I was there to see the rabbi. She entered his office and when she came out, she said that the rabbi did not want to see me. I left. Later, Rabbi Tal sent me a message saying that he had not meant it personally, but that he had refused to meet me because of what I represented. It was not clear to me which was worse.

Since the evacuation, Rabbi Tal has chosen a road of personal detachment. He has led his pupils toward a deeper alienation from the state. Though he seems to belong to the Religious-Zionist movement, his philosophy and his attitude are actually similar to those of the ultra-Orthodox Jews who only show tolerance toward the state because of the material benefits they receive from it. Rabbi Tal, who is a great believer in the Land of Israel, does not have any faith left in the State of Israel; he does not celebrate its independence and he regards it as a foreign regime that must be tolerated and exploited. This can be illustrated by the way he led an aggressive and open struggle against the authorities while simultaneously secretly negotiating with those same authorities for a new yeshiva complex in exchange for a peaceful and orderly evacuation.

After the evacuation, several students from Rabbi Tal's yeshiva approached me and asked to enlist in the Netzah Yehuda Battalion, a special IDF unit set up to accommodate ultra-Orthodox Jews. I faced a serious dilemma. On the one hand, the army prefers not to enlist recruits to those Orthodox units if they do not belong there. On the other hand, I suspected that if they were not allowed to do so, they might not enlist at all. Additionally, allowing them into the Orthodox units would be another step toward obtaining the legitimacy these units needed.

In the end, I decided to approve the request, under the condition that the rabbi himself would come and discuss the issue with one of my officers. I thought that by meeting with the officer, Rabbi Tal would, in some way, be recognizing the legitimacy of the IDF and the State of Israel, even if as a foreign regime.

The officer who attended the meeting later told me that the rabbi had explained to him that his motto was, "I am against the state and the army, but I will take from them as much as I can get." This type of attitude is familiar to me. I witnessed the same attitude in other yeshivot in different sectors, in institutes that approve lying as long as it is done in order to avoid enlisting in the army.

In the case of Rabbi Tal's yeshiva, they were allotted fifteen spots in Netzah Yehuda, but only three were used by his yeshiva's students. Rabbi Tal used the army's good will to help twelve students from other yeshivot, who did not deserve to enlist in the ultra-Orthodox unit. The students fictitiously joined his yeshiva;

he received larger budgets for them and they were able to enlist in the ultra-Orthodox unit. I observed with a heavy heart how the art of shady business prevailed in this case over the sacred biblical rule: "Thou shall keep away from false words."

I Accuse (2)

I accuse members of the religious community who degraded themselves and their religion with their patronizing, insulting, humiliating, and ugly behavior toward me and my friends – IDF soldiers and officers – prior to, during, and after the evacuation.

I accuse them, not just because they hurt me; I accuse them because they demonstrated to our children and to their children, to my neighbors' children and to their neighbors' children, a narrow-minded Judaism, one that is frightening and threatening. They represented a Judaism in which only love or contempt exist; they represented a Judaism that forces one to think only one way.

All of those connected to the evacuation – religious and secular – experienced the foul tongues, and sometimes also the violent arms, of certain members of the religious crowd, who made themselves intentionally blind. I say blind, for they failed to see the values with which they were raised, values they learned long ago and they themselves taught. They failed to see the desecration of God that evolved and will continually evolve from their acts – all done allegedly for the love of the land.

I witnessed endless examples. Months after the evacuation was complete, when I was on a trip with several families from Hoshaya to a hostel in Dimona, I entered a conversation with one of the more recognized figures of the Gaza Strip settlements. Our dialogue was interrupted when his sister in-law approached and said in a loud voice, "Abraham, it is prayer time – leave him. It's not worth missing the afternoon prayers because of him!" We said the prayer together, and after we finished, Abraham told me that whenever he hears someone speak against me, he tells the person how I, with all my heart, attended to every single request he and his friends asked from me prior to and during the evacuation. I thanked him and refrained from mentioning the venomous remark we had heard before the prayer.

Another time, Dorit and I attended a Torah scroll dedication in memory of Gilad Fisher, the son of our friends and neighbors. When the synagogue ceremony ended, a friend of Gilad's mother approached her and informed her that she would not be joining the banquet following the ceremony because I would be there, and she refused to sit with me in the same room. That is how low things got.

The community to which I belong is supposed to follow scriptures' commandments. Many of the people believe that insulting someone in public is equivalent to shedding his blood, they denounce slander, they practice the commandment to "love your fellow man as you love yourself," and they pride themselves on their social compassion. Yet they failed over and over to fulfill each one of those commandments. Among those who failed, many believe that phrases such as "Observant scholars increase harmony in the world" and "*Derech eretz* (common decency) is a prerequisite to observing the Torah" are but a testimony to our ancestors' sense of humor.

For many months, when I was invited to secular weddings, I went like all other guests, but when I attended a religious wedding, I had to be accompanied by security guards. Often, this insulted my hosts, but I could not change that.

Dorit, my wife, works in the town of Sachnin. When asked if she was afraid to go there – to a place surrounded by Arabs – she replied that she is more fearful of the religious community. Though both the question and the answer use broad generalizations, we, unfortunately, felt this way. It is hard to comprehend how a military man can feel alarmed by his fellow countrymen and people who are considered first-rate citizens. Maybe some of the following episodes will shed some light.

Violent Encounters

During one of the very charged visits I made to the Gaza Strip, my staff suspected that I might have been kidnapped. Although this may seem a bit hysterical now, given the atmosphere of those days and several violent incidents, their fears were not completely irrational. That same logic perhaps lies behind the hesitation I feel today before I offer my handshake to a religious person whom I do not know. How did we reach a state of such distrust?

At the time, I was escorted by car to discuss some issues with a leader of one of the settlements. At the entrance to the head of the Gaza settlement council, some people signaled to us with their hands that we were marked men and should expect the worst. The meeting itself was completely peaceful, and on my way out I met all kinds of different people: some were familiar people who treated me like an old colleague, but others wore the faces of extremists facing a military officer who will soon come to banish them from their homes.

When we reached our armored jeep we found that its four wheels had been punctured. A second car was brought, and when we tried to enter the car, a large crowd showed up and blocked the doors of the vehicle. A fortified wall of people surrounded me from all sides, blocking me so that I could not move. Some cursed at me; others called me a "criminal" and other names. We managed to push our way into the car with all our might, but the mob encircled the car and did not let it move. It took a lot of resourcefulness on the part of my driver and my aide to get us out of there. Pictures of this incident that were published in the newspapers illustrated the anger and hatred on the mob's faces.

After the incident was broadcast on television, I was asked how I managed to control myself. I replied again that I know what we demand from our regular soldiers and officers who are going to serve in the inner circle of the evacuation. I can easily predict the curses and spitting they will, unfortunately, face, and nevertheless, we demand that they remain completely in control of themselves.

If I did not show restraint when facing provocation, how could I demand it from my soldiers?

A True Rabbi

On the day after I was attacked at the Kotel, an incident I described in the introduction to this book, I was on my way to a ceremony celebrating the completion of several handwritten Torah scrolls donated by Ira and Inge Rennert. The semi-annual ceremony always takes place in the Netiv Aryeh Yeshiva and includes the writing of the last few words of the scrolls. I am invited to these ceremonies because of my friendship with the contributors, as well as with Rabbi Aharon Bina, the head of the yeshiva, and because there is always at least one scroll for which I had the honor to help decide in whose memory it was to be dedicated. That year, one of the five Torahs was dedicated to the memory of the soldier Gilad Fisher from Hoshaya.

When I passed Jaffa Gate on my way to the yeshiva, I received a telephone call from Rabbi Mordechai Eliyahu's assistant, who said that the former chief rabbi wanted to have a few words with me. When the rabbi got on the line he let me know that he is sending me words of support following the violent incident I experienced a day earlier at the Kotel. I was, of course, both surprised and honored by the rabbi's call.

When I climbed the stairs leading to the yeshiva, my guards reported that the situation was fairly calm inside the building. "The atmosphere inside is tranquil," reported my guards, "aside from one woman who lost her husband in the settlement of Homesh." They added that they would keep her away from me.

In the middle of the ceremony, my daughter Liron told me that one of the woman's friends had asked her to convince me to speak with the woman, describing it as a small service for this poor woman. Liron beseeched me to agree, thinking it might serve to comfort the widow, and I agreed. The guards were concerned and did not want to permit it but I insisted, and we were led into a small office, surrounded by glass walls. The woman asked that we remain alone and when my guards refused, I convinced them that they would be able to see everything through the glass walls. Eventually, they agreed and we were alone.

The woman looked silently into my eyes for several minutes. She observed me and I observed her in sort of a psychological game she tried to play until, at last, she said, "Tell me, who is your rabbi?" I asked her what she meant. "Who is the rabbi that you listen to?" she continued.

I said I do not have one such rabbi, but that Rabbi Aviner, for example, is a rabbi that I highly respect. To that, she replied, "Elazar, I asked you about a *rabbi*!" I went on to say, "Rabbi Moti Elon..." and she continued as if she had not heard me. "Name a *rabbi*!" I said that on my way to the ceremony I had received a call from Rabbi Mordechai Eliyahu, who wanted to let me know he sends me his support. "Is he also not a rabbi in your eyes?" She was taken back by this name and could hardly believe it.

"Who *is* a rabbi in your eyes?" I asked her. "Someone who says only what you want to hear?"

We spoke some more. I understood her boundaries and we parted in peace. I was glad that I agreed to do what my daughter had asked, but altogether I was saddened – not only because of the woman's personal tragedy, but also for the terms of her expression, her way of thinking, her entire philosophy. I even felt sad for her unusual interpretation of the phrase "Make for yourself a rabbi." In her eyes, the phrase meant one should find himself a rabbi who mirrors his own opinions.

The Same as Explosives

Several weeks after the evacuation, Rabbi Dudi Dudkevitch, the rabbi of the settlement Yitzhar, one of the rabbis who issued calls for soldiers to refuse their orders during the evacuation, was invited to spend Shabbat in our town of Hoshaya. He was the first person invited to our village after the evacuation, and it seemed strange to me and many others in the village. I could not understand why of all rabbis, Rabbi Dudkevitch was chosen.

Soon after I became commander of the education division, I was forced to intervene in a very grave matter. Newspapers had published reports that a commander in the Nahal had told his subordinates that Reform and Conservative Jews were worse than Nazis. According to him, Nazis had killed six million Jews, but the Reform and Conservative movements had caused the extermination of eight million. Rabbi Dudkevitch wanted to meet me in order to speak in favor of this commander.

I came to the synagogue in Hoshaya to meet Rabbi Dudkevitch together with my friend and relative, Sidney Teichman. It was shortly after I was attacked at the Western Wall. Sidney had been with me when I was attacked, and the incident left a deep scar on his soul. After Rabbi Dudkevitch finished his sermon, Sidney asked him what he thought about the Kotel incident. Rabbi Dudkevitch justified the attackers, saying that their response must have been a physiological response, some type of uncontrolled biological reflex, even though none of them had been evacuated settlers. Rabbi Chaim, the rabbi of Hoshaya, kept silent while Rabbi Dudkevitch spoke. Rabbi Dudkevitch went on and told us how Rabbi Chaim had said in one of the rabbinical assemblies prior to the evacuation that "maybe the time has come for us to regard ourselves, the religious people, as a community and not as a state." Our rabbi remained silent and did not object to his words.

I was not altogether surprised. I had heard our rabbi, whom I respected and liked, talk on earlier occasions about the possibility that ultra-Orthodox Jews are right. We do not know that the state will exist in the future, he said, and the ultra-Orthodox have proven in the past that they know how to preserve their religion even without a state. Maybe we can do without a state. I tried to ignore those words, hoping that they were said in response to momentary pain of some kind, or as a fleeting philosophical thought that was meant only for a few carefully chosen ears. But I was now disillusioned.

A community rabbi is a very influential position, especially when he is as loved and respected by his congregation as Rabbi

Chaim is. A rabbi is in a position, at least in the eyes of children and teenagers, that what he says reflects the Lord's own words. I am afraid that a mixture of religion and politics, in the hand of such a person, has highly explosive potential.

The rabbi raised a black flag over his house and hung posters objecting to the evacuation. His house was provided to him by us, the inhabitants of Hoshaya, as part of the compensation he receives for his religious services. Officers in the army receive a car from the state for their own use, and an officer would not think of – and regulations prohibit – putting political stickers on that car, even when it is used for recreation.

Rabbi Chaim is hardly the only rabbi who served as a community or settlement rabbi who used his status to promote a political agenda. In many synagogues one could hear, instead of the expected Torah words, political statements ranging from denunciations of the evacuation to denunciations of our prime minister.

I asked the rabbi why he uses this platform, and my arrival at the synagogue to pray, to force me into listening to his political opinions against our prime minister. He claimed that I do the same. He said that I use my position to make statements on issues that are not directly within my responsibility. I answered him, and I will say it again here, that I never do that. Nobody, not even my family, and certainly not any of my subordinates, know what my opinion of the evacuation is. This has nothing to do with my strong objection to all kinds of insubordination in the military.

I am not the only high-ranking officer who lives in Hoshaya. During the evacuation at least three other high-ranking officers serving in significant posts lived there: Brigadier-General Menashe Goldblatt, a decorated hero of the 1973 war, Colonel Ehud Nusen, and Colonel Yuval Biton. I am afraid that to this day, all three carry spiritual scars inflicted upon them by their neighbors' aggressive attacks and by the silence of other neighbors during the days of the evacuation.

On the eve of Rosh Hashana, Rabbi Chaim preceded us by coming to our gate and greeting us. I greeted him back, and the rabbi added, "You should know that I am still angry with you!" I was surprised and replied that I was also still angry with him. I asked him where he found the courage to promote such an explicit opinion against the evacuation. I understand that scripture forbids us from giving away parts of the land and I realize that the rabbi considered the Gaza Strip to be a part of the Promised Land, but is it a prerogative of an authorized settlement rabbi to promote such a position? Did he consider other sound opinions in the world of scripture?

Did he inquire how much money could be saved each year from a different military deployment – money that perhaps could be added to the health ministry and used to save lives? Did the rabbi ever speak to a bereaved family, whose son died defending those settlements, and hear his parents testify about how he considered our stay in the Gaza Strip unnecessary? How much do rabbis know about the rational considerations of political decision-makers regarding state affairs? I do not claim that those things would necessarily change anyone's opinion. I myself have no clear stand on this matter. But if I were asked to state my opinion, I would go and examine all the aspects, some of which may be commandments from the Torah that are just as important as the issue of the land.

I asked the rabbi what he was thinking when during a conference – organized by him – of opponents of the evacuation in our settlement, while one of my daughters was sitting in the crowd, he had said that the low-ranking soldiers sent to evacuate the settlers may be forgiven, but never the high-ranking officers.

It was very hard for me, during those holidays, to concentrate on the prayers. I thought of Rabbi Chaim, reading the prayer book and blowing the shofar, weeping with absolute sincerity, yet knowing that he did not fulfill the basic commandment "Until you first request forgiveness from your neighbor," one is not forgiven by God.

The following year, the rabbi came to me on Yom Kippur evening and asked me to forgive him. In the final prayer of Yom Kippur, the rabbi made an extraordinary gesture. I do not remember whether he asked the cantor to say a prayer for the health of army soldiers or the security of the state. I just remember that it was a prayer that was not in the regular order of prayers, and I thought when I stepped out of the synagogue that a big step had been taken toward reconciliation.

Unblessed Soldiers

One day, in a youth magazine, I noticed an essay written by Rabbi Yaacov Ariel, the municipal rabbi of the town of Ramat Gan and the president of the local Hesder yeshiva. The rabbi wrote, "I now omit the word 'all' from my prayers for the IDF soldiers. I used to pray, 'Bless all the soldiers of the IDF' and 'Bless everything they do,' but today I do not pray for all the soldiers and certainly not for all they do. I do not pray for those who took a part in the inhumane expulsion of men and women from their homes...for them – the soldiers who did those things – I will not say prayers. What's more, I denounce every soldier who took part in the evacuation, for doing an inhumane deed."

I wrote a letter to the rabbi, saying that I understood from his essay that soldiers who go out to fight in Lebanon or in Nablus do not receive his blessing if they took part in the evacuation from the Gaza Strip. I also gathered that as a municipal rabbi, he only prayed for the well-being of part of his town's soldiers.

I added that although I searched the prayer books, I did not find any version of the prayer that includes the word "all" in the prayer for the soldiers. The original version is "He who blessed our forefathers, Avraham and Yitzchak and Yaakov, He will bless the soldiers of the IDF," without the word "all." Did the rabbi add a word to the prayer, only to spread controversy and hatred?

I also wrote that I long for the old days, when rabbis were less occupied with the questions of whom they bless, whom they should excommunicate, who will manage to evade enlistment, and who will not be invited to take part in the priestly blessing or pray at the Kotel.

I concluded my letter to the rabbi saying that we, in the army, will continue to do all that is in our power in order to bridge the gaps, and we hope that the Master of the World will support us and bless all the soldiers.

A WILD GUESS

Again and again, I found myself upset by random encounters with religious people before and since the evacuation. If I had not been religious, I would not have had to suffer the many remarks and rebukes said with a tone of, "But it was we who sent you" or even "You are there to do our work."

One day, I was sitting in a restaurant in Tel Aviv with Dorit's father and two other acquaintances. I was dressed in civilian clothes, as I usually am when I am not on duty. Suddenly, the owner of the restaurant handed me an envelope with a letter inside. She told me that one of the restaurant patrons gave it to her and asked her to deliver it to me. When I asked who he was, she said it was not important.

I put the envelope in my pocket to read later. When I opened the letter, it said: "Elazar Stern, this is the second time I have seen you in this restaurant. Officers like you should be busy training and correcting the failures from the Second Lebanon War. I do not understand what you are doing here at such an early hour." It was signed, "a captain in the reserves."

When I asked the owner again who gave her the note, she replied that he requested to remain anonymous and that he had already left. I asked her if he wore a *kippa*, and she confirmed that he did. I was dismayed that I immediately realized he must have been a religious man.

Several months later, while at another restaurant with a friend, I was approached by someone with a big smile who told me that he was the one who had sent the letter.

I told him that I did not understand why he was smiling. He was embarrassed, and I informed him that I considered him an insolent fool. In response, he asked me why I assaulted yeshiva graduates. I said I didn't, and I asked him what made him think that he could pass me such a rude note while I was in civilian clothes in a restaurant, and if he sent the note, why did he hide behind the owner? Several minutes passed and the captain approached once again and asked for forgiveness.

I asked him why he did not send notes to other officers in the restaurant – those not wearing yarmulkes on their heads. Why did I immediately know that he was religious? Where does that arrogance, insolence, and lack of boundaries come from?

He asked me again to forgive him and I did.

Later, he told me that he served on the board of the Hesder yeshiva in Ramat Gan. Two years later, I read in a pamphlet usually dedicated to Torah and distributed in synagogues on Saturdays, words written by the head of that same Hesder yeshiva, Rabbi Yehoshua Shapira, one of the most dominant rabbis in the Religious-Zionist community. The rabbi wrote about the people who founded the State of Israel as follows: "We returned to our land through the efforts of people whose hearts were made of stone – people who were estranged from the Torah and its commandments." They might have been estranged from scripture and its commandments – but hearts of stone? Why? Where does this arrogance come from? How did Rabbi Shapira, and unfortunately others too, associate estrangement from the Torah and its commandments with a "heart of stone"?

A Rebuke in Beijing

We were in Beijing on an official tour and had some free time on Shabbat. The folks in the embassy knew, of course, that I ate only kosher food, and they put us in a hotel a short walking distance away from the local Chabad house with its synagogue and restaurant. Though the other officers who were with us on the tour were not observant, they all preferred to accompany us to the prayers and the kosher Friday night dinner.

When we came to the Chabad dining house, I was asked to say a few words. More than eighty guests usually attend each of those Friday dinners in the Chabad house, including embassy personnel, businessmen from countries around the world, backpackers, and students. Customarily, each guest introduces himself before the meal starts. I learned from those introductions that there were people there from Australia, Switzerland, New Zealand, and naturally, Israel. One of the guests introduced himself and said he lives in Elkana.

I imagine that when I stood up to speak, the audience expected to hear about the military situation or something along those lines, but I chose to talk about Rabbi Shimon, the Chabad representative in Beijing, who raised his children in Beijing together with his wife and catered to the needs of all the different people who came to the Chabad house. He does not touch a morsel of bread before he sees that each of his guests is comfortable and has a seat and a plate of food. I spoke first about the beauty of the hospitality, about Chabad and their dedicated volunteer activity, and I finished with a few words from the weekly Torah portion.

When the meal was over, many of the guests approached me to thank me for my words. The tourist from Elkana came over and asked me why I supported the evacuation. He then added that he was a retired colonel from the Ordnance Corps and now lives in Elkana. He said, "I did no less for our country than you – maybe even more than you! Why did you support the evacuation? Because of you there are eight hundred families without homes!"

I replied that I did not know whether I had supported the evacuation or not, but I certainly did not approve of insubordination. He went on to ask why the entire high command had supported the evacuation. I asked him how he knew that, and he replied, "It's a fact that none of you resigned!" I pointed out that he paid taxes and his money served to finance the evacuation. He said that was different and continued with his insolent tone. Dorit was already outside and returned to get me. I could see the contempt on her face when she discovered what had delayed me. She, like me, was fed up of encounters with Religious Zionists who tried, in every place they met me, to tell me who is more religious, who did more for our country, and what, in their opinion, I should do.

I ask myself sometimes how people who turn to me in a restaurant or in Beijing – when I travel with my family or when I am on some official errand – feel completely comfortable trying to educate me. What do they tell themselves? Do they expect me to suddenly change all my opinions, or do they want to punish me? What uncontrollable impulse drives them? What sort of Judaism do they represent? What kind of love of the land do they have – love combined with arrogance, insolence, and scorn? This is not the Judaism that I believe in.

CHAPTER 11

HESDER

One Saturday morning, my daughter Adi was the officer on duty on her base, and she went to pray in the synagogue. When prayers ended, the soldiers sat down together to eat breakfast, and at the meal, Adi met five yeshiva boys from the settlement of Peduel. The boys asked her what her name was and where she was from. She answered, "My name is Adi and I'm from Hoshaya." The soldiers responded immediately, "The village where that filthy Stern lives?!" and proceeded to curse me out.

Adi asked them calmly if they had ever learned any manners or at least not to gossip. Then she cut them off and said, "You didn't ask me what my last name is. It's Stern. Now, thanks to you, there is another issue on which I disagree with my father. He should have kept the Hesder students in separate units, so that I wouldn't have to be around any of you."

I was cursed because of my outspoken position on the issue of the Hesder yeshivot. I was regarded as an enemy of the people. It was my idea to abolish the separate platoons for religious soldiers and to merge Hesder soldiers with secular soldiers. I imagine the fact that the idea came about around the time of the Gaza Strip evacuation made the reaction harsher than it might have otherwise been, though I am certain that it would have been met with harsh resistance anytime.

What guided me on this issue was part of an overall philosophy about the role of the army in our life as a nation. This philosophy is based on the belief that the IDF has a larger and more encompassing task than just looking out for the security of our people; I believe it also has the responsibility of looking after the spiritual well-being of the people as well. Ever since I was in Bahad 1, this philosophy led me to promote knowledge of Judaism and the education of soldiers, and to be involved in projects like the conversion of non-Jewish soldiers to Judaism.

I must emphasize here that I do not have and never have had any intention of breaking up the Hesder yeshivot. I was once asked this question at the Knesset Committee for Foreign Affairs and Defense. The representatives of the Hesder yeshivot were also present at the same meeting, and the Knesset members spoke in favor of dismantling the Hesder program altogether. I told the members of the Knesset committee that the IDF, which allows special conditions for athletes and musicians in order to ensure the future of athletics and sports and music in Israel, should also look after the yeshiva students, to preserve our spiritual future and even more importantly, the future of Judaism in Israel. The Knesset members responded by saying that the number of Hesder students is far larger than all of the other "special" soldiers put together. Although this is correct, I countered by telling them that, unlike in the other frameworks, more than 80 percent of the Hesder students serve in combat units.

One of the reasons I came out in favor of Hesder is that one cannot take a three-year hiatus from learning scripture and return at the same level. The same applies to soccer players and musicians who cannot reconstruct the same abilities after long breaks and therefore receive special service conditions. The MKs replied that if one could take a break from chemistry and biology and return after army service to study medicine, one can probably do the same with scriptures. This was a strong argument. There are certainly those who return to yeshiva after completing a full three years of service and later become dominant rabbis. I could not come up with a good answer.

FACE TO FACE

In chapter 2, I wrote what my reasons were for enlisting as a regular soldier instead of as a Hesder student. As a boy, I could not understand – and I still cannot understand – how an observant young man who sincerely cares about the Jewish nature of Israel, would give up the opportunity to serve with secular youth.

In one of my discussions with cadets in Bahad 1, one cadet who was a Hesder student stood up and asked me about my intentions regarding Hesder and why I had abolished the segregated units. He mentioned the deep commitment the religious students showed after finishing their service. As an example, the cadet mentioned a project called "Face to Face" which proposed bringing religious and secular Israelis closer. I told him that the ultimate opportunity for a face to face encounter is in the army service, when there is not a single, carefully planned encounter, but rather a true chance to get to know someone. I think this is important for both religious as well as secular youth; everyone benefits from it.

When Hesder students encounter secular soldiers during their service, it can not only open their minds and broaden their perspective, but it can also strengthen their own Jewishness. Getting to know secular soldiers adds new dimensions to their thinking. Understanding that a person who does not fulfill all 613 commandments can still regard himself as a proud Jew and that Rashi and Maimonides are not the only noteworthy figures, but that Agnon and Shakespeare are also valuable, can ultimately positively influence the religious soldiers. I think that when yeshiva students serve in mixed units, they have a better chance of realizing that, in the end, each of us has his own personal "rabbi" – whether it was a teacher in high school, a mother, or an influential novelist – someone whose advice and philosophy he respects. Everyone has individual core values that should always be respected by the other.

During our military service, walls that normally separate religious from secular (separate kindergartens, elementary schools, high schools) come down, and we have a long encounter with those who are different from us. But this encounter is crucial and ensures our Jewish army, and by doing this, guarantees a better Jewish state.

One of the principal reasons for the strong reluctance heard in religious circles to allow a mixture of the Hesder soldiers into regular non-observant units is the unspoken fear that their religiosity will suffer a blow. Rabbi Shlomo Riskin, the rabbi of Efrat, said about this fear, "If, after eighteen years in our religious kindergartens, elementary schools, high schools, and yeshivot, we are afraid that when our soldiers are out on their own in the army – not alone, but with many of their peers around them – they will lose their faith, then it is not the army we should check, it is ourselves!"

QUANTITY VS. QUALITY

Though the main reason I oppose Hesder in its present form is because I consider the mixed units important for the future of our lives here, I also think that Hesder should be smaller. In recent years, the number of soldiers in Hesder rose by more than 20 percent. This increase in Hesder actually detracts from the number of soldiers manning combat regiments at any given moment, thereby forcing the army to mobilize eighteen additional reserve regiments each year in order to fulfill all its necessary security tasks.

A combat soldier who serves in Hesder units serves only sixteen months in the IDF, less than half of the full thirty-six months that his fellow soldiers serve. Upon closer examination, it seems the contribution of Hesder soldiers to the army is even more limited. Each soldier needs seven to eleven months of basic training. If one assumes nine months of basic training for soldiers, the effective contribution of Hesder soldiers to the army is barely seven months, about a quarter of the twenty-seven-month contribution of a regular soldier in operational units.

The reduced Hesder service could be more easily defended when we were faced with short-term, high-intensity wars that erupted every few years, which were fought with a mix of regular and reserve forces. But since the Lebanon War of 1982, all the conflicts in our region have been relatively low intensity. Most of the fighting takes place in Lebanon, Gaza, and the West Bank and the daily burden lies mainly on the shoulders of the regular soldiers. It is a war against terror that demands continuous sacrifice and fierceness from the fighters.

There are two arguments usually used to defend the shorter term of the Hesder service. The first claims that the Hesder platoons are exceptionally high quality. This is true in many cases, but we must remember that it is a homogenous unit, while the other platoons include recruits from many different places. I am certain that if we constructed platoons from the graduates of an exclusive high school in Ra'anana, Karmiel, or one of the kibbutzim, we would also get exceptionally high-quality platoons.

The second argument is that the burden is balanced out afterward, during the reserve service of the Hesder soldiers. According to this argument, the number of Hesder soldiers that show up for reserve duty is so high that it balances the shorter regular service. It is true that the Hesder soldiers appear for reserve duty in high numbers, but what about secular soldiers who also never miss reserve duty? What shall we say to those who join pre-military institutes for a year after high school, then serve a full term, and still continue to answer every reserve summons? It is also worth pointing out that the twenty months missing from the Hesder soldier's term of army service are equivalent to more than twenty years of reserve service (based on being called up one month each year).

The situation should be judged for the way it is: the length of service in Hesder is short and in some ways it is an inconvenience to the army. It is permitted because the state recognizes the importance of having students who study Torah.

Devoted Almost Exclusively to Torah Study?

As far as I and many others are concerned, it is very important to have devoted Torah students studying in yeshiva. The question that should be asked is how many of those who are registered as Hesder students are really devoted and therefore deserve special consideration. In all other specialty fields in the army, for example musicians and athletes, there are objective tests that clearly prove the exceptional talent of the soldier in question. In each of the categories there is a strictly limited quota of soldiers. It is different with Hesder. Anyone can become a Hesder soldier, even one who does not know how to learn, even one who does not learn at all. Though many might disapprove of my last sentence, I think that we in the Religious-Zionist movement all know that even if you do not devote yourself exclusively to Torah study, you can still be a registered yeshiva pupil.

I am not removed from my community. I see students who lack the ability to study scripture for the major part of the day joining Hesder yeshivot. Their rabbis, who consider these yeshivot to be a kind of haven, let these kids roam about at their discretion and hurriedly summon them when an army inspection comes to the yeshiva. One of the many understandings reached by the heads of the Hesder yeshivot and the army's authorities was that the yeshivot are informed in advance about any such inspection. I think this understanding in itself is problematic.

The somewhat artificial increase in the number of Hesder recruits complies with the philosophy of the Hesder rabbis, who regard the program as a civic service. I visited one of the Hesder yeshivot located in a rundown part of the country. There I spoke with the head of the yeshiva, who was opposed to the idea of mixed units. He told me that he feared his students would be influenced by the secular soldiers in the units and would abandon their religion. I asked one of the institute's rabbis if he would accept those kids to one of the non-Hesder yeshivot and he replied that he would not, thus proving that the Hesder yeshivot serves only as a haven for those kids.

Many consider this to be a legitimate approach, but in my opinion, it is wrong. I feel that this is how we lose those youngsters twice: once, when they serve less than half the mandatory term in the army, and a second time when they do not join the military framework that best suits them. The army offers great opportunities. These soldiers could learn a trade for their future.

This could also be rewarding for society if they return to this trade upon their discharge. Also, when it becomes clear, to the boys themselves and to everyone around them, that they are not going to become rabbis or teachers, their rabbis should realize that by keeping these boys in yeshiva, they are not helping the boys' future prospects of integrating into the workforce and becoming proud family men.

In such cases, I feel as though the conduct of these rabbis, as well as that of their institutions, is a type of thievery: they are stealing potential soldiers from the state. One can also regard this behavior as a symptom of the assimilation of an ultra-Orthodox form of behavior into the Religious-Zionist movement. It represents a frame of mind that says, "We will take into our haven as many as we possibly can and Israeli society will fill the missing positions."

In a way, this equation is not entirely fair to the Hesder people. Sixteen months of training prepares a soldier for combat missions, for participation in the defense of his land, and sometimes for paying the heaviest price. Still, I cannot shut my eyes to how the mass registration to Hesder resembles ultra-Orthodox society, which does exactly the same to avoid recruitment, knowing that there will be someone else who will stand up and protect them.

I certainly do not intend to make a sweeping statement here. Among the Hesder graduates one can easily find great scholars and pedagogues. But even that does not compensate for the many others who do not have the strict devotion required from Torah students and who would be much better off contributing their time to the army – as most of their compatriots do.

The Reason No One Will Talk About

Between the years 1999 and 2003 there was an increase of more than 35 percent in the number of soldiers that enlisted through the Hesder program. This is not evidence of a sudden learning craze that took over the Israeli Religious-Zionist society. It is not a result of a demographic explosion either.

The significant growth since the start of the second Intifada proves that behind the ideology lies the basic instinct of parents to want their offspring to be safe. Many parents convince their sons to join Hesder because they know that they will be safer there. Recent wars have lasted long periods of time; some have lasted years. In wars, the reserve forces are no longer just as dominant as the regular soldiers. Now, battles are continuous and take a toll mainly on the regular army. A soldier who enlists for sixteen months, about ten of which are spent in training, hardly spends time in the monotonous daily fighting and thus is naturally much more protected. These are the conveniences and relative safety that Hesder offers its soldiers and another reason for parents to choose it over regular army units.

Mothers always comfort themselves: "My boy is safe right now because he is in a course!" When a soldier is posted in an area of conflict, that is when his mother really worries. A Hesder soldier will participate in about seven months of combat activity while a regular soldier partakes in twenty-seven months – more than four times as long.

A Religious Soldier in a Secular Platoon

After the process of the assimilation of religious soldiers in mixed platoons was launched, I visited the Einhorn family from the village of Gimzo, whose son Yehonatan was killed in the Second Lebanon War.

The parents of the fallen soldier, who was very devout in his religious observance, mentioned that their son had started in Hesder but left to go join the regular army, and he had suffered many difficulties being a single observant soldier surrounded by secular soldiers. I said I understood that it must have been difficult for him, but that it would have been much easier for him if all Hesder soldiers were integrated into regular companies. That way, instead of keeping all thirty-six Hesder soldiers in one separate platoon, there would be twelve in each of the company's platoons.

When I left their house, one of their neighbors, a woman who was once my counselor in the Bnei Akiva youth movement, followed me out and told me that she shared my opinion.

To be an observant soldier in a secular platoon is not an easy matter. I know this from my own experience. But if there were no separation to begin with, there would be a better chance that the religious soldier would experience normal religious life, including public prayer services and a Shabbat atmosphere. Therefore, dispersing the Hesder soldiers throughout other units would make life easier for religious soldiers who do not enlist through Hesder.

When I launched the first mixed platoon project, I issued a strict rule that the number of religious soldiers in each such platoon could never be fewer than twelve soldiers, in order for them to be able to continue their religious practices. In addition to this minimum number of twelve Hesder soldiers, the platoon's religious soldiers who did not enlist through the Hesder yeshivot would also be present.

This number cancels out all the usual arguments about the problems a young religious soldier faces when he serves amidst secular soldiers. Even the issue of the use of foul language is no longer pertinent, due to the large number of observant soldiers who are expected to have a positive influence on their peers, forcing them to use cleaner language in their presence – influence that a single religious soldier could never have. At the same time, the integration could have the desired effect of mutual understanding that Israeli society so desperately requires.

I once met an elderly gentleman named Kurt Rothschild, president of the World Mizrachi movement. He had been following the Hesder program closely since its inception and felt great pride at the success of the project. He attacked me for the mixed platoons project, declaring that his organization felt responsible for the Hesder soldiers. I replied that I understood his fears but that if his organization chose to identify with one sector of the recruits of our army, it should, at the same time, consider the many thousands of religious soldiers that do not necessarily enlist through Hesder and are scattered throughout the army. His organization has the same responsibility toward all the other religious soldiers and to their parents' concerns regarding the difficulties of the course their children have chosen to follow.

OFFICERS AND YESHIVA STUDENTS

Since the Hesder program does not provide its students with enough service time to become officers, many of the Hesder soldiers who are officer material remain in Hesder and never achieve this goal. Thus the army often misses potentially talented commanders. I do not intend to promote the idea that soldiers should abandon Hesder, but I do think each soldier should reach an individual decision on how he can best contribute to the state. As I mentioned before, not every student has the making of a rabbi; similarly, not everyone is fit to become an officer.

With regard to this matter, the mixed platoons have a clear advantage over the homogenous units. Each platoon commander marks four of his finest soldiers as potential commander material and starts instilling them with a commander's mindset as soon as basic training begins. When we integrate the yeshiva boys in mixed platoons, a soldier who might have been somewhat less outstanding in the homogenous Hesder platoon might then be singled out in the mixed platoon as one of the outstanding four soldiers chosen to be a future commander.

In order to avoid all possible criticism of the army being opposed to learning, and to encourage religious officers to remain longer in the service, I issued an order that each religious officer be entitled to four months of vacation in order to learn. Officers who take this leave are entitled to a full salary during this period.

"JOIN THE PARATROOPERS"

When I was appointed the commander of the paratrooper training camp in 1984, the late Menachem Zaturski, the Paratrooper Brigade commander, came to me with an idea to send Hesder soldiers to the paratroopers. He believed that they would make good soldiers, especially because he knew the Brukental brothers from Kibbutz Hafetz Haim and Israel Gur Aryeh from Kibbutz Yavneh. I knew all three of them. They all became colonels during their reserve service.

The Brukental brothers did not actually serve through Hesder, though they were religious. Until my conversation with Zaturski, the Hesder students were regularly sent to the Givati Brigade. It was only two or three years after the brigade was organized, and it still lacked prestige. Recruits hardly agreed to join it, so the yeshiva boys were sent there to fill the lines.

When I spoke with Zaturski, I realized that he had a good idea, and I immediately decided that Hesder soldiers should no longer enlist as full homogenous companies, but rather in separate platoons in regular mixed companies. I already intended on having mixed platoons someday, and I considered this the first step in that direction.

A year later, I approached Rabbi Yehuda Amital, head of the Hesder yeshiva in Alon Shvut, and presented the idea to him of disseminating Hesder soldiers throughout regular units. He wanted to know why. I told him that when I studied economics and Israel Studies in Bar-Ilan University, there were many yeshiva kids who studied economics with me but only one who studied Israel Studies. I asked the rabbi if after attending religious kindergartens, elementary schools, yeshiva and then Hesder yeshiva – is that what all the young men intended to do, go and study economics? Is it logical to serve only half the army service for economics studies? I asked the rabbi, if we are separated from the rest of the nation from kindergarten until we finish our military service, when will we become influential?

Rabbi Amital found two more reasons for spreading Hesder soldiers throughout regular units. He claimed that many students were killed in the war because they were all in the same company, and maybe, if they were disseminated throughout many units, the burden would fall more equally. "Second," he said with a smile, "our students were not always treated fairly by Givati; when there is competition between Givati and Paratroopers, Givati will have to behave better toward them..."

Things began to move quickly and we had a conference with all the yeshiva principals. One of the rabbis attacked me intensely, saying that I was responsible for the fact that for several months now, all his students have been spending their time preparing lists of who is going to the paratroopers, instead of devoting their time to Torah study.

Rabbi Druckman said that he could provide me, by the following August, two full companies of Hesder recruits. I replied that I could be ready for six mixed platoons (a company consists of three platoons) but not for two homogenous companies. Those were the first Hesder platoons in the paratroopers corps.

A month and a half later, I participated in a memorial ceremony in honor of Major Sefi Shauman, commander of the armored corps officers' school regiment, who was killed in the First Lebanon War and who served as a role model for many of us as a religious man with a career in the army as a combat commander. There, I met General Matan Vilnai, then the head of the Human Resources Directorate.

Vilnai told me that he opposed the plan to let the Hesder yeshiva students integrate in the paratroopers. He claimed that our goal is not to enlarge Hesder, but rather, to limit its size. He feared that if we open up new possibilities of army service to its students, it might tempt kids who refrain from joining Hesder in order to volunteer for the paratroopers and other units that are now closed to them. I replied that if they join Hesder and come to the paratroopers, they might want to remain in the army as officers and leave Hesder.

Sadly, I realize now that Matan Vilnai was correct.

WHO WILL COME TO WHOM?

The dialogue with the leaders of the Hesder association commenced soon after I became head of the Human Resources Directorate in the summer of 2004.

Toward the end of that summer I presented to them my plan to enlist their students into mixed platoons. They asked me if I would be willing to present the plan in a meeting with all the Hesder principals and I agreed.

Meanwhile, the talk about the evacuation of the Gaza Strip began to sound believable, and the papers published reports stating that several of the principals of the Hesder yeshivot implored their students to reject their army orders.

The conference of the yeshiva principals took place inside a military recruitment camp. They arrived there in the morning and I planned on joining them toward midday. At approximately ten o'clock in the morning a string of phone conversations began with Rabbi Druckman, who said that some of the rabbis had remarked that it would be better for me not to come.

The rabbis were afraid that I would choose to focus on the call for insubordination. Although the discussion was not intended to deal with refusing orders, since it had been brought up by the rabbis and I was a high-ranking officer, I answered that it would probably be unavoidable. I promised him that I would refer to the issue in only one sentence and afterward we would focus on the issue for which we had assembled.

Rabbi Druckman passed on my words to his colleagues but failed to convince them to meet me. Rabbi Druckman apologized at length and explained that for him this whole issue was very painful, but that his hands were tied due to the democracy of their organization. I asked him if he did not think there should be leadership on top of democracy and we ended our conversation. An hour later, I heard on all the radio stations derogatory expressions referring to my "stupidity," coming from the principals and their spokesperson, Rabbi David Stav.

Later, when the murky relationship between the Hesder association and me began to damage the entire Hesder idea, Rabbi Shlomo Brinn asked me if I would agree to meet with Rabbi Aharon Lichtenstein, head of the Hesder yeshiva in Alon Shvut, together with Rabbi Amital. I said that I would be honored. A few days later, because Rabbi Lichtenstein was sick, I traveled to his house in Alon Shvut, where we had a sincere conversation that cleared up all the misunderstandings and misinterpretations.

The most meaningful lesson I learned from that conversation was the fact that Rabbi Lichtenstein attributed the decline in my relationship with the Hesder Association to the behavior of the rabbis during the conference on the recruitment base. According to him, he did all he could to dissuade them from their decision to disinvite me, but it was made because of the false democracy that they practice. It is false because the vote of Rabbi Lichtenstein, for example, a rabbi with tens of thousands of devoted students, like Rabbi Druckman and Rabbi Tzfanya Drori, carries the same weight as the vote of the head of a yeshiva founded a week ago with twenty-five students. That, coupled with the fact that the Hesder association has no mandate to make enforceble decisions, makes it an institution that is unpleasant to deal with.

A few weeks later, a meeting with the yeshiva principals did take place in the same recruiting camp. It passed without any problematic incidents, except for when a famous yeshiva head told us that he has secular friends who invite him to come to them on the Shabbat to smoke marijuana with them, implying that this is the nature of their Shabbats. I was ashamed that a rabbi in Israel, who is admired by his followers and respected by many, promotes his Torah way of life by describing others as pot-smokers. I was especially ashamed because I knew he was lying, and because he sincerely thought that I and others in the room were stupid enough to believe him. I was also ashamed for the serious rabbis who sat in this room and did not reprimand him; I was particularly ashamed for the secular officers who sat in the room and had to listen to these ignorant lies.

After this conference, more meetings were held, all of which were futile, including a meeting at the Hesder yeshiva in Ramat Gan. My assistants were shocked to hear that I had accepted the invitation, since they remembered that the leaders of this institution openly supported insubordination and were active among those who denounced me.

One of the rabbis in the yeshiva was the rabbi in my parents' neighborhood. He is a few years younger than I am, and one day he announced to the entire congregation, in my elderly father's presence, that he cannot feel proud to have learned in the yeshiva from where he graduated, because I and two other generals also graduated from there. Later, following protests from many members of his congregation, he apologized.

During this meeting I learned once again something that I have known for a long time. The Hesder association has its agenda. They bring up all kinds of requests and the army usually complies, but when the army comes to them with some request, they notify us that, according to the decision of the yeshivot rabbis, the association does not have the authority to make a decision in the matter. "So what is the association good for and what do they hold meetings for?" I asked them, frustrated. From their answer, I understood that they have the authority only to receive benefits on behalf of the yeshivot, but not to give anything.

Nahal in the Same Boat

The same reasons that drove me to integrate Hesder students into regular and not segregated platoons later made me promote a similar plan for the Nahal group.

Nahal is a Hebrew acronym loosely translated as "Fighting Pioneer Youth" and refers to a program that historically combined military service with the establishment of new agricultural communities throughout the country. The program later branched out to other welfare projects, but what made it unique was the fact that the members of the program later served together within the Nahal Infantry Brigade.

We had a number of major arguments against the preservation of the Nahal Program. First was the plain military interest – the service in Nahal was shorter then service through the regular military track, lasting twenty-four months instead of thirty-six. In addition, their time in active duty was split into two segments – eighteen months in the beginning, then a year of volunteer service, and then another six months in the army. Splitting up the service encouraged a large number of the Nahal members to do all they could to avoid returning to the army for the second six-month stint, and at times 20 percent succeeded in evading the completion of their service. The remaining majority also lost its motivation to complete its service during this year of national service.

The second argument against retaining the Nahal Program was of a social nature – Nahal troops don't establish new communities like they used to. Nowadays, their year of national service is more welfare work in the Israeli periphery, in underprivileged towns and neighborhoods.

If that's the case, I don't understand why soldiers who go help kids in underprivileged cities should insist that when they return to the army, they serve only with their own kind. Why shouldn't they join the general military and its so-called melting pot like all regular soldiers? And this question can really be asked about their entire service. Why is the issue of social integration neglected all of a sudden?

I'll give you an example. Let's take Eran, a nice kid from Ramat Gan, who does his community service with his Nahal group in Dimona. He will help Rafi from Dimona prepare for his matriculation tests at school and talk to him about serving in a combat unit and contributing to the state. But when both will arrive at the induction center and Rafi will ask Eran to join him in the Givati Brigade, Eran will answer, "I don't serve with you in the army; I'm in a segregated unit..."

Isn't that hypocritical? Are those deprived kids like Rafi only good enough for them when they come down from Ramat Gan to Dimona, and then stop being good enough for them once the loftiness is taken away from their position, in the daily, equal, military life?

The final argument against the preservation of the Nahal Program was that in the past, the national service the Nahal soldiers did took place in remote frontier settlements and communities, places often used as forward bases by the IDF. That was a good enough reason to keep soldiers with combat training there. Nowadays, when all their projects are inside towns without real military value, their combat training is hardly required and is even wasted.

For all those reasons I thought it was justified to integrate the Nahal groups with the regular army units, instead of assembling them in one unit – Battalion 50 of the Nahal Brigade. I felt that such a move, similar to the one I fought for with regard to the Hesder yeshivot, would have social and military value. I wanted to see Nahal soldiers in Combat Engineering units and places like the Artillery Corps.

One of the youth movements whose members joined the Nahal Program opposed my plans, and people said that I didn't stand a chance in pushing the initiative through. The movement – called "Hano'ar Ha'oved Ve'halomed" – was closely associated with the defense minister at the time, Amir Peretz.

I met with Peretz and asked him if he didn't think that the idea behind segregated army units negated Ben-Gurion's idea of the IDF serving as a melting pot? Did the idea fit Peretz's own social ideology? He couldn't come up with a good answer and instead supplied legal advisors who claimed that we couldn't change the arrangement with Nahal since the members of the program had enlisted with the stipulation that they would serve in a segregated unit.

As a result, we all agreed that next year's recruits would be informed about the intended changes and that we would discuss the issue once again. The following day, my office issued a letter to all of the Nahal recruits, saying that they would be assigned to units in the IDF upon their enlistment based on the army's requirements as well as each recruit's personal qualifications.

Toward the summer we started feeling pressure from the direction of the defense minister's office. A month before the Labor Party primaries, I was informed that officers under my command had received a letter from the ministry, telling them that Peretz had assured the head of the Hano'ar Ha'oved Ve'halomed Movement that the recruitment for Nahal would not be changed without his consent.

Apart from the issue under question, the procedure itself was highly problematic. It's hardly appropriate for a minister of defense to neglect to first update the head of the IDF's Human Resources Directorate and then bypass him and send a letter to his subordinates. The official who had written the letter later apologized.

A month later and the day before the Labor party primaries, the recruits again received a letter in the name of the minister stating that Peretz had decided to leave the Nahal program intact.

For me, it was particularly disturbing to see how Peretz, whose main political agenda was social equality and concern for the weak, completely ignored the fact that he was helping to preserve an elitist program, which kids from the lower class – whom he claims to represent – will never be able to join.

No Double Standards

As the debate continued on the future of the Nahal Program, the Hesder yeshivot continued to loom in the background. I learned from the defense minister's aides that he supported the idea of mixed platoons, but my instincts told me that since these two issues were very similar, if the subject came up Peretz would be careful not to let anyone attack him for holding double standards – mixed platoons for Hesder; segregated platoons for Nahal.

The way Peretz accomplished this was to announce that Hesder students could serve in all IDF Infantry Brigades. I knew exactly what Amir Peretz had in mind. He knew that Hesder was connected to Nahal and he decided to be the knight in shining armor on the Hesder issue so no one could blame him for having double standards.

I asked the Defense Minister's aides what they expected me to do since the draft orders were about to be mailed out; I would have to move things around if Hesder students were going to be allowed to serve in the Golani and Paratroopers Brigades. I was told to issue the draft orders and not to change anything, which meant that after all the publicity surrounding the issue, the Hesder soldiers would still not serve in Golani or the Paratrooper Brigades. The important outcome was that the defense minister did not appear to hold double standards.

"Be the First to Welcome Every Man"

It is very easy to be content with your self-righteousness if you never listen to the other side. Why should you let yourself face conflicting opinions, when you can block out any inconvenient ideas? When you can isolate yourself from hearing any outside voice and believe that yours is the only truth? There are numerous institutions, yeshivot, and groups of teachers from the religious community who prefer not to listen to other opinions. Unfortunately, in many cases, the basic philosophy that lies behind the religious education system is that other parties aren't worth debating with. Perhaps they are simply afraid of another truth.

During the work to establish mixed religious-secular platoons, I had dozens of conversations and arguments with different rabbis from the Hesder yeshivot, some of which ended in agreement. There were rabbis who wanted me to come to their yeshiva and explain my project to the students themselves. Some students even showed up at my offices for more intimate conversations. One day, a group of students from the Hesder yeshiva in the northern town of Kiryat Shemona arrived and requested to meet with me. My staff officers were surprised and some of them even angry at my consent to meet the students, who had not yet even enlisted into the IDF. They reminded me once again that I'm not only a Religious-Zionist Jew but am also a general in the IDF, and that such unscheduled meetings were insulting to the organization I represented.

Some of the things that were said during that meeting deeply troubled me. The students tried to convey to me the great importance of their yeshiva and maybe also how important they themselves were. They quoted from the second chapter of Isaiah, about the mountain of the Lord that is high and lofty and how all the gentiles will flow to the place to pay their tribute. They explained to me that their yeshiva in Kiryat Shemona was the "mountain," and that all of the secular communities nearby look up to them to lead the way. They even went as far as to hint that just as the people of Israel had to stay united when entering the Land of Israel, so too, they had to stay united in segregated units during their military service to also serve as a "light to the nations."

I listened to them and was shocked by their arrogance and closed-mindedness. Who made them the bearers of the light? I was ashamed to hear them refer to themselves as the true Israel while comparing the rest of the army's soldiers to gentiles.

Even more distressing was another example of closed-mindedness that came from a head of a yeshiva, when I was in the northern town of Beit She'an to attend a ceremony in memory of Brigadier General Erez Gerstein, who fell in Lebanon. The ceremony was scheduled for 3:30 in the afternoon. I was expected to speak before Golani commanders in the morning, and in the several hours in between I had planned another meeting.

During my lecture before the young Golani commanders, I suddenly remembered that Rabbi Sugarman of the Hispin Hesder Yeshiva in the Golan Heights had asked me several times to come speak with his students about the mixed platoons. Rabbi Sugarman used to call me every time there was an argument among the different Hesder rabbis, usually after midnight, and we would talk. Every now and then he would ask me to come to Hispin and talk to his students. I saw that I had just enough time to make it there, knowing that my other meeting would manage quite well without me.

I finished my lecture before the Golani commanders and called Rabbi Sugarman to confirm, but I was now informed that since the Purim holiday was coming up his students wouldn't be back until 1:30 p.m. and it would be best be if I could delay my arrival to the evening. I told the rabbi that though this was my only free evening at home that week I was willing to spend it at his yeshiva.

I called Dorit and told her that our evening out was going to be spent at the yeshiva (she was by then used to the strange forms of recreation my career often dictated).

Later I received another call from Rabbi Sugarman, who told me of a new problem – the students, he explained, threatened to demonstrate against my visit, and several police cars had already been summoned to the yeshiva. I said that this shouldn't be a problem and that I would come with my personal bodyguards. A few minutes later the rabbi called me again, this time to inform me that the students from the nearby high school had arrived on the scene carrying posters against me. "As much as I want you to come, I don't think you should," Sugarman said. "It will lead to undesired hatred."

I called Dorit and informed her of the change of plans and that I was coming home after all, but since I was so disturbed I decided to call Rabbi Moshe Egozi, the former principal of the high school in Hispin, where my own son had studied several years earlier. I asked the rabbi cynically if it would be more convenient for him if I stopped mentioning the fact that my son had graduated from his yeshiva, because perhaps my connection to the school was causing them damage.

Rabbi Egozi was surprised to hear my story and didn't understand what I was talking about. He asked me to give him a few minutes to look into what was happening. A few minutes later, I received a phone call from Rabbi Palti Granot, the current principal of the Hispin high school, who said that while he wasn't on the campus, he had spoken to teachers who were and there were no demonstrations, banners, or protests against me. A few minutes later I received another call from Rabbi Egozi who told me that he himself went and checked the yeshiva grounds, and confirmed that there were no banners or protests.

I went home confused. At 10:30 at night someone knocked on my door. It was Zahalon Sidi, my neighbor from Hoshaya and the secular studies principal at the Hispin high school. He came holding a flowerpot in his hands to apologize for what had actually never happened. He said that he didn't know where the story had come from, but assured me that no one in the school had protested my planned visit to the campus. I told him what Rabbi Sugarman had told me, and Sidi was extremely embarrassed.

Instead of telling me directly that he didn't want me to come speak to his students (even though several times he had asked me to come), Rabbi Sugarman preferred to make up a story and while doing so smear the name of another yeshiva. I wasn't angry; I have a lot of respect for Rabbi Sugarman. It was just unfortunate and regretful.

One day, a man with two sons in the army – one from the Hispin yeshiva and the other from the yeshiva in Eli – approached me and started talking about the Hesder program. Until that conversation, he had the impression that I was "the liquidator of Hesder." Now that we talked, he realized that the reality was far more complex. Towards the end of our conversation, he said: "I don't know why I was told that you are such a difficult person. You are actually quite nice."

I asked him where he had heard that I was such a difficult person. "Rabbi Sugarman," he answered. I again felt regret.

A few months later, I met a friend of mine at a wedding, chatting with someone who had a *kippa* on his head. My friend shook my hand and asked me if I knew the man he was talking with. I said I didn't and reached out my hand while saying, "It's a pleasure to meet you, my name is Elazar."

"I don't see any pleasure, and I don't want to shake your hand," the man replied. I said a few more words to my friend and went on my way.

Later my friend came up to me and apologized. "I didn't know he would act that way," he said, explaining that the man's name was Dani Sugarman, brother of Rabbi Sugarman.

Ever since that event, and even though my mother taught me that I should always be the first to greet someone, I am careful not to greet religious people whom I don't know. I wait for them to reach out their hand first.

Nevertheless, there is a somewhat brighter ending to this sad story. One day I received a call from Rabbi Avihai Ronsky, the IDF chief rabbi until 2010, who was visiting the Paratroopers Brigade's training base. The rabbi told me that a squad commander had just told him how he had met with me several years before as part of a delegation of Hesder students who tried to convince me to retain the segregated platoons.

The commander told Rabbi Ronsky, "I enlisted, in the end, to a mixed platoon, and I just want to thank him and say that he was absolutely right."

He was one of the boys from the Kiryat Shemona yeshiva who quoted Isaiah to me to prove their point. Apparently, sometimes "the mountain" comes to you.

Mixed Platoons and Success

One day, I received another call from Rabbi Ronsky. Rabbi Ronsky was one of the most senior officers in the IDF, and the one who spent the most time in the field among combat soldiers. This time he was in a Combat Engineering Corps base in southern Israel, and he called to tell me that he had just met several soldiers who serve in a mixed platoon; he couldn't find words to describe to me how happy they were. I was actually familiar with the platoon in that base and I knew that the Hesder students were from Yeshivat Hakotel in the Old City of Jerusalem

I believe we had Rabbi Moti Elon, the head of the yeshiva at the time, to thank for that. He had supported the program from the beginning and traveled often to that base to spend time with his students. After spending a Shabbat with them at the base, Rabbi Elon called me one Saturday night and said that in all his life he had never encountered such exuberance as he met in the mixed platoons down there. Not even in the yeshiva itself.

Rabbi Ronsky told me that what thrilled him the most was a story he had heard from one of the company commanders. Anxious to see the mixed platoon program succeed, the battalion commander decided to put the yeshiva students and the secular soldiers in separate rooms over Shabbat. He assumed that this would ease some of the possible tension and make it easier for each side to respect the other. In response, the yeshiva boys rose as one and declared that they weren't interested in such separation and that they would manage without such measures.

The secular soldiers didn't like the idea either and decided that on Saturdays they would refrain from listening to music in the rooms and use of their cellular phones outside the rooms. I was overjoyed by the story. If a major part of what we wanted to achieve by the mixed platoons was tolerance, we seemed to be on the right path.

And then there was another similar story. On a nice spring day in 2008, Rabbi Ronsky called me after a visit he had just made to a company from the Nahal Brigade, in the Nablus area. The commander of the company was the son of a well-known rabbi and one of the company's platoons was mixed. Rabbi Ronsky said that he had asked one of the secular soldiers how he got along with the Hesder soldiers and was told: "Everything is great. I don't know how it happened, but apparently we got special religious soldiers."

Ten minutes later, Rabbi Ronsky met one of the Hesder soldiers with a large *kippa* on his head. The rabbi repeated his question and the yeshiva student replied: "Everything is great. I don't really know how it happened, but we must have received some very special secular guys."

Nobody selected special soldiers. No extraordinary observant guys and no special secular kids. Regular people were assembled and put together with other regular people and they were then given the opportunity to get to know one another.

For Our Sins

My relationship with Rabbi Shmuel Eliyahu, the rabbi of the town of Safed and son of the former Sephardic chief rabbi Mordechai Eliyahu, was particularly bad. Until today, I have to restrain myself from calling him "Shmulik" since I hardly think he deserves the honorable title of rabbi.

On several occasions, friends of mine were shocked to learn that I was still in touch with him, particularly after a neighbor told me that he had heard Rabbi Eliyahu say that he didn't know even one girl who had served in the army and come out in "good shape." I was insulted not just for my own daughters but for countless decent girls who served in the army and were much better than in just "good shape." I despised this generalization that was insulting for numerous young women who serve and served in the IDF.

One Friday morning I received a call from Rabbi Eliyahu asking to have a few words with me. I gave my consent, not knowing that this conversation was about to cost me dearly. Shmuel Eliyahu wanted to ask me why we were not permitting pre-military academies, where soldiers learn for a year before their three-years of service, to also open a parallel Hesder program. I didn't quite understand what the issue had to do with the rabbi of Safed and why he was interfering in something that had nothing to do with him.

I have always been on good terms with the various heads of the pre-military academies since their establishment in the early '90s. I knew for a fact that they didn't need Rabbi Shmuel Eliyahu's help, and I figured he simply regarded this as a good opportunity to gain some publicity for himself through an issue that wasn't really any of his business. I also knew that in the few cases in which the heads of the academies thought one of their students needed to be given an opportunity to continue his yeshiva studies, I gladly gave them my full assistance. I explained to Rabbi Eliyahu very patiently that the army had no interest in promoting such an idea because the state needs soldiers. The soldiers of the pre-military academies have a reputation for being excellent soldiers, and unlike their colleagues from the Hesder yeshivot, they serve a full term of three years, so why would I promote a program that would cut the length of their service?

Our conversation continued and we moved on to the subject of the Hesder program. I claimed that religious soldiers in regular companies found their military service easier because there are many more religious soldiers today in the IDF in command posts. As a result, I said, the IDF is much more considerate toward religious soldiers than when I was drafted, for example. In response, he chose to give me an example that was supposed to prove me wrong. He told me that his son was forced to guard a certain post for seven consecutive hours together with a female soldier. I said I couldn't believe that such a thing had happened, but if it did, it must have been a very unusual incident.

Toward the end of our conversation, I asked Rabbi Eliyahu why certain heads of yeshivot intentionally spoke against the IDF Rabbinate and its chief rabbi Avihai Ronsky. When a soldier has a religious question, I said, Rabbi Ronsky should be the natural address for him. The heads of the yeshivot should explain to their students, I said, that when they serve in the army the head of the Military Rabbinate is the *Mara De'atra* (in ancient Aramaic, the Rabbi of the Land), essentially the rabbinical authority to whom one turns with questions.

To my surprise, Rabbi Eliyahu answered me that the issue of *Mara De'atra* wasn't as straightforward as I had made it out to be. I was sorry to hear his different interpretation. He implied that being the chief rabbi of Safed, he should enjoy the privilege of having all his town's soldiers turn to him with religious questions even when they are far away from home and that, if necessary, the entire army should wait patiently for his rulings. But still, I was more surprised by the story about his son who had been forced to guard a post for seven hours with a female soldier. I just couldn't believe it.

A week later I spoke with Rabbi Ronsky, who told me that Rabbi Eliyahu had been invited to speak before bereaved religious families at an official IDF event. I told Rabbi Ronsky that I thought it was a mistake to invite Rabbi Eliyahu to speak, due to his opinions and his reputation for being an instigator. Rabbi Ronsky replied that Rabbi Eliyahu had promised to give an emotional talk based on Torah teachings. I still thought that we were providing the rabbi with a kind of legitimacy by giving him such a platform, because when he will later continue to spread hatred his voice will be heard louder.

I also asked Rabbi Ronsky to check for me whether it was possible that a Hesder soldier would be forced to guard a post for seven hours with a female soldier. The rabbi said he was sure this couldn't have happened but he would check out the story. I said to him that if he spoke about the subject with Rabbi Eliyahu, he might also ask his opinion regarding the Military Rabbinate's authority.

Rabbi Ronsky returned looking a little embarrassed. It seems that the incident with the rabbi's son had happened ten years earlier, before the army had withdrawn from Lebanon. When Shmuel Eliyahu had spoken to me, he made it sound as if the incident had happened just a few days earlier. Even then, Rabbi Ronsky said, it wasn't clear that the soldier was forced to do this guard duty, but Rabbi Ronsky didn't want to embarrass Rabbi Eliyahu so he didn't ask him any more questions. I asked Rabbi Ronsky if he had forgotten that female soldiers were not stationed in military outposts in Lebanon. Rabbi Ronsky said that when he asked Rabbi Eliyahu about religious authority in the IDF, he was told that the Military Rabbinate was the sole authority. At least that.

I was naive enough to think that the story was over. A few weeks passed and during the ten days between Rosh Hashana and Yom Kippur, Major Yael Wolf, the spokesperson for the Human Resources Directorate, entered my office and asked me if I had read Rabbi Shmuel Eliyahu's letter on Hesder yeshivot, since a newspaper was asking if I had a response to it.

I was somewhat surprised because I hadn't received any letters. I wasn't totally surprised, though, because by now I knew that delivering a letter first to the press was a standard, cheap, political move.

This happened, as I said, during the sacred Ten Days of Repentance between Rosh Hashana and Yom Kippur, and the rabbi apparently had no moral difficulties as long as his name got in the press.

Several hours later, I was asked to respond to the letter by a popular radio news show. He tried to convince me to talk by saying that the rabbi had already agreed to speak. I was determined not to participate in this charade. I decided that it would be wrong to confront him on radio, he being the rabbi of the town of Safed, and the time of the year being what it was. I knew that it wasn't going to be a conversation about atonement, and I also hoped that if I forfeited the right to respond, the rabbi might also give up the whole story.

But Shmulik didn't think of giving up a chance to go public and spread hatred. He spoke on the radio and said that it was widely known that I wanted to dismantle the pre-military academies and the Hesder yeshivot, and that I told him that I believe that the number of Hesder soldiers should be limited. This was the only true statement he made during the entire broadcast. I never claimed that Hesder was unnecessary, just that the numbers were too high – just like I never claimed that I wanted to cancel the pre-military academies. The truth was that I was a big supporter of the academies, which produced some of our finest soldiers and commanders. The rabbi simply lied for his large audience.

The highlight was when the rabbi was asked about the incident involving his son and the female soldier. In contrast to what he had told me, he said that his son was forced to ride in a military jeep with another soldier and a female driver.

This time, his story might have been a true one, and though it might not be an ideal situation from a religious point of view, it could easily be changed if more male soldiers from religious communities decided to serve in the IDF. If the number of Hesder students was limited and fewer kids were spending their days in the yeshivot – where many of them prepare for the psychometric test (the Israeli equivalent of the SATs), as many Hesder soldiers told me they do – they could serve a full three-year term in the army and maybe one of them could replace the female driver.

I must confess that during the Yom Kippur services I couldn't stop asking myself how this rabbi could preach to his congregation that an offense against another person will not be atoned for on this holy day until one has apologized and obtained forgiveness from the person he offended. How can one go to the press and publish a false letter without giving the other side a chance to respond first to his accusations? How much hatred does this rabbi spread around him while he waves the flag of love and unity?

If I had the opportunity I would tell him that for his sins against me I have forgiven him and I hope that God will too. I cannot say the same about the rest of the IDF since I do not have the authority to forgive him on behalf of all soldiers, especially not the female ones.

A Lesson from Rice

We all hope our children will follow the path we have tried to put them on throughout their lives. This is especially true for the religious communities in Israel. Service in the IDF is indisputably one of the most difficult tests for observant Jews. Like any other father, I don't know whether I do the right thing when I ask my son if he remembered to put on tefillin or if he put on his *kippa* when leaving the house.

But I found that I have reasons to be proud of my children. When my son Ilan was discharged from the army, he traveled to Turkey with a friend from his combat unit and they returned a few days before the Sukkot holiday.

We all sat in the sukkah, and a few of Ilan's ex-squad members came for a visit. He and his friend began talking about their trip to Turkey, while everyone passed around the food on the table. At one point, Shacham, Ilan's travel mate, tasted the rice and turned to Ilan saying, "Ilan, this is rice!" Someone asked what he meant and he told us the following story: Being a good friend, Shacham decided from the beginning of the trip that he would eat what Ilan ate. One Friday, he and Ilan came to a hostel late in the afternoon and quickly started cooking rice on a small camping stove they had brought with them. Ilan, meanwhile, went to the bathroom and noticed from the window that the sun was setting. He yelled out to Shacham to shut the stove since Shabbat was beginning. The rice, however, was not cooked enough, so they ended up eating uncooked rice in honor of the Shabbat.

Now Ilan sat and enjoyed his mother's rice, and his mother and I enjoyed the story and what it revealed to us about our son and his friend. The story illustrated for me, once again, why I prefer mixed platoons over segregated ones.

Chapter 12

Draft Dodging

I neither launched nor designed the public campaign against dodging the military draft. Things just started to move by themselves after a routine visit I made with the Chief of General Staff Lieutenant General Gabi Ashkenazi to the Tel Hashomer Induction Center.

I had made the same visit with three different chiefs of staff. Each time we arrived at the base, the chief of staff spoke with the fresh recruits and then usually took a few of the journalists' questions as well. While the questions were supposed to deal with that day's event – the new draft – there were always several reporters who used the opportunity to ask about other issues. I was usually a passive companion on those visits.

On this particular visit in 2007, a year before my retirement as head of the Human Resources Directorate, the chief of staff was in a hurry to reach another engagement and couldn't stay to speak to the reporters. Seeing that, the IDF's spokesperson asked me to fill his place and to speak to the reporters. I claimed that I did not have much to say, but the spokesperson insisted that I say a few words about the draft.

One reporter asked me what I thought about the increasing draft-dodging numbers. At the time, we were reaching the point where a quarter of all eighteen-year-olds were somehow avoiding military service.

I said what I thought. Another reporter asked me if I blamed the government for the rising figures, and I said that I did. When the reporters asked me to be more specific, I said that I would prefer to see the government talk less and do more for soldiers who serve in the IDF. I also added that in my opinion the state should pay for discharged soldiers' university education and that if I was asked where the money for this should come from, I had several suggestions.

My remarks were made on the eve of the ninth day of Av – the annual fast day to commemorate the destruction of the two Jewish Temples in Jerusalem. I didn't watch the news that day but that night I received a call from the chief of staff's office asking me if what was published under my name was accurate. I confirmed that it was. I was told to expect queries from various politicians and government ministries to clarify my remarks and my implicit criticism of the government. I said that I would back every word and, if asked, I would also be happy to explain my statements.

Things escalated and the topic remained in the headlines for several weeks. A week after the chief of staff's visit to the recruitment base, Defense Minister Ehud Barak also came to visit the base and said to me in front of a crowd of people, "Stern, though I do not disagree with you about the concern with the rise in draft-dodging numbers, I must nevertheless censure you, since an officer cannot criticize the parliament and the government."

I replied, "You are absolutely right; I expected a censure from you. But I believe that I had to say exactly what I did."

He said, "Then, consider yourself reprimanded."

Later his military secretary told me that my response took the minister by surprise, because nobody else would have dared say to him that he expected a reprimand. This was another lesson for me that my candor has its pros and cons – but I wasn't the issue. Since the political establishment was reluctant to award those who do their duty and serve, and since it also failed to pass legislation that would punish the draft dodgers who were caught cheating their way out of the army, it became the Human Resources Directorate's duty to try and stop the state from drowning under this flood.

And a flood it indeed became. When I was appointed commander of the Human Resources Directorate, the draft-dodging rate stood at 23 percent. It later climbed and reached 27 percent. Eleven percent were on religious grounds, and 40 percent of all female recruits didn't enlist, claiming also that they were religious.

Such an enormous wave threatened to negatively affect the level of motivation of those who actually enlisted in the IDF.

One of the first steps I took was to hold a meeting with all of the IDF psychiatrists and psychologists. I asked them to cut the number of soldiers they discharged on psychological grounds and to toughen the criteria that warrant a discharge: not to be as lenient in releasing new recruits, some of whom took advantage of the mental health officers. I assured them that they would have my full support if one of the soldiers ended up harming himself. The massive release from service also had its price, I explained. Every platoon commander in a field unit, I said, takes decisions that influence the lives of his subordinates, no less than the decisions made by the mental health officers. Take responsibility, I said. I have your back.

When I came out of the meeting, I saw a mother pushing her disabled son in a wheelchair to her car; he was wearing a soldier's uniform. I approached them and thanked the mother for bringing us such a soldier. "I'm the one who should thank you," she said, "for accepting my son to the army." She went on to ask me for a favor.

"I bring my son to his base and take him home every day, and I have no problem doing that. But if you could arrange for someone to bring him back home once a week so that I could have time for other activities that I don't have time for now, I would be most grateful," she said.

I thought about her devotion, her graciousness, and her sacrifice. I then thought about all those who were willing to do almost anything to free themselves from service. The difference between the heartwarming encounter with the soldier and his mother, and the conference I had just left with the army's mental health officers was a mirror of our problem in a nutshell.

Toughening the criteria helped somewhat to minimize the number of draft dodgers. The Military Police also increased their efforts and tracked physicians who forged medical papers for the draft dodgers, and that also helped a bit. But the main battlefield was and still is the public arena, where we still need to fight against indifference and the legitimacy draft dodging has received from different sectors in society.

Bereavement in Tel Aviv

Toward the end of the Second Lebanon War, the press began writing about how chief of staff at the time Lieutenant General Dan Halutz had called his bank just hours after the reservists Eldad Regev and Ehud Goldwasser were kidnapped on July 12, 2006, and ordered his banker to sell his stock portfolio.

I said that I thought the whole issue was distorted and blown way out of proportion, and that in my opinion the chief of staff was treated unfairly. I agreed to express my view publicly.

The next morning, while I was visiting a military unit on the Egyptian border, I received a call from a radio station. I made it clear that I didn't want to take part in a conversation that was only about Halutz, because it would look like all I had come to do was defend my direct commander. The talk show host asked me what other issues I had in mind. I said that I wanted to talk about my visits to bereaved families during the last war. The talk show host gave his consent. I began my bit of the broadcast saying that I was willing to speak on behalf of Halutz even though the man had never appointed me to any position in the army and would never do so in the future. The talk show host asked me if I implied by that that my present assignment was my last one in the military, and I replied that I did not have to make such a declaration because it was known to everyone.

I established my defense by explaining that air force pilots like Halutz, who was a former head of the Israeli Air Force, entered a war in a different mindset than infantry and armored commanders. Pilots take off in their aircrafts and within minutes they reach and attack their targets. They go on these missions together with pilots who sometimes do not return, and those who do return land, rest in the squadron club, and then enter the cockpit once again.

The constant and rapid changes – from the intense concentration of the cockpit to the off-duty relaxation after the mission – force pilots to learn how to divide and compartmentalize their attention and emotions. On the other side are the regular infantry soldiers, for example, who once they enter the battlefield are focused just on fighting until they come back home.

I thought that this line of defense was not just important for helping out Halutz but was also important for all IDF soldiers to understand. Nonetheless, I was concerned that once again my remarks would be distorted by the media.

After a few more questions, the talk show host asked me about the fallen soldiers. I wanted to tell him about Benaya Rhein's tank crew – a story I told in the introduction to this book.

I also planned to tell about the request that I received from famous Israeli novelist David Grossman when I visited him during the shiva – the traditional Jewish seven days of mourning – to receive his "verdict." I didn't quite understand, and he explained that he wanted the sheet of paper that the IDF officer read from when he came to his house to inform him about his son's death. I asked him if he referred to the first message or to the second one, since during the war there were a number of cases when we had to inform families that their son was killed even before we had the complete information in our hands. As a result, I found myself writing with a shaking pen death notices that said that sons were probably killed, which meant that certain families received two visits.

I also wanted to speak about Yossi Yasemau Yaleo from Ethiopia, whose family I visited and whose mother had just arrived for the first time in Israel the day before. When I entered she was dancing a mourner's dance, accompanied by a heartbreaking song, while holding the picture of her dead son in her hands. I was already familiar with the Ethiopian mourning dance from earlier visits to soldiers' families. Yossi Yasemau Yaleo's sister showed me his packed suitcase; he was supposed to go on a visit to Ethiopia to meet his mother but he knew that he would be called up for reserve duty in the war. His sister had said to him, "Go to Ethiopia. You have a mother waiting there." He had replied, "But I also have a country that needs me here."

The sister also told me that his nickname in the army was "The Russian," because they lived in a building with a large number of Russian immigrants and Yossi had learned Russian from helping his neighbors. So he became a "Russian-Ethiopian," and then his country summoned him and he didn't return. I thought that if people heard these stories they would realize that no one could ever defeat us.

I wanted to say all of this, but in his next question the host of the show asked me, "Elazar Stern, I understand that you mainly go to houses of settlers."

I replied, "You are wrong."

So he said, "Religious families and settlers," to which I replied that he was again mistaken.

"But you primarily visit settlements and moshavim," he insisted. I said that more young people from the settlements, moshavim, and kibbutzim enlisted in combat units than boys from the religious public schools. I said that there were houses that I visited and there were other houses that I would never visit because they do not have the risk of losing a son in the IDF.

He asked me, "Are you referring to homes in Tel Aviv?" and I replied, "You said it – but the truth is that I rarely visit homes in Tel Aviv." That was how the uproar began.

The fact is I didn't really intend to name Tel Aviv. I was referring to a completely different population that lives in the center of the country. A week before the interview, while the war in Lebanon was raging, my niece Meital got married to an officer in the elite Duvdevan Unit from the town of Kochav Yair. The groom's brother, also an officer, was fighting in Lebanon at the time and of course couldn't come to the wedding. I tried to get him on my encrypted secure military-issued cellular phone so his parents could at least hear his voice during their celebration. I can only imagine what must have been going through the heads of parents who were marrying off one son while the other was fighting in Lebanon.

Part of my family is ultra-Orthodox, and a few days after the wedding we all met again in a hostel in Jerusalem on the most difficult Shabbat of the war, when the soldiers were fighting deep inside Lebanon. Among the guests were also three families from the ultra-Orthodox side of the family whose sons, unfortunately, do not serve in the army. When I spoke on the radio about houses that I did not have to visit, I meant those houses – the houses of the ultra-Orthodox who do not serve in the IDF. But since the issue of the Tel Aviv "bubble" was already in the headlines, everyone thought that I referred to Tel Aviv.

I do not regret anything I said during the program. I do regret that some other journalists attributed statements to me that I never made – like "there is no such thing as bereavement in Tel Aviv." Whoever knows me knows that I visited Tel Aviv's cemeteries far more often than those who criticized me. I visited bereaved families in Tel Aviv two days before and again the week after the radio broadcast. I was born and raised in Tel Aviv, and naturally I frequently had the grim duty of visiting Tel Aviv cemeteries.

But I am not sorry for the statement that was falsely attributed to me, because, even though I didn't say it, the ensuing controversy shed light on a state of affairs that needed attention. I knew that if I turned the focus to my denial, the issue itself would be neglected.

As the controversy over my false statement attributed to me continued, I decided to publish the official numbers of soldiers who serve in the IDF based on their residence per municipality and local council. The information included service periods and the type of service and also singled out specific schools from which the soldiers graduated. The Ministry of Education joined the battle against draft dodging and today publishes those figures in their annual evaluation of high schools, together with the percentage of students who complete their matriculation exams.

A year and a half after I retired, the IDF published a list of the fifty schools that send the largest number of graduates to combat units. Not one was in Tel Aviv. This time I refused to be interviewed. The numbers speak for themselves.

"A TRUE ISRAELI DOESN'T DODGE THE DRAFT"

A number of people joined forces to fight draft dodging. Some of them established new NGOs with the sole purpose of increasing the enlistment numbers.

Ronny Kobrovski – president of Coca Cola in Israel – who served under me when I was a brigade commander, invited several friends to a housewarming party in Ramat Hasharon. The people at the party all declared their readiness to help. Rami Yehoshua, the owner of a large advertising company whom I had never met before, told me that he was willing to launch a campaign. All he asked was that we look over the slogans before they go public to ensure they would not cause damage to the IDF.

Several weeks later I was invited to a meeting in his office. Sitting in traffic, I arrived an hour late. But all my frustration disappeared once they started their presentation. Their slogan was: "A true Israeli doesn't dodge the draft." The campaign included bumper stickers, billboards, newspaper ads, and even short films for the Internet. Their creativity and concern filled me with confidence.

The campaign was launched with an initial budget of NIS 5 million (approx. $1.5 million), financed by private donations. On the occasion of Israel's sixtieth year of independence, Rami's office published large ads that said, "If we had evaded the draft then, you wouldn't be celebrating now!"

EYAL GOLAN

In 1999, soon after I was nominated to be the IDF's Chief Educational Officer, I was asked by the Golani Brigade for a special grant of 45,000 shekels (approx. $12,000).

When I asked what the money was for, the Golani officers told me that they had decided to bring the famous singer Eyal Golan to perform for the troops. I asked why they were paying him so much and didn't prefer to call him up for a day of reserve duty, during which he would be paid but far less than what he was currently asking. The answer was that Eyal Golan did not serve in the reserves. My response was that he should not be rewarded for not serving and that we had enough singers who serve in the IDF. "Should they be punished while those who do not serve are rewarded?" I asked.

The answer was: "But the soldiers like him."

"So the soldiers should like someone else," I replied, rejecting their budget request.

The phone calls began immediately. The education officer of the Northern Command, which was responsible for the Golani Brigade, called and said that the brigade had planned an entire day full of education activities and that Eyal Golan was supposed to be the highlight of the night. She added that the whole concept of the day was taken from a day I had once designed when I was a deputy division commander and that the lectures would be delivered, like I always preferred, by the immediate commanders and not the education staff. I guess this was said to insinuate that if my fantasy was coming true I might be willing to compromise. But I didn't.

I was then informed that the brigade soldiers had declared that if Eyal Golan did not perform, they were going to boycott the whole day. I said that as far as I was concerned they could cancel the day altogether.

A call came from the brigade commander Shmuel Zakai. "Zakai, are you insulted?" I asked. I asked him why he had to have Eyal Golan, and he said that the soldiers liked him. I reminded Zakai what we both taught when we were commanders together at Bahad 1: It isn't our duty to give the soldiers what they want. It is to teach them to want what *we* think they should want.

I then asked if he thought the army should reward people who do something wrong. He didn't understand what I was talking about. I said, "Don't you know that Golan does not serve in the reserves?"

"Oh, my God," Zakai said about three times. I asked what had happened, and he finally explained: "What am I going to do now with all of his CDs?"

And so it happened that Golan didn't perform for the Golani Brigade.

Two nights later, I was sitting in a restaurant when a young man with dreadlocks came over to our table and congratulated me for standing strong and preventing singers who do not serve in the IDF from performing before soldiers. It was the famous singer Idan Raichel. He asked me not to cave in to public pressure. We developed a strong friendship, and in the end Idan himself went public and spoke out against draft dodgers.

A couple of months later, I noticed Eyal Golan talking on a TV night show. He told the host that apart from his singing career he also played soccer. The host asked him how he managed to find time for practicing and Golan said that he hardly ever practiced and that the team's doctor couldn't believe that he didn't need to and was in such good shape.

I sat down and watched the show, and then I called the host. I asked him too why he encouraged evading the draft. The man almost choked, and after he stopped coughing, he told me that his son serves as an officer in a combat unit. I commended him for his son and said that in that case I found it even stranger that he supported draft dodging. He again said he did not understand, and I said that by interviewing Eyal Golan – who didn't complete his regular service and does not serve in the reserves – he is supporting draft dodging.

Several months later a senior official from the Defense Ministry called to say that the office was organizing an annual evening for the staff and that they wanted to invite two or three hundred soldiers to participate. I reminded him that by planning to hold the event on a Thursday evening, we would have to either delay soldiers' arrival at home for the weekend or provide for a very expensive transport for soldiers back to their bases. He said that the Defense Ministry would pay for the transportation. I asked about the program, and he finally said that Eyal Golan was scheduled to perform. I said that in that case we would not send any of our soldiers. "I was told that you would not give your approval," he muttered quietly.

The next morning I called one of the defense minister's aides and asked him how the defense minister could be present at the performance of a draft dodger. The aide said to me, "Stern, don't start this, you're wasting your time. Let it go..."

I told him that he should know me better than to think that I would give up.

I quickly wrote a letter to the chief of staff stating that while the ministry could do whatever it wanted I will find it harder to encourage youth to serve in the IDF if he and the minister go to hear Eyal Golan.

Now all hell broke loose. A friend of mine, Victor Bar-Gil, the deputy director general at the Defense Ministry, called and informed me that Golan was willing to donate his revenues to the military unit where Victor's son served. I said that I wasn't interested in his donations and that I would not agree to send soldiers to the event. Victor asked me, "What do you want?" and I said, "Only one thing – the man has to enlist and start serving in the reserves." Military service could not be redeemed by cash.

After some negotiations, terms were agreed upon for the performance to go ahead. Just before Golan began singing, the defense minister came on stage and announced that Golan had requested to enlist in the reserves.

Several months later, Eyal Golan got married and I was even invited to the wedding. When I arrived, people stared at me in complete shock. But when I entered the hall, Golan's father approached me together with the father of the bride and they both said to me, "You were absolutely right."

From Jaco the Singer to Bar the Model

The episode with the singer Eyal Golan was the first encounter I had with the phenomenon involving artists who dodge the draft.

Later, I found myself boycotting the concerts of Jaco Eisenberg, winner of the Israeli competition *A Star is Born* – the Israeli equivalent of *American Idol* – for not serving in the army, and then I would not authorize military support for the film *Beaufort*, featuring several actors who evaded military service.

Some of the incidents, like that of model and singer Maya Buskila, ended well, when the artists enlisted; other cases were unsuccessful. When I heard that the model Bar Refaeli, who evaded the draft by marrying fictitiously, was selected by the Tourism Ministry to lead its tourist promotion campaign, I called the minister of tourism at the time Yitzhak Herzog. He told me that the story of her evasion was incorrect and asked me to talk to the model's mother, Zippy. She told a very complicated tale about the trick her daughter performed to evade service. When I later heard that Bar was selected to represent two major Israeli companies, I called the companies' directors to ask why she was chosen. The answer I received was that she was a role model for the younger generation. I informed them to not be surprised to read that I will no longer be using their products because they promote evasion from military service. I was glad to hear that a few months later, she no longer represented one of the two major companies. I meticulously refrain from buying the second company's products.

More than once, I have been asked why I spend so much time on this subject. I am determined to win this struggle, first of all, because of its importance to the army, but especially because it encompasses much larger issues. The real matter is what kind of a society we are and what we will do for each other. What do we neglect to do because we trust that we will find somebody else who will do it for us? And how will we manage to survive here, in the center of the Middle East?

Liking a singer is not just about liking his songs. The singer represents something larger and becomes a role model for his admirers. Inviting a singer who evades army service to give a concert for soldiers lends legitimacy to his evasion and thus legitimacy to an unequal society where some fulfill their duty to the country and others do not. This is wrong. I hate it when anybody evades being drafted to the army, but when it comes to people who significantly influence others, the damage is much greater. The state's support of artists who evade the draft, or its purchase of tickets for those artists' concerts, creates a platform for somebody who does not hesitate to act against the state.

Creeping Evasion and Slanderous Headlines

Another front of this struggle was opened when I was invited to speak on a panel at Bar-Ilan University. The panel also included the minister of defense, Ehud Barak, and the chief of staff, Gabi Ashkenazi. It was my turn to speak after the chief of staff, and I noticed that he did not leave the auditorium after his speech but instead took a seat among the audience. I was flattered, but when I passed by his seat on my way to the podium, he told me, "I stayed to watch over you." I opened my speech with the words, "The chief of staff stayed to watch over me, so I will have to choose my words carefully..."

Later, on my way out, some reporters followed me and asked me for a sound bite. They did not find anything extraordinary in my speech and I also did not think I had said anything out of line.

The next day, I reached my office at 6:15 a.m. At 6:30 the newspapers were brought in, and to my amazement I discovered a large headline that read, "The commander of the Human Resources Directorate claims that draft dodging has spread into the Religious-Zionist movement," and under it was a large sub-headline stating, "The religious general attacks the Religious-Zionist movement."

I confess that I swore quietly. What do they mean when they write, "Stern against the Religious-Zionist movement"? Am I not a part of the movement?

When I started reading the article, I was not surprised to find the name of Rabbi Shmuel Eliyahu among the rabbis who supplied those juicy headlines to the newspaper. He also claimed that I put girls into combat units of the army, a claim that was absolutely false. Knesset Member Uri Ariel, whom I once considered a decent fellow, said that I spit into the well we all drink from. I cannot understand why what I said is regarded as spitting and not sincere concern.

Here are the words I said in the panel: "When I report to you that the evasion from duty is spreading, or if you prefer, is being given legitimacy, in places that we used to regard as the best communities, I'd rather refrain from going any further. I don't think I should make any sweeping statements and say anything more on this issue, but let me just say that it has even spread into the Zionist religious movement, a community whose continuous great contribution is well known to everyone in this hall."

The fact is that the numbers prove there is presently more draft evasion in communities identified as Religious Zionist than there was in the past. Do those statistics make me an enemy of the Religious Zionists? Religious communities should learn from those figures. Is every criticism a reason for a skirmish and a reason to ostracize me?

More than anything, I was enraged to read that the head of the Hesder yeshiva in Petah Tikva, and the spokesman for Hesder, Rabbi David Stav, said angrily in reference to me, "He provokes the Hesder soldiers, and has no appreciation for the problematic aspects of serving together with female soldiers." I learned from a rabbi who knows Rabbi Stav well, that he spoke with Rabbi Stav, who denied initiating contact with the reporter. According to him, the initiative was Ethan Ozeri's, the CEO of the Hesder association.

I called Ethan Ozeri. He told me that the public relations representative of the Hesder association had called him and asked if he had heard "what Stern said." Ozeri responded that he had and that "he agreed with every word"! When I asked him what could be done now with the false statements, he replied that there was nothing we could do. I again spoke with the rabbi who knew Rabbi Stav and said to him, "Tell me, this Rabbi Stav of yours – if you want to refer to him as a rabbi – must be teaching about the importance of refraining from gossip and slander. How can he talk like this about other people? How can he say that I provoke the Hesder soldiers? Did he investigate the matter?"

If he would have listened to my speech, instead of running to the press with hateful headlines, he would have heard the many other things I said, such as, "We believe that an officer who cannot give his subordinates a twenty-minute speech on what Judaism means to him, will not emerge victorious from battle, and that is why we spend so much time on these subjects."

The secular and liberal sectors in Israel were by now accustomed to me and my methods, and they learned to carefully analyze my words and maybe even appreciate and discuss them. They certainly did not hurry to make headlines out of this statement. But the Religious-Zionist movement, or at least a minority of its leaders who pretend to represent its silent majority, prefer to "shoot the messenger" rather than honestly confront the figures that indicate an alarming rise in the number of evading youngsters in their community. They would rather close their ears to most of what I said instead of examining themselves and thinking earnestly about how to correct this problem.

Rabbi Stav can continue to perform wedding ceremonies for thousands of couples without demanding payment; he can also pray intently on Yom Kippur. But what is all that worth if he contributes to slanderous headlines in the newspaper? Rabbi Stav is a municipal rabbi, a head of a yeshiva and the spokesperson for the Hesder association. One who understands only a little of what the task of a spokesperson entails and the amount of discipline involved in its execution would realize that the job does not suit the head of a yeshiva.

Thelma Yellin High School of the Arts

The Thelma Yellin High School of the Arts was for many years described as an institute where students drew on the creativity and freedom they derived from their art and applied them to their military duty.

I have visited this prestigious high school several times and met a lot of the faculty and students there, and I can gladly report that I enjoyed most of these visits. My last visit to the school was toward the last days of my role as the commander of the Human Resources Directorate of the army. I came following the invitation from a mother of one of the students, who felt that my visit would be essential to "both sides." As the principal escorted me to the auditorium of the school, we passed through corridors adorned with impressive pieces of art created by the students.

I conducted the meeting the same way I usually do. First, I presented the subject for fifteen minutes and then allowed time for the audience to ask questions. When no one raised a hand, I said, as I do on such occasions, "Okay, let's start with the second question..." but they still did not participate. I then told them that since no one had a question for me, I had a question for them.

I mentioned that on my way to the auditorium, I had walked through two long corridors and was impressed by the quality of the artwork on display. I told them that their principal had proudly given me a short summary of each of the pieces and I had noticed the names of the young artists that were printed next to the works. I said that my own children attend religious institutions and my daughters attend Ulpana (a religious high school for girls). I told them that I could easily tell, from the way they dress, that none of the girls in the auditorium learned with a daughter of mine in Ulpana or in any other religious school for girls.

I then asked them if it was possible for someone to erase a name from one of the pieces of art hanging in the corridors and put someone else's name on it instead; what would happen to a student who presented a work he or she had not created?

The young students and their teachers did not understand where I was leading them. I told them that according to the records in my hands, 15 percent of the female students in that auditorium had declared before the army authorities that they are religious and are therefore exempt from military service. The teachers in the hall knew, of course, that there was not even one female student in the room who was too religious to serve in the army. I asked both the faculty and the students what the difference is between signing your name on a piece of art that is not yours and does not truly reflect your values and talent, and signing your name on a declaration that is false and similarly, does not reflect your values and beliefs.

I had not planned this question. If I had, I probably would not have come up with such a creative analogy. But after I asked them this question, many hands came up with all sorts of questions, and finally I had to stop them because my time was up.

Thelma Yellin is not the only school where female students falsely declare that they are religious to avoid enlistment, nor are its teachers the only teachers who watch their students make false declarations, yet refrain from saying anything. There are several schools that offered to provide us with a list of the female students who made false declarations, but the majority of the schools prefer to close their eyes to this phenomenon.

The ease with which girls are released from their military duty under false pretenses has the blessing of the legislators, and there is nothing the army can do about it. We did all we could to make the legislators correct this outrage, or at least deal with those girls whose lies were exposed, but the furthest we got was the government approval of several corrective steps, which, for political reasons, were not brought for a vote in parliament. I hope the time will soon be politically "ripe," and at least those few corrections will pass.

I used to say that in order to be released from army service, a girl only has to say that she went for a stroll in the city's streets and saw a Hanukah lamp in a window and the sight gave her a feeling of exhilaration. She would be released immediately, because the rabbis, who authorize such releases for girls, do not believe that girls should serve in the army. Many of those rabbis have also not served.

One of the most ironic and moving incidents that I witnessed was a case of a young man who wanted to marry a girl who had immigrated to Israel from abroad. The municipal rabbinate refused to authorize their marriage on the grounds that the girl was not Jewish. All the testimonies and the documents from her birthplace could not change the rabbi's mind. The absurdity was that this rabbi who was now rejecting their marriage by declaring her a gentile was the same rabbi who had signed her release from military service on the grounds of her being religious. He did not even flinch when they showed him the document that he himself had signed. I tried to help them as much as I could; I was simply ashamed.

I was often asked by teachers and principals how they should deal with the issue of evading military duty, or what they could do to persuade their students to choose a more significant form of service when they enlist. I usually told them that all they have to do is influence those kids to assist their friends, to volunteer at a nearby hospital, or to participate in some other activity for the benefit of their community in order to get them into the habit of contributing. If they learn the value of selfless contribution, then, it will be easy to explain to them the value of military service as a similar contribution.

I was asked on many occasions why the children of the Religious-Zionist movement and those from the settlements have a much stronger motivation when they enlist. I replied that these two communities educate their youth to know that there is something external to them that is more important than their personal convenience. For some it is the kibbutz or an ideology or a movement, while for others, it is God and the community. Once they learn that there is something more important than themselves and that they have unselfish goals, explaining the role of the army becomes much easier.

LIFE-SAVING ARMY

Even before I became the educational division commander, I always carried around an organ donor card from the Adi organization. I wanted to recommend the idea to soldiers and thought the best method was to address all the recruits and suggest it to them upon their enlistment. I proposed my idea to the Human Resources Directorate, which directed me to the headquarters of the Medical Corps and the Military Advocate General, who strongly opposed the idea.

The IDF legal department claimed that the excitement a young person feels when he reaches the recruiting base should not be utilized for something that is not one of the basic purposes for which the army exists. Second, a big part of the excitement of the young recruits and their families stems from their natural fear that something might happen to the young soldier. Having them sign the Adi organ donor card on their first day would appear to make the statement: "You came here to die, so just sign this card that allows us to make a productive use of your body parts."

I had to admit that their arguments were reasonable.

Several months later, I was asked for my help in contacting the commander of the Human Resources Directorate, and in asking him to permit the distribution of a request to recruits asking them to give a blood sample in order to include them in a national database for bone marrow donations. I was asked to meet Dr. Bracha Zisser from Ezer Mizion. I told the organization that although I believed it was an important issue (and had already donated my blood sample for the benefit of this database), such a meeting would be to no avail. I had already tried a similar move with the Adi organ donor cards and learned not to take advantage of the soldiers' sensitive disposition when they enlist.

Two years later, when I was the head of the Human Resources Directorate, my friend David Hager, the philanthropist, asked me why I had refused to meet with Dr. Zisser. I told him my thoughts. He accepted my answer but then began to tell me about Dr. Zisser. "She does a lot of kind acts for children who suffer from cancer. But, you should know, that when such a child is on his deathbed, when even his parents find it difficult to remain beside him, or when they are in need of comfort for themselves, even if it's four o'clock in the morning, she leaves everything and rushes to the child's bedside."

This story stirred a very particular association for me. I once was in a similar situation and will never forget it for the rest of my life. And I cannot understand how some people can endure this experience several times.

When I was a student in Washington, DC, I met the IDF non-commissioned officer Meir Vaknin and his wife Miriam through another couple, Avi and Esther Zemmelman. The Zemmelmans' entire existence is devoted to charity. Every Israeli who comes to Washington, DC, can find more than just a listening ear in that family. The Zemmelmans "adopted" every despairing Israeli family who arrived at the National Institute of Health. This hospital tries to help people with medical problems that conventional medicine hardly dares to confront, and the Zemmelmans would help by providing families with everything from sleeping facilities to regular medical assistance.

The Vaknins' son, Idan, had been brought to the National Institute of Health. One day Avi Zemmelman asked if I could speak to someone in the army to help the father receive enhanced service conditions (a longer vacation, etc.). I told him that I would be glad to meet the family and went to the hospital with my daughter Adi, who was ten years old at the time.

We stood next to little Idan Vaknin's bed, while I spoke with the boy, and his parents described his situation to me. After a few minutes, my daughter Adi fainted and I had to carry her out from there. If I had stayed inside any longer, I would have fainted myself.

I visited the family in the hospital several times. During one of those visits, the famous Jewish singer Avraham Fried came from New York to sing for the boy. A secluded room was arranged and we stood there, ten of us, while Avraham Fried gave a private concert for the child.

Weeks passed, and on the eve of Independence Day, while I was on one of the tours that the university had organized for us, I was informed that little Idan's condition had deteriorated and that night might be his last night among the living. I was scheduled to speak for the Washington Jewish community that night, and I planned on hurrying to the hospital as soon as I finished speaking. We went to the hospital with the Zemmelmans. We stood around the bed with the parents and several other friends. I found myself avoiding the difficulty of the bedside experience by taking the Vaknins' other children, one at a time, with me to the adjoining room and entertaining them as much as I could. From time to time, I approached the bed and learned the significance of the various monitors surrounding it.

By three in the morning, we were signaled to approach the bed for Idan's final minutes. We stood there with Idan's parents and a few members of the dedicated medical staff, who were also attached to the dying boy and his noble family. Someone started to softly sing one of the songs Avraham Fried had sung for Idan just a few weeks earlier. The power of the assembly, together with my clinging to the bedside, gave me the strength to join the singing. I choked, I sang, and I clung to the bedside tightly so as to hold back my tears. The parameters on the monitors grew weaker and the singing grew stronger, until at three o'clock, the lines on the monitors went flat. I will never forget that night as long as I shall live. Ever since then, whenever I hear and sometimes even manage to sing that song, I mentally return to the tenth floor of that Washington, DC, hospital.

When my friend Hager told me that Bracha Zisser goes through this kind of ordeal every time it is asked of her – and often without her being asked – I could not refuse her anymore. I told Hager that I would meet and assist her as much as I could and invited her to my office. I knew what her request was going to be, and to save time I summoned to our meeting the military advocate attorney, the head of the Medical Corps, and the commander of the central recruiting base.

Dr. Zisser asked us to let the soldiers donate, on their enlisting day, a sample of their blood. All the attending commanders opposed this idea, each for his own reasons. One said that there are several bone marrow donation organizations, and we cannot demonstrate partiality toward one of them. Another said that this will be taking advantage of the soldier's most sensitive state during his recruitment – when he is still unable to differentiate between a request and an obligatory order. The commanders of the recruiting base said that the first day's schedule is very tight as is, and they would not be able to find the time. Summed up, it was neither the right place nor the right time.

I told the assembled officers that although I had heard and understood all of their arguments, the project was to begin in three months from that day. I told the attorneys that I knew they were capable of defending alleged rapists and killers, and I had faith that if I were to be prosecuted for adding the blood sample request to the first steps of soldiers' recruitment, they would know how to defend me as well. "Besides," I said, "I like bananas and I checked – they can be passed through prison bars...."

Ezer Mizion donated a large sum of money to build a high-speed facility and it was entered as a part of the first day trail of the recruits. To address the problem of taking advantage of the sensitive psychological state of the fresh recruits, letters were sent out to them several days before they were due to join the army, informing them that the donation is not mandatory and if they do not want to donate, it will not be held against them in any way.

The soldiers donate in large numbers. A significant percentage of donors are recruits who eventually go to combat corps, a finding that did not surprise me. Thanks to the soldiers' donations to the bone marrow bank, the bank developed rapidly. Before the army recruits' donations, the bank had 200,000 donors. Four years later, their list had increased to 340,000 donors.

In that case, we are not just the Israel Defense Forces; we are becoming the Jewish people's defense forces, because the bank provides donations to Jews all around the world.

Through this program, a fascinating fact was discovered. According to the professional literature, the standard probability of finding a matching donor is one for every 10,000 to 30,000 donors. In the soldiers' samples, the probability suddenly jumped up to one for every 297 donors – 3,000 times better than standard. The reason for this revolutionary change is being checked right now by researchers. It may be due to the numerous marriages between men and women from different countries of origins in recent years, which has rewarded us with a better genetic diversity and richness. Another added benefit of the soldiers' donations is that because of the young age of those donors, the shelf life of these donations is much longer than average.

We identified, during this period, seven hundred potential donors for cancer patients in need of a life-saving donation. One hundred seventeen people have already donated and 40 percent of those donations went to sick people outside Israel.

There is a clear lesson to be learned from this story. Everyone said it would be impossible; I was told there is no available space in the recruiting base and that it goes against the goals of the army. But, in the end, many lives were saved due to the goodwill of a voluntary organization, as well as Bracha and Moty Zisser, and to the axiom that says, "For sitting idle you'll find a hundred reasons, but for action there is only one reason and this single reason prevails."

Later, Bracha took me on a visit to a hospital ward, to meet children who suffer from cancer. Bracha inspected the quality of the medical treatment, and even more, its sensitivity. She caressed, wiped a burning forehead with a cold damp cloth, and said a few encouraging words. I watched her strength with admiring eyes; I was in pain and could not utter a word. To my embarrassment, and my good fortune, she noticed my distress and signaled for me to wait outside. I went out and waited for her outside the room.

I have never understood where her strength comes from. It is even more difficult to understand when you consider the possibilities that are open before her and the luxurious life she can enjoy. It is difficult to understand, especially when you know that as far as contributions and donations for the community go, the Zisser family has long ago given much more than their share.

I participated in several celebrations of the Zisser family. They know how to celebrate and get others to rejoice. After one of those celebrations, the army's spokesperson received a question from a reporter asking what Elazar Stern was doing at a celebration of the Zisser family. The spokesperson contacted me and I wrote a reply, which, to my disappointment, was not published. I wrote that Moty Zisser paid me a million dollars in exchange for my arranging service in a combat engineering unit for his son.

David Zisser served in a unit in the Combat Engineer Corps, a unit that is not known for being desired or prestigious. His parents could have asked for him to be transferred to some other combat unit, like many parents do. I could never imagine them asking for him to be transferred to a non-combat unit. But they never asked for anything and he remained in his unit until his release. He finished his service as a captain and company commander, and he even signed on to serve longer than he was required. It is needless to mention the comfortable life he had waiting for him in the civilian world while he finished his voluntary service.

Chapter 13

Broken Communication

My turbulent relationship with the media began even before I left the army for the first time. A press conference was held in Ramat Gan in honor of the thirtieth anniversary of the paratroopers' drop at the Mitla passage in Sinai during the 1956 Sinai Campaign.

For the press conference, the paratroopers were represented by the chief paratrooper officer, the paratrooper brigade commander, a reserve brigade commander, a young company commander and me, a regiment commander. We sat on a panel, questions were asked, and I kept my mouth shut; I did not utter a word. Then, Tally Salinger, a reporter who later married chief of staff Amnon Lipkin-Shahak, stood up and said, "I have a question for Stern." I was taken aback. I had never spoken to her before that day. She asked me about the large number of officers who left the service in those days, four years after the First Lebanon War. She must have known that I was leaving the service myself. I do not know how I came up with my answer, but what I said was, "Vanunu is probably right!"

The room fell silent. A regiment commander in the paratroopers who claims that Vanunu did the right thing?! After the initial astonishment subsided, another reporter asked me to please explain my answer. I said that if we did not have ninety-two atomic bombs that we believe will save us, as Vanunu told the British *Sunday Times*, people would not ignore the shamefully low salaries of army officers.

Those days, we were earning $700 a month. I added that whoever had decided that officers should earn that amount must have taken into account the fact that he would have worse officers in the army, and as a result, each year, twelve additional casualties among soldiers on the northern border and three children killed in one of the northern kibbutzim and, in the event of another full-scale war, an additional two hundred and fifty casualties. That same person must have taken the extra money and invested it in education and health, telling himself that though in the short term, this decision carried a hefty price, in the long run, the state would benefit and lives would be saved. That is the prime duty and prerogative of every prime minister, and I am certain he considered all the options very carefully.

The press conference was over, everybody asked to interview me but I did not want to answer any more questions. The chief paratrooper officer, Shmulik Arad, told me, "Stern, you are going home anyway, so give these interviews for the benefit of all the officers who remain in active service."

I found myself giving a chain of interviews in the garden of the Paratrooper Pavilion in Ramat Gan. The next day, the radio broadcast an interview with me. I did not hear the broadcast, but when I came that afternoon to practice parachuting, in honor of the thirtieth anniversary, I met a senior officer who was, at the time, the head of the staff department in the Human Resources Directorate. He told me that when he was sitting in his car during the morning commute, someone knocked on his window and suggested he listen to the broadcast of my interview. He said, "I heard your answers. When I reached my office, I called the head of the Human Resources Directorate and told him that you should take my place as soon as possible."

The first to fully embrace me were the NCOs (non-commissioned officers). It was extremely unusual – almost taboo – for officers to discuss their salaries. Two months later, Yitzchak Rabin, then the minister of defense, visited the northern border and among other things met all the battalion commanders. My good friend, General Udi Adam, who was then a battalion commander, said to him, "If you want to have the best battalion commanders, I can line them up for you within several minutes, but be prepared to pay each of them a salary of $3,000."

My opinion had not changed when, later, I became the head of the Human Resources Directorate. I accept the fact that officers are paid less than what they earn in the civilian market; the sense of contribution and accomplishment compensates for the lower wage. But if this gap becomes too large, values will not bridge it. The sense of mission is expressed in the willingness to take upon oneself such a task, with all its difficulty and its risks. But this feeling cannot counteract the feeling of discrimination and disrespect from government; no amount of determination will stop the more gifted commanders from leaving when they are treated this way.

These were things that directed me in the many negotiations I conducted with the treasury officials, as well as in my negotiations within the army, on the conditions provided to officers and on budgets for salaries, though I never ignored issues like values, education, and the sense of mission.

The spontaneous stunt I pulled by mentioning Vanunu's name taught me an important lesson about the immense power of the media and how essential it can be when one wants to convey a clear message and draw the public's attention to an issue. But over the years, more than once, I also learned painful lessons on the superficiality, lack of understanding, arrogance, and problematic ethics one confronts when dealing with the media. I am not referring to all reporters, or even the majority of them, but unfortunately in many cases instead of being a serious platform for a productive and practical discussion of some of the most important issues of our life, the media prefers to use a distorted quote taken out of context, in order to suppress such a discussion and thus squeeze the life out of any original and non-conformist opinion, even before it has a chance to be fully expressed. The following examples shed some light on this aspect of the media.

The Carmela Menashe Syndrome

Years ago, while I remained on a base for a weekend during Sukkot, acting as a duty commander of the northern division, the telephone rang on Friday night. When I am on duty on Shabbat,

I answer the telephone out of concern that it may be a matter of life and death. On the other end of the line was a staff member of the IDF spokesperson's office. When I heard that it was not an operations officer, I asked him if he was absolutely convinced that this phone call justified desecration of the Shabbat. When he replied that it did, I let him talk.

He told me that the veteran radio correspondent Carmela Menashe had issued an urgent question to the spokesman. At that time, in 1988, Carmella Menashe had already achieved a reputation for being a very serious and determined correspondent. I stopped him and told him that I was certain that our conversation could wait until after the Shabbat ended, but he hurried on, saying that a reserve soldier from one of the battalion posts on the border had called her and informed her that the post was left without any provisions and that they had already been forced to open their emergency rations. I told the man that I had personally visited the post in question that afternoon and had left the place an hour before Shabbat, and I was told by the battalion commander that all was well. Therefore, I told him that I did not intend to deal with his information until the end of the Shabbat. Although he tried to convince me that the issue was urgent, I cut him off, said good-bye, and hung up the phone.

Doing what was expected of him, the officer from the spokesman's office did not stop there, but rather, called the commanders of the relevant reserve unit. Before sunrise on Saturday morning, supplies made their way to the post, accompanied by the brigade commander, the battalion commander, and every other available commander. An immediate inquiry was then conducted revealing no shortage of any kind. The soldier who had telephoned Carmella Menashe admitted his actions, apologized, and even called the reporter again and confessed to her that his story was untrue.

This incident stimulated me to write letters to the chief of staff and the head of the Northern Command and initiated my complicated thoughts about the relationship between the army and the media.

Two days before this incident, I had spoken with one of the division's brigade commanders. He had asked me what I thought about certain results of an inquiry committee in which he was found guilty and was rebuked. What bothered him much more than the rebuke was the fact that two or three minutes after he was informed by his commanders about the committee's results, he heard all the details on the radio. I do not want to discuss the rebuke itself, but I think that this soldier should have enjoyed the privilege of telling his family the news instead of having them hear it on the radio. A wife who pays a daily price for her husband serving in Lebanon has the right to hear such saddening news from him directly. What makes us give our consent, and sometimes even support, to such a hurried publicity?

I am sure that the officer who telephoned me on Friday night is a dedicated officer, as are those commanders who hurried to the remote post in the middle of the night. They are all innocent victims of blind devotion to the godhead of the media to whom we blindly sacrifice many values and standards that are otherwise dear to us. We frequently idolize correspondents, building them up in the eyes of our subordinates until they serve as commander-substitutes. I feel that we are losing the normal and productive contact with the media.

How did this frenzy enter our lives? How did we become susceptible to a hysteria that drives us every once in a while to forget our primary goals and moral values that we acquired during long years? How did we ourselves assist in inflating the role of the media and diminishing at the same time the position and the functioning ability of our commanders?

Screaming Headlines

In March 2001, several days after the announcement of my program to assist soldiers who want to convert to Judaism, I was summoned to the Knesset's Absorption Committee to provide explanations. I arrived a few minutes before the discussion was scheduled to begin. I was surprised by the large number of participants; the hall was filled with Knesset members from all the parties, and many members of non-political organizations for immigrant rights, organizations for civil rights, and organizations that fight religious coercion.

Just before the debate began, MK Ophir Pines approached me, gave me a friendly slap on my shoulder, and told me that he used to carry out his reserve service in my education division. Minutes later, before the leader of the committee had formally opened the debate, Pines stood up to speak. In his speech, he accused me of stigmatizing an entire community and called for my immediate resignation. While he gave his statement, I asked the committee's leader whether I was summoned there to inform them about what I had actually said or just to hear Pines' accusations in this improvised field court. She agreed and tried to stop Pines' monologue. He added a few "compliments," apologized for being in a hurry, and left the hall. He did not have any intention of listening to me once he had finished putting on his show.

The discussion itself was lively. It started with MK Galon, who accused me of being a missionary – thereby finding herself in agreement with ultra-Orthodox MK Gafni, who objected to my intention of conducting a parallel, friendlier system for conversion. Others came to my defense. It was a long and serious discussion, and at the end I believe that most of the members, even if they did not support my program, understood it. Pines was not there, of course.

The next day I read an article in *Yediot Aharonot* that falsely quoted me as saying that more than 50 percent of all young immigrants who serve in the army are not Jewish and therefore their motivation to enlist into field units of the army is naturally weaker. Next to this outrageous headline, they brought Pines' accusations. The editors even found a picture of me with a sulking face to appropriately accompany the article.

After this publication, I immediately became the target of all media correspondents in a manner that no other officer has ever experienced. I contacted the army's spokesman and said that unlike in past incidents where I was falsely quoted, this time I did not intend to remain passive. I demanded to meet Moshe Vardi, the editor of *Yediot Aharonot*. The spokesman tried to placate me by telling me that it was only a newspaper; by the next day it would only be good for wrapping fish. I told him that I did not intend to let this go. Avi Benayahu, commander of Army Radio at the time and later the IDF Spokesman from 2007 until 2011, also tried to stop me by telling me that newspaper rooms are the places where Israeli prime ministers are crowned and that I should not start a battle against them. I was not moved and still demanded a meeting with Vardi.

Concurrently, I obtained the transcription of the committee debate. I called the Knesset chairman, Avraham Burg, who told me that it usually takes several weeks to print a transcript. "Avrum," I said, "I have never asked you for any favors in return for the many years of not telling on you when you skipped classes in high school. But, now I need a favor. Please make this happen as quickly as you can." He promised he would do his best.

Two weeks later, when I went to a meeting at *Yediot Aharonot*, I came with the full transcript of the committee's session. The army spokesman, Moshe Vardi, and a news editor from the paper were all in the room.

I laid the transcript on the table without looking at it; I did not need to check. I knew that I had never said anything of the sort. I told the people in the room that I had heard that this was the room where prime ministers were crowned, but, since I had no ambition to become one, I intended to see this matter through till the end, and I explained why. My wife, Dorit, was the director of a retirement home in the town of Tivon at the time, and most of her staff consisted of immigrants from the former Soviet Union. They were very fond of her and many of them had visited our house more than once. But ever since the newspaper had published my false quote, they hardly gave her the time of day. "Even if it means a five-year-long battle in court," I said, "I am determined to do what must be done!"

I would not accept any proposed compromise. I explained that I was falsely quoted as saying things that upset a community that I would never dream of hurting. I flatly refused a suggestion that I write a four-hundred-word article and present my position. This was not compensation in my eyes.

I demanded that they publish an article on the same page and of the same size that would make it clear to everyone that I never said the things that were published under my name. I said that I realize that it might be too much to expect that an apology headline be the same size as that of the original offensive article. Instead, I suggested that they send a correspondent to the Knesset right away. The chief of staff was scheduled to appear in front of the Foreign Affairs and Defense Committee, and I knew that he was going to say some things about this issue. If this happened and the chief of staff was asked a direct question on what the newspaper published, he might supply them with a headline that I would regard as sufficient.

Vardi looked at me and said, "You didn't want to consider our offer, but we want some time to consider yours." I asked only that they bear in mind that my wife had to go to work the next day.

Everyone said that I had asked for the impossible. They said that if *Yediot* agreed to my demands it would be the dawn of a new era in the media – army relationship. After a few hours, the news editor of *Yediot* called me and informed me that they had decided to accept my offer. They sent a reporter to the Knesset, and he quoted the chief of staff who said some nice things about me in this context. They even offered to send me the article by fax for my approval. I have been interviewed quite a few times during my life, but I had never been allowed to view any of these interviews before they were printed, and I had certainly not received an offer to correct a possible error. It was, indeed, a historic day.

Two years later, I was appointed the commander of the Human Resources Directorate. In honor of the nomination, *Yediot Aharonot* published several controversial sentences that I had said on different occasions. One of the quotations was the same false quote for which they had already apologized. This time I did not bother demanding a correction.

A Confrontation with *Haaretz*

During the last years of my military service, when I worked as commander of the education division and as head of the Human Resources Directorate, I was required to sleep in Tel Aviv several nights a week. I never used the hotel room that the army offered; I preferred to stay with my parents, and later, in my Tel Aviv office.

One night I arrived at my parents' home at 11:30 p.m. My mother had just turned off the television and she noticed me changing into my jogging outfit. She tried to stop me, as she always did, from running at such a late hour. "You are truly crazy," she remarked, as usual. "Aren't you afraid to go out at such an hour? Who knows what types of characters are out so late at night!" Or she would say, "You know that I can't fall asleep until you get back. You should put an end to this nonsense!" The two of us knew perfectly well that I was not going to stop.

I left the house at 11:40. Five minutes later, while I was parking my car beside the park where I intended to run, my telephone rang and at the other end of the line was the chief of staff's aide. This was just before Mofaz was to finish his term as chief of staff and Ya'alon was to begin. To my surprise, Mofaz's aide's voice had a tone of reproach. He wanted to know why I had sent a letter of complaint to the press council against Amir Oren, a reporter from *Haaretz*. I asked him why I should not send such a letter, and he told me that the reporter had threatened that if I did not withdraw my letter by midnight, he was going to publish everything he knew about the IDF. I was actually a little surprised to learn that Amir Oren, quite the prolific writer, knew something about the army that he had not yet published. I did not understand why we should worry about a threat like that.

Ya'alon's aide interrupted the conversation and asked me why I was causing the incoming chief of staff trouble even before he entered office. I did my best to calm down both of them, to no avail.

The aide of the outgoing chief asked me why I had not requested the chief of staff's permission to send the letter. I explained that before I sent the letter, I had checked with the military attorney. Since the press council is not considered "press," I was free to send any letter I wanted. I added that since I expected the letter to initiate a crusade against me in the reporter's paper, it would be better if everyone knew that the chief of staff had not authorized the letter, otherwise he might also become a target of vengeance.

My complaint against Amir Oren followed an article he had written on the new chief of staff, entitled "Ya'alon's Next Battle." In the article he wrote, "Even at this moment, in his capacity as chief-of-staff-elect and before he is sworn in to office, he established several teams, headed by senior officers, mostly dealing with significant issues. Only one team is headed by a superfluous commander of a superfluous corps, the commander of the education division Elazar Stern, to deal with an issue on which the military should not intervene: 'Judaism and Israeliness.'"

The combination of "a superfluous commander" and "a superfluous corps" seemed exceptionally malicious to me, but that was not why I complained to the press council. A deliberate omission appeared in the paragraph. The name of my committee was "Judaism, the IDF, and Israeliness." "One may argue whether or not the army should be intervening on those issues," I wrote, "but the prerogative of the chief of staff to discuss the aspects of these subjects is as clear as day. Omitting the name of the IDF from the name of the committee turns its mandate into something completely different. Oren chose to put the name of the committee between quotation marks, pretending to quote the committee's name accurately. Being an experienced reporter, he must be completely aware of such nuances, and therefore I believe that he distorted the name deliberately."

I decided to write my letter of complaint because I actually knew very well that behind the article hid a deliberate intention to persecute me. He had openly threatened that this was going to happen.

Two years earlier, I had given my consent to have Avi Benayahu work for a limited time in the Education Corps. Just before I gave my consent, I received several phone calls from Oren on this matter. In the most embarrassing call, Oren told me that he had a good opinion of me, but if I authorized Benayahu to join the corps, he would realize that his positive opinion of me was a mistake and he would "move me to the other side."

I hardly believed my ears, and naturally this did not affect my decision on the issue of Benayahu. Oren's hatred toward Benayahu was so overwhelming that ever since this episode, my name had been mentioned over and over in *Haaretz* in unflattering ways. Many people raised eyebrows at the surprising frequency with which the commander of the Education Corps was mentioned by the newspaper, but I viewed this as a compliment. I knew very well that no education commander in history had ever been mentioned so often by *Haaretz*.

Within a short time, this open animosity intensified. Oren was the only military reporter I knew of who demanded and received payments for his appearances before soldiers. "First," I wrote to the council, "I find it awkward that a reporter, who should remain free of any prejudice, receives payment from the organization he covers. Second, what happens to a military figure who decides not to invite Oren as he is used to?"

In the couple of years after I put an end to this complicated relationship, Oren must have earned less than he used to. It seems to me that in the years prior to my term as the "superfluous commander" of the Education Corps and prior to my decision to stop his payments, Oren never wrote that the Education Corps was superfluous.

Chapter 14

Toward a Better Future

In 2006, the number of people who dodged the draft by claiming they were students in ultra-Orthodox yeshivot reached over 10 percent of all eligible young Israelis. More than fifty thousand youngsters now enjoy the status of Torah students and are exempt from the military duty that is mandatory for all other Jewish Israeli citizens. It is common knowledge that not everyone who receives such an exemption devotes all his time to learning Torah.

The following ideas, which are my personal opinions and do not reflect the army's position, are the result of a painful compromise. From my standpoint as an officer and a citizen, I have no doubt that the right thing to do would be to recruit everybody. A limited number of scholars should receive an exemption to continue their Torah studies, because these scholars have a significant impact on the continuity of Judaism in Israel and the Jewish nature of the State of Israel.

In the past, I fought every program that created a service exemption bypass. In a way, I also objected to programs that directed ultra-Orthodox recruits to special logistics and technological units. I have always said that what all these programs have in common is that they never involve the privilege to risk one's life for the safety of the State of Israel, the safety of its inhabitants, and the preservation of the Jewish nation. One does not go there for combat service. To put it bluntly, we were being fooled. Not only did these kids not enlist in combat service, but we provided them with special courses for their future economic welfare. The establishment of the Nahal Haredi – now called Netzah Yehuda – and the novelty of an ultra-Orthodox combat unit, however, enabled me to support and even initiate non-combat units for other ultra-Orthodox recruits.

Today, you can find ultra-Orthodox kids who serve in the air force, the navy, and the Intelligence Corps, some even as officers. Those recruits arrive from the best yeshivot of the Orthodox world and their service is less restricted than that of the soldiers who serve in the Netzah Yehuda Battalion.

I accepted another compromise – an even bigger one – when I realized that the ideal of equality in the face of the recruitment authorities is something that, for the time being, should be laid aside. I reached this conclusion when I realized that we are dealing with a whole culture of evading military service among the ultra-Orthodox. This culture guides its followers into a life of unemployment and poverty, within an atmosphere of contempt toward external obligations. Further acceptance of the ultra-Orthodox evasion has the potential to cause the army major difficulties when recruiting other communities that witness this phenomenon, leading to a natural decline of Israeli motivation to enlist.

One day I met a high-ranking official of the Yeshivot Committee, an institute that confirms the list of Torah students who will receive an exemption from service. The man said to me, "Thanks to you, Elazar Stern, more people study Torah in Israel." I understood perfectly well what he meant, but he continued, "Since every Orthodox kid who is not registered in a yeshiva must join the army, and he is not allowed to work anywhere or learn other trades, all the kids register at yeshivot."

I told him that it was not my responsibility to add Torah students to the nation of Israel. Besides, I added, I wish he were right, but due to my activity there are more who are registered at yeshivot: I do not think that there are more who actually study Torah. I suddenly visualized this man's world: the yeshivot were some type of prison, the people on the Yeshivot Committee were the wardens, and we, the IDF, was the stick the warden holds over his prisoners. Being a religious Jew myself, I do not believe that an eighteen-year-old should study Torah out of fear that he will otherwise be recruited to an army. As an officer, I do not wish to be considered a stick in some warden's hand.

We could say that we should not intervene, that we should bury our heads in the sand. We could say that the ultra-Orthodox Jews belong to a secluded community that lives by its own rules, and even if they are somewhat impoverished, let them follow their chosen destiny. We, those who serve in the army, will carry the collective burden, follow our destiny, and if along the way, we defend them and their way of life, so be it.

As soldiers and as commanders we could turn a blind eye to this issue. After all, recruiting policies are not our concern; they are the concern of the civilian authorities. The state has the responsibility of providing for the army's needs, whether they are financial needs or human resources.

But I have no doubt that as long as we are the people's army, and as long as service in the military is the entry ticket to adult Israeli society, we must take a stand on this issue or at least come up with a proposition for action. The destiny of the ultra-Orthodox Jews is the destiny of us all. We are brethren and cannot afford a cultural and economic alienation from one another.

The present situation requires us to give up (hopefully, for a short while) our ideals of equality. We are forced to come up with a new program and present a solution, even a limited one for the next few years, so that at least the younger generation of ultra-Orthodox will serve the community, work, and become full partners on this journey, in the military, in the financial world, in education, and in all other issues that make up a state. We cannot desert the ultra-Orthodox Jews because their destiny is linked to ours.

A Court Injunction the Community Cannot Live Up To

The decision of the High Court, accepted in February 2012, regarding the cancellation of the arrangement known as "their Torah learning is their profession," as anchored in the Tal Legislation, is indeed dramatic. But in the absence of any groundbreaking ideas, it may be a case of "a rose by any other name."

"The legislation to defer military service for yeshiva students whose Torah learning is their profession, which has previously been found harmful to the right of equality, does not fulfill measurable conditions and is, therefore, illegal," wrote Justice Benish in her argument for cancelling the legislation. "It seems to me," she continues, "that very few in the State [and that may be an exaggeration] are convinced that we can anticipate a massive enlistment of ultra-Orthodox yeshiva students to Tzahal [Israel Defense Forces]. Will a court judgment bring about the hoped-for enlistment?"

Justice Groniss wrote the minority opinion. "And if the author of the 'Book of State' had not been wary of extraneous matters, he would have said both sides are true." Shai Agnon wrote the 'Book of State' at a time when there was similar discord amongst Jews that also typified his era.

Both of the respected judges are correct – but at the same time, they are both incorrect.

Dorit Benish is correct from the point of view of justice and morality upon which Israeli society is based. Asher Groniss is correct because there is no way to apply obligatory draft legislation, or even civil service legislation, on everyone. Civil service (even in its present form, which includes hundreds of ultra-Orthodox individuals and requires very little of them, and certainly does not include them all) will only intensify the inequality. Should civil service become a required service, the ultra-Orthodox will relate to it as they relate today to military service.

But they are both wrong: Benish is wrong in her pretense to change the reality by brandishing a court decision. Groniss is wrong in thinking that it is possible to live ideologically and socially with the law as it stands now. And in the meantime we, along with all the petitioners who perhaps went out momentarily ready for a fight, will continue to carry the burden and not be compensated. Like the prime minister's equation, but in reverse: You give – you don't get; you don't give – you get more.

CONTEMPT IS NOT A WORK PLAN

I have had a considerable part in the campaign against the evasion of army service for the last few years. On my car, as on the cars of my other family members, I still have the sticker, "Real Israelis Don't Dodge the Draft." But I also know that cancelling the status of the arrangement "their Torah learning is their profession" and at the same time enforcing an obligatory draft of ultra-Orthodox – whether it is to Tzahal or to civil service – cannot be used by the state. It will require building large holding cells, more than are required to hold the many Arab infiltrators.

I have met a lot of petitioners who are from the organizations who carry on their shoulders the battle against the ultra-Orthodox evasion of army service. I enjoyed their naivete, their pure intentions – but I did not find any solution to the problem among them. Contempt is not a work plan. I can't see a better solution than what I propose here – to swallow hard for the next ten years and give the ultra-Orthodox a general exemption to do whatever they wish from age eighteen. Whoever wants, can remain registered in the yeshiva. Whoever wants, can go to work. And whoever wants, can serve the country.

The process will be supported, of course, by a gradual yearly reduction of 5 percent in the support of the principle "their Torah learning is their profession," and the assumption of my work (which is supported by many leaders of the ultra-Orthodox community) is that in three years, half of the *avrechim* (yeshiva students) will leave yeshiva of their own accord – for the threat that "the army will grab them" will be removed. This idea will save about a billion shekels ($500 million) annually, from the cutting of the compensations that they and their yeshivot receive and by their contributions to the Gross National Product. This same amount will be invested in the regular soldiers: they will benefit doubling of their salaries and be able to complete a bachelor's degree paid for by the state. When they are ready to purchase an apartment, they will receive benefits worthy of someone who has given all he can to his country. At the same time, the resources that are saved do not rule out improvement of the conditions of the ultra-Orthodox minority, for it is indeed appropriate that they should sacrifice themselves in the "tent of Torah."

In order to reduce the opposition of the leaders of the ultra-Orthodox community, we can reach an agreement with them that when the number of yeshiva students is reduced to 50 percent of what it is today, the budget will be fixed and not reduced even if the number of students diminishes. The Board of Yeshivot will know that there is a set sum, but they can divide it among their students in any way they wish, even double or triple the salaries for the true prodigies. Why should a prodigy have to necessarily be poor? He could live like an academic, for learning Torah is also important for the Jewish people.

A set yeshiva budget will serve as an effective filtering tool. Instead of sheltering yeshiva students and hiding them away in cities of refuge, the *roshei yeshiva* (heads of yeshivot) will send the loafers home, in order to make the budget that has been wasted on them available to the sincere learners. And what about the ultra-Orthodox who choose to enlist? In my opinion, the best solution is doubling the entity of Nachal Haredi that today has only one regiment – a fighting regiment that is prepared for any operational mission and is on par with current security – but regrettably is not growing. If other regiments like this were established and provide their soldiers with all their particular needs as ultra-Orthodox fighters: time for prayers, no contact with females, Torah lessons, professional kashrut certification, completion of higher education, food that is stringently kosher – each regiment would save the drafting of more than twenty reserve units per year (and among them thousands of students who are in the middle of their academic studies and young employees who are in the process of adjusting to new jobs). This would be an important contribution of sharing the burden, even if in the first years in these regiments, there would not be a melting pot according to the full meaning of such.

Inequality Exists Anyway

I am aware of the painful concessions involved and the inequality inherent in my suggestion, but in the present reality, inequality exists anyway. As an officer and a citizen, there is no doubt in my mind that the correct and fair thing to do is to draft everyone, but the understanding that we have to deal with the culture of evading military service overrides that feeling. Sometimes that culture leads to real poverty at a later stage, poverty that causes religious, political, and national extremism. Continued acceptance of evasion of military service may also cause the IDF serious problems in the future. According to predictions, it will find expression in other sectors of the population and affect the general motivation to serve.

If we continue with my suggested arrangement, at the end of ten years, there will be a lot fewer fictitious students in the yeshivot, and the fear of the IDF will perhaps pass from ultra-Orthodox society. Due to this arrangement, we will be able to reach other logical arrangements in the future, like limiting the number of students. The IDF will then cease to be the doorman, or more accurately the prison guard, of the yeshiva world, and the quality of life in ultra-Orthodox society will be better. They will encounter us in the workplace and see that the demon isn't so bad after all. They will then understand the importance of service and also its ideological and material worthiness and enlist more. They will discover the advantages of a higher standard of living as a result of being proud providers. We will have a different reality here.

Small Compromises

Even the ultra-Orthodox know that Judaism has preserved itself for the course of years because it was wise enough to know to adjust to reality. This was proven to me again when I was in the Chabad House in Bombay for Shabbat. Around the Shabbat table, under the direction of Harav Chanoch Guttman – who, with his wife, replaced Harav Gabi and his wife Rivki Holzberg, of blessed memory, who were murdered in the terror attack on the house in 2008 – sat fifty Jews from all over the world: men, women, tourist, businessmen, religious, secular, and ultra-Orthodox.

The next day, a discussion on the topics of drafting the ultra-Orthodox and the principle of "a woman's voice is immodest" ensued. A ultra-Orthodox Vishnitzer hassid told us that when he was a yeshiva student in Israel he conducted business while he was registered in the yeshiva. When he had to travel to Spain for business, he had to make a special effort to convince the army authorities, and he succeeded. In order to accommodate his travels, he told us unabashedly – and he knew exactly who he was speaking to – that he had gone to the mental health officer and received an exemption. He told us with pride that the ultra-Orthodox in New York work for a living and also learn.

I asked him about them and himself: In order to earn a living it is permissible to encounter women all over the world with exposed legs and shoulders, but for the defense of the Jewish people in Israel it is not possible to make a small compromise?

He was dumbfounded but did not lower his gaze. From his point of view, we are the beast of burden that must carry him. He presented himself as unstable in order not to defend the Jewish people, but for his personal income he has no problem traveling in the promiscuous world.

I asked Rav Chanoch what he did when the female traveler next to him sang the Shabbat songs (*zemirot*) with him. He told me he would raise his own voice, and he had to agree with me that, though not all behave this way, there are certain things, such as unity amongst the Jewish people and bringing people closer to God, that are more important than "a woman's voice is immodest."

In the end, most of the ultra-Orthodox will understand the obligation to live in today's reality and to live with us – not only for income but for the existence of all of us as one people.

FIVE YEARS OF RESOLUTION

In 1992, the percentage of recruits who received an exemption from military service by virtue of learning in yeshiva was 5 percent. Today, it has reached 11 percent. In order to comprehend what awaits us in the future we should consider today's numbers of first-grade students.

In 1990, 7 percent of all the first graders in Israel were pupils at ultra-Orthodox educational institutions. Ten years later, the number of ultra-Orthodox children grew by 400 percent. In 2000, they comprised 20 percent of all first grade students. In 2006, they were already 23 percent of all first-graders. By 2018, when today's first graders enlist, the percentage of those who will be eligible for an exemption is expected to be over 13 percent.

The devastating implications of this rapid growth, for the entire state as well as for the ultra-Orthodox Jews, are quite obvious to all the decision-makers, and yet they continue to avoid this issue due to short-sighted coalition considerations.

As in so many other cases, the story of yeshiva exemptions began full of noble intentions. Prime Minister David Ben-Gurion remarked on the issue of the exemption that was provided to yeshiva students for the first time, in a speech he made in October 1948: "There are four hundred yeshiva students, all young, and I was informed that if they were to be forced to enlist in the army, the yeshivot would be shut down, that they aren't recruited in other countries either, and that there was a previous understanding that they will not be recruited."

In 1949, the prime minister published, for the first time, a pronouncement blocking the future recruitment of yeshiva students. In 1968, in accordance with a request by Minister of Defense Moshe Dayan, a ministerial committee was organized to investigate this issue. They reached a decision to prolong the routine exemptions and a quota of eight thousand yeshiva students per year was set. In 1975, all restrictions on the number of participating yeshivot in the exemption program were withheld.

In 1977, the limited annual quotas of exemptions for yeshiva students were canceled.

In 1986, a subcommittee headed by MK Rabbi Menachem Hacohen was set up within the Knesset's committee for foreign affairs and security, and this subcommittee delivered its conclusions in 1988: "We must return to the quota system and set it at 3 percent of each year's total recruitment."

In December 1998, the High Court of Justice ruled that the arrangement allowing the exemption from military service for yeshiva students is illegal and allowed the state one year to enact the necessary legislation for this matter. In 1999, the Tal Committee was assembled to discuss the legislation and in April 2000, the committee published its conclusions and drafted a bill. The Knesset accepted the new law.

Among others, the committee's conclusions suggested "a year of decision making." This mechanism allows each ultra-Orthodox youngster four years of yeshiva study, after which, at the age of twenty-two, a year of decision-making commences. During this year, he must choose among several options: continue to learn in yeshiva, go to work in any field he chooses, enlist in the army, or join some other form of national service. When the year ends, he has to make a final decision to continue to study Torah or to choose one of the other options.

The president of the high court of justice, Judge Aharon Barak, after hearing a complaint from the The Movement for Quality Government against the Tal Resolution, called the resolution, "a social concession." He declared that although the resolution contradicts the value of "human dignity and equality," an opportunity should be given for it to prove itself and its concept of the decision-making year. He announced that the resolution would have to be discussed again, in time.

My proposal includes an even more painful social concession, but today, the reality is much more distressing than it was when the high court discussed the issue. I propose now, with apprehension, that the year of decision at age 22 for an ultra-orthodox youngster be prolonged to five full years. He would be allowed to make his decision any time between age eighteen and twenty-three. In other words, I suggest that ultra-Orthodox kids who graduate from one of the ultra-Orthodox institutions should be free from any duty until the age of twenty-three. Then, they would have to choose between serving in the army or one of the other forms of national service, or remaining in yeshiva. I realize that the main significance of such a late military service lies less in its usefulness to the state and more in the sheer fact that it exists. If he were to choose military service, he would be free to join any of the enlisting programs that he finds fit: the ultra-Orthodox Nahal, regular service, Hesder, or one of several other forms designed especially for these youngsters.

The IDF takes into consideration the family situation of its recruits, as far as duration and conditions of service are concerned. We could establish several new service tracks for recruits that would provide them with basic military training and then send them to perform tasks as civil guards, assistant policemen, and other regular security tasks. The yeshiva students who prefer to renounce the five-year exemption program and enlist in one of the army units would receive a three-month-long course in English, computers, mathematics, etc., to help them adapt to the current requirements of the IDF and the civilian job market. The IDF would establish several service frameworks and the state would establish new forms of national service, all designed especially for this community. The national service would be for two consecutive years or for a shorter consecutive period and then continue as reserve service until the age of fifty.

According to the proposed plan, all ultra-Orthodox youth, even those who do not learn or enlist in the army, will be able to enter the regular job market and become productive citizens, who earn their livings through their own efforts. This will put a stop to the disgraceful practice of near-automatic registry to yeshiva of every young ultra-Orthodox Jew as a shield against "forced" recruitment.

Ultra-Orthodox youngsters who choose not to learn will be free from the velvety prisons that their political leaders have built for them. They will integrate more smoothly into Israeli society, and maybe they will discover that the devil is not as dreadful as they were told. This program should have a trial run for ten years, and at its conclusion, even if we decide to return to the old system, the number of registered Torah students will drop to reasonable numbers; and maybe the bias that ultra-Orthodox Jews have against the army will disappear. The IDF will stop serving as an agent that helps acquire students for yeshivot, and the living conditions of the ultra-Orthodox community will improve. We will enter a new reality.

THE BUDGET OF THE YESHIVOT

Apart from their religious objection to recruitment, the principals of the ultra-Orthodox yeshivot have another incentive for bulking their student body whether with genuine or fictitious students. The budget of each yeshiva is determined according to the number of its registered students. My suggestion is to cancel this policy and instead allot a fixed budget each year based on the amount received the previous year. This enables principals more flexibility and they can avoid the temptation to add fictitious names to their students' lists. This way there will also be a larger budget for the remaining students and their families. I believe this is also the desire of the yeshivot principals.

This will also put an end to the staunch opposition to military service. The existing opposition indirectly leads the ultra-Orthodox community to a lifestyle reminiscent of the Talmudic proverb: "One who does not teach his son a trade, it is as if he has taught him banditry."

Stealing is stealing, even if it is from state funds.

If my initiative is adopted, the program I suggest will continue for eight to ten years, and afterward a new reality will prevail that will enable new assessment and decisions. To avoid a situation in which children register in ultra-Orthodox institutions only for the benefits of the program, I suggest that it only include children who are already registered in one of those institutions at the time my initiative is accepted.

These suggestions, whether accepted in full or in part, could significantly contribute and have a long-term influence on the social structure of the ultra-Orthodox society, and the entire social and economic future of the State of Israel.

Professional experts estimated the annual increase to state revenue as a result of my initiative at a billion and a half shekels (approx. $400 million), as of the third year, when some 40 percent of those registered in yeshiva renounce the exemption from military service. This extra income will be generated due to the reduced budgeting for ultra-Orthodox yeshivot, and mainly because of the growth to the GDP. I suggested that one quarter of a billion shekels be taken from this money and given back to the same yeshivot, in order to improve the economic status of those who remain there and study, so that they will no longer have to live in such poverty as they do now. I suggested that another billion shekels be added to the budget of the veteran soldiers so that at last every discharged soldier will be entitled to a free university education, or an equivalent benefit, and the remaining sums would be returned to the treasury. This would also promote equality.

WE HAVE NO ALTERNATIVE

The chief of staff, Dan Halutz, gave his consent to my sending the letters with my proposal to the prime minister and to the minister of defense. Many people told me that my initiative was both very impressive and very important. My friend David Hager, who heads the voluntary association that supports Netzah Yehuda, organized a Saturday night tour of Jerusalem's bars and public houses for religious and secular Knesset members. Everyone knows that tens of thousands of those young boys who are exempt from military service on religious grounds are the best customers of those bars and pubs on Saturday nights. These kids sit in bars and not in the yeshivot learning halls. The only dispute was exactly how many tens of thousands.

When I explained my initiative to an ultra-Orthodox member of the Knesset, he said that I was right but that they, the ultra-Orthodox ministers, would never let it pass, because such a move could empty the ultra-Orthodox yeshivot completely. Naturally he was right.

I asked him how he would explain his objection. "You are getting everything that you ever requested with this initiative including a complete and easy release from military service," I told him.

The minister replied: "We'll find a way to explain our objection." And we both knew that the decision makers would accept those explanations without serious opposition.

I remembered the response of the minister of defense when I told him that I pay ultra-Orthodox teachers – soldiers in regular service who don't even agree to wear army uniform – more money then I pay my NCOs, whom I was then forced to fire and render unemployed. The minister asked me why I do it, and I said, frustrated, "You force me to do it!" Political agreements, some from many years ago, which no government has found enough courage to cancel, force us to recruit fictitious teachers from the ultra-Orthodox communities.

The minister looked at the chief of staff and said, "We have no alternative. We've got to dismantle the state and reconstruct it correctly."

Chapter 15

Only What I Lost Remains Mine Forever

Over the last thirty years, there hasn't been a single week in which I didn't act in some way to help bereaved families. There are long periods of time in which I am occupied with these matters almost every single day. Once you choose to become a soldier, especially a commander of combat units, you must be aware of the fact that deep feelings of camaraderie develop for your soldiers and accompany you throughout your life. This is very fulfilling when these friends are alive, but the value of camaraderie becomes especially compelling when it comes to friends who were killed – be they your subordinates, commanders, or comrades in arms.

Naturally a relationship with a bereaved family is very hard to keep. It requires a lot of time and energy; it affects your disposition and oftentimes the atmosphere at home. At times, you leave a house of a bereaved family with a frustrating sensation that you did no good. Other times, you feel a sense of guilt, not because you failed to bring the dead son or husband back home, but because it wasn't you who perished out there in the battlefield.

As life goes on the relationships become harder and harder to maintain. You have moved on and have a family of your own, and you do not like remembering those sad and morbid events – and anyway there are memorial days especially meant for that. But I believe that these connections with the bereaved families are the purest demonstration of the moral value of camaraderie. If risking your life for a friend is the highest manifestation of camaraderie, maintaining contact with the relatives of a fallen friend is the second highest.

Fortunately, though I live in a bereaved family, I cannot say that I myself live in bereavement. Still, from my own experiences having been close to many bereaved families, I feel that I could describe it, in a sensitive and careful manner, in order to maybe bring happiness to bereaved families.

I think that when a child dies, his parents' world turns black. From that moment on, they try their best to find some small area within this engulfing blackness that lets itself be painted white, even if for a short while. It takes tremendous strength for such parents to be able to participate in a "regular celebration," silently praying that that moment might become another "white" spot in their bleak existence.

When there are other children, their very existence is part of those areas painted white, with the anniversaries, birthdays, and weddings still to be celebrated and the grandchildren still to be born. Waiting for these happy moments is by itself a white area that helps soften the daily life of a bereaved family, once it has begun to move beyond the blackness.

Another white element is the family's pride in what their dead child was or did, and I believe that contact with and certainly visits to families of fallen comrades create a similar effect – maybe even a stronger one after many years have passed.

We should ask ourselves if, when we gently but firmly assure a bereaved family "We are with you!" it is genuine or just cliché. Is this "We are with you" meant only for the funeral and mourning period and perhaps later memorials, or is it intended for the days in between those memorial days? Is it only meant for the first and the second yearly commemorations, or is it for years and years to come?

The way I see it, there is no end to the camaraderie. Our duty toward our fallen friends, and even more so, toward our fallen subordinates, remains with us until our final day.

On the other hand – and I don't see a contradiction in this statement – I detest some of the mourning rituals that we have witnessed in recent years; all those orgies of collective weeping on the edge of open graves, by both male and female soldiers, crying on each others' shoulders openly, for the entire world to see. I am one of those who can easily be observed shedding a tear during a military funeral and other sad events. Nevertheless, I think that we have gotten carried away in how we publicly express and expose our emotions. The sessions of howling and collective weeping harm us.

As fighters, we are required to have firm control over a whole range of emotions: Fear, hate, and pain of all kinds. The howling next to open graves signifies, more than anything else, a lack of self-control. When I go to commemorations for friends, sometimes many years after they were killed, I never see enough comrades. Sometimes I feel that in a way, those collective expressions of lamentation around the grave serve as an exemption from a longer term participation in the bereavement of the family. It is a sort of a declaration saying: "See how much it hurts me now," and then you are free from the need to demonstrate it again.

I think it is better to remain in control during the funeral and then stay committed and loyal in the future as well.

Ilan

Ilan was a soldier under my command when I was a young platoon commander. He came to the paratroopers after spending several weeks as a flight cadet in the air force's flying college. I soon found out that his parents' house was a hundred yards away from my parents' home, in the same neighborhood of Tel Aviv. Like myself, he was a graduate of the Netiv Meir Yeshiva; I vaguely remembered him from there. He was two years younger than me. Though I knew who he was at the yeshiva, I never paid much attention to him, until he joined my platoon.

He quickly stood out from all the other soldiers of the platoon. He was strong and clever and well liked by all of his peers. I naturally chose him to be my runner, a task I myself had filled before I became a commander, and he quickly became my trusted secret advisor in all matters.

Apart from all his qualities, God had given Ilan such beautiful features that you could hardly take your eyes off him. I said on several occasions that he was the most beautiful soldier who ever served under me. And what's more, he was one of the only two observant soldiers in the platoon, something that was quite rare in those years.

Though Ilan was an outstanding and ethical soldier, and maybe because of that, I didn't give him any special privileges. Once, when we were lying in an ambush in Lebanon, I caught him dozing. I asked him whether he noticed something just passing by. He replied that he didn't. I asked him if he were certain, and he confirmed that he didn't see anything passing. I said that it's a pity because it was his weekend leave that had just gone when his eyes were closed...

In the beginning, when military protocol required a distance between us, serving under my command was complicated for him. It was especially complicated when we went home for weekends. I wasn't strict on maintaining my commander status, certainly not when we were at home, but he, as I learnt later, was deeply embarrassed whenever our paths crossed or when we met in the neighborhood's synagogue.

After his basic training our ways parted. He and the rest of the platoon were sent off for advanced training while I was promoted to the rank of deputy company commander with new cadets. This was where I received the tragic message that Ilan had been killed in a training accident. It was supposed to be the last exercise of his training and he had already been chosen by the course's staff as the outstanding graduate of the course.

The next day was Friday and I went to Ilan's parents' home. We lived in the same small neighborhood and I knew their faces. But on that Friday they were different from the people I thought I knew. I had met bereaved families before that day (a friend died in my hands not long before), but this was the first time I had accompanied mourning from so close.

Ilan's parents did not have a family of their own, no parents and no siblings. They had only their two daughters, Bracha and Dorit. Dorit, who is the person to be thanked for everything I have, intended on enlisting in a Nahal unit. At the time, she was engaged to a boy seven years her senior. I had not met her until then, the four-year difference between us being too large for her to enter my range of interest in the neighborhood inhabitants.

Several months after Ilan's death, Dorit decided that she wanted to serve in the same unit in which her brother had served. She came to the battalion as an education NCO. In her first months in the battalion, my company was training in the West Bank while she served in the Golan Heights. Avner Talmon, the deputy commander of the regiment, takes credit for being our matchmaker.

I had had two or three company clerks until then, women who did not get along with me and what they considered my harsh demands from them. Talmon decided, baselessly, that I was bound to drive away every secretary sent to me until I got Dorit. The surprising truth was that he proved to be correct; Dorit became our company's enduring clerk.

At the beginning of her service in the regiment, my relationship with Dorit was completely devoid of romance. She was engaged to be married and wore an engagement ring on her finger. Then one day she informed me that she had broken off her engagement.

I paid careful attention to that fact.

Dorit was an extraordinarily devoted company clerk. Whenever the company was engaged in combat or other activity, she would not sleep for weeks. Everyone in the regiment and brigade knew that whenever they climbed to the posts on the summit of Mount Dov, each soldier, commander, and guest would be welcomed with a pastry, hot beverage, and pleasant word.

That was where love flourished. My mother says that it was Dorit who initiated our relationship. For proof, she shows paintings that Dorit painted in our house from when she came, according to my mother, to get close to me. Dorit does not deny my mother's account, but she adds that if she had not taken matters into her own hands, I would still be a bachelor to this day. I do not know whether she is right, but at least we agree about how it all started.

My relationship with Dorit and Ilan's parents had a crucial impact on my understanding of the world of bereavement, something that later led me to develop the IDF's policy toward bereaved brothers and sisters. Such a policy was previously not considered necessary. Dorit described to me how army representatives knocked on their door at 6 a.m., and informed her father that his son was killed, without paying any attention to her at all. Her father had lost a son, but she had lost a brother and, at the same time, also a father.

Grandfather Shlomo, Dorit's father, was extremely agitated after his son's death for two reasons: First, he was concerned about who would say Kaddish for him and his wife, Rina, after their deaths. Second, he was worried about who would carry on the family's name. I personally do not see the major significance of the family name; we are all destined to be forgotten in two or three generations. The only ones who will be remembered will be the killed soldiers; their names will be recalled every year, at commemorations and memorial ceremonies held in schools and cemeteries. Flowers will be placed on their graves and young children will carry on their heritage. But, still, when we got married, Dorit added her family's name to mine – a practice that has become quite common in our society.

What's less common is that our eldest daughter, Liron, upon her marriage to Shimon Abuhatzeira, also kept her name from her parent's home, but we were proud when she did not choose to keep the name Stern, as is usually done. She kept her mother's maiden name, and she is now called Liron Abuhatzeira Mannes, as are my grandchildren Roi and Zohar.

As for Kaddish, Dorit researched the issue thoroughly. She discovered that women are permitted to say Kaddish after a father's death and that this practice was actually quite common in Europe. So today, with the approval of the rabbi of Hoshaya and several other rabbis, women in Hoshaya who wish to say Kaddish are welcome to do so.

Bereavement as a Permanent Resident

Bereavement resides in our house because Dorit is a bereaved sister. Our children lost an uncle and they always see his photograph on the shelf in the living room. We are forever torn between our desire to describe to the children what kind of man their uncle was and the fear, on the other hand, that we will accustom them too much to grief and death.

We are very close to several other families who suffered fatal losses, like Penina Kenishbach, and Nono (may he rest in peace) and Malka Mizrachi, the parents of Zion, who was a company commander killed in Lebanon. They have all been integral parts of our daily lives for more than twenty years now. While we moved through the years, we gathered more and more bereaved families into our family circle. More recently, we assembled several new bereaved families from our son Ilan's squad: Jonathan Evron and Yosef Goodman, and Gilad Fisher from Hoshaya. Shlomo Vishinski became a regular guest in our home after his son Lior was killed in the Philadelphi Corridor on the Egyptian border of the Gaza Strip together with Aiman, the grandson of Abu Sallach Gadir, who is truly a member of our family.

When I was promoted to the rank of Major General, the Gadir family held a large celebration in honor of the promotion, in their home in Birr El Machsur, and there, Chief of Staff Moshe Ya'alon congratulated them on the first "Bedouin" general.

All those encounters and events have placed bereavement almost at the center of our home. These families are with us whenever we celebrate, on Shabbats and at holiday dinners, and we cannot deny the impact this must have had on our children. In one of the events organized after my retirement, Dorit mentioned this issue and concluded that, to our great relief, the kids have grown and left the house, and thank God, they seem perfectly alright.

A Family's World Shattered

During my military service I had, to my great misfortune, several cases when the names of soldiers I was personally familiar with landed on my desk in the casualties list. They were soldiers whom I had met over the years or whose families I knew. Sometimes I knew about the death of such soldiers before their families were notified, and I was consumed by the thought that this family didn't know that their world was about to be blown to pieces.

As head of the Human Resources Directorate, this became a sad routine for me. I learned that being among the first to know sometimes carries a very heavy toll.

During the Second Lebanon War in 2006, I received numerous reports about soldiers either injured or killed, but usually I would first find out the numbers before the identities. I remember one night when I stopped my car on the side of a highway after receiving a report that five soldiers from the elite Egoz Unit had been killed in a battle in southern Lebanon. Since rumors were already spreading like wildfire, I knew what awaited me at home so I decided to wait on the side of the road until I received the list of names.

Minutes after I entered my house, two of my neighbors who had children in Egoz knocked on my door with pale faces. I told them that their sons weren't among the dead soldiers but that I could not give them the names since the families had yet to be notified.

Unfortunately, there were other incidents as well. On the first night of Sukkot one year, at 3:45 a.m., my phone rang. It was Brigadier General Yossi Peretz, the commander of the IDF Adjutant Corps. "Sir, I am sorry for the late hour, but I need your advice. A soldier from Hoshaya has been killed in the Gaza Strip," he said. I took a deep breath, and he continued, "I wanted to ask you if we should inform the family during the holiday, or should we wait until it is over?"

I asked him what the routine procedure was in such cases, and he said that usually the families were immediately notified. I asked him what was the dead soldier's name, and he said that he didn't know yet. He only knew at that point that he was from Hoshaya, my home. I started to think about the young men who were not at the holiday services that night. My own son was among those who didn't get off for the holiday.

Holding the telephone in my hand and only half dressed, I stepped outside so as not to wake up Dorit. Yossi asked me for a few minutes to receive an update, and after five minutes he called me back and said that the soldier was from the Nahal Brigade but that he still didn't know his name.

I now tried to recall who from the community served in the Nahal Brigade. At synagogue, I usually sat next to Gilad Fisher, a soldier who served in Nahal, and he wasn't there that night. But, I thought, Hoshaya is already a large community and maybe there were other Nahal soldiers who I couldn't remember. A few minutes passed and Yossi called again and said that the dead soldier's name was Gilad Fisher.

Gilad lived very close to our house. His parents, Hedva and Hanan, were among the founders of Hoshaya together with us. We have lived together for more than twenty years, and Gilad was one of the children to be born in the community together with our daughter Liron and some others.

I went into the house, quickly dressed and went straight to the rabbi's house. It was now 4:30 a.m. Rabbi Haim opened the door himself, perhaps sensing that something had happened. He looked silently at me and I said, "Gilad Fisher was killed." He covered his face with his hands, moaned, and leaned heavily on the doorframe. I waited, and he finally asked me if the family had heard the news. "No," I said, "that is the reason I came to you."

I explained to him the dilemma. His immediate response was to wait until the holiday was over. I explained to him that such a decision was problematic since, by the end of the holiday, news of a dead soldier would be spreading around the country and would make its way to Hoshaya as well. As long as we do not inform the family we cannot publish the name of the soldier, which means that thousands of other families will be sitting at home terrified that the rumors they had heard were about their son.

The rabbi thought for a moment and we decided together to give the family a few more hours of grace and to inform them after the morning service at about 11 a.m. I called Yossi and told him of our decision. I sneaked quietly back into the house, tiptoed to the bedroom, and found Dorit sitting up in bed. She asked what happened, and I said that someone was wounded and that one of the officers wanted to consult with me. She looked me in the eyes and said, "You are not telling me the truth! What happened?" I don't want to think what thoughts must have been going through her mind.

I asked her if she really wanted to know, and even before I finished asking I realized how stupid the question was and told her that Gilad Fisher had been killed in Gaza. She started crying and asked me if the parents knew. I told her that they didn't and that we had decided to give them several hours and to notify them after the morning service.

Dorit was shocked. "You can't do that!" she said. "You have no right! You don't know what they will think afterwards. Maybe they will think that while their son was lying dead they went to synagogue services, prayed, sang, and enjoyed a good breakfast. You have to inform them immediately!"

I realized she was right.

I went back to Rabbi Haim's house and he also agreed with Dorit. The rabbi asked me to pick him up when the IDF delegation arrived to inform the family. I called Yossi and told him that I had changed my mind and that the family needed to be informed as soon as possible. It was by then 6 a.m. and Yossi informed me that it would take a while to get the officers to Hoshaya. I asked him to do his best to get there before 7:00, since by then, people were already making their way by foot to the synagogue. He said he would do his best.

I returned home and found Dorit dressed. When I asked her why she had gotten dressed so early, she said that she intended to accompany the officers to the Fisher house. I tried to stop her. I reminded her of the scar that she still carries from the loss of her late brother. I asked her why she needed to go through it again. But Dorit only said that she knew that Hedva would need her there.

Half an hour later, I saw out the window that the officers were approaching the main community gate. I went to meet them, stopping briefly at the rabbi's house on the way to inform him that we would soon pick him up. Dorit said that she would wait outside our house. It was a race against the clock. It was now 7:15 a.m. and while I led the officers, who were in uniform, through the sidewalks of Hoshaya, I almost panicked when I stumbled onto a friend who was on his way to the synagogue. I didn't want to leave him enough time to think so I asked him why he was heading so early to the synagogue. He said that he needed to arrange some things.

"Certainly you also intend to come soon." he said.

"As you can see," I said, "I have some guests with me. I'll be there soon." He later explained to me that he really thought they were guests since I always had soldiers and officers over at my house.

We carried on walking, collected the rabbi, and then picked up Dorit. At this point, I excused myself by saying that I had to go inform some other friends of the Fishers, so they could get ready to come and assist.

And the convoy of angels marched on their way to shatter another family's world.

A Souvenir

One evening, I took Dorit to the theater. During the break, I spoke with our son Ilan who said that his squad was in the middle of routine arrest operations near the West Bank Palestinian city of Jenin. We returned home after the show in a restless mood. I woke up at around 5 a.m. and took my beeper with me to the other room. The message read that a soldier was killed during a routine operation in the West Bank. I hurried to the living room and called my bureau chief Amir and asked him for information on the incident. Amir told me that the soldier was from the elite Maglan Unit – Ilan's outfit – but that as far as he knew Ilan was fine. Amir requested some more time and promised to call me as soon as he had more information. For me, it was eternity.

He finally called and said that the soldier's name was Yonatan Evron. I recognized the name from Ilan's stories.

I returned to the bedroom and found Dorit sitting in bed and crying. She only wanted to know who it was. I told her that it was Yonatan, and she covered her face with her hands, wept, and told me that just this week she and Yonatan's mother Talilah had spoken several times on the phone. Talilah had called to say that she was putting together a souvenir book for the squad, and she asked Dorit for a picture of Ilan. She had done the same for all of the soldiers in the squad.

I was at a loss for words.

Later that day, Talilah said to me over her son's open grave: "Remember that we will still put out the souvenir booklet."

Several days later I saw an early draft of the book. I asked Talilah why it didn't mention that Yonatan was killed in action and with her extraordinary sense of nobility, she said, "I don't want this to spoil the soldiers' memories."

I tried to convince her that the tragic death of Yonatan was an integral part of the soldiers' service. She promised me she would think it over.

Eventually, Talilah carried on preparing the booklet and refused to make any changes. When I saw the printed booklet I realized that I had failed to convince her. She only added a short statement saying: "Yonatan was killed during an operation against terrorist infrastructure in a village near Jenin, on the second day of November, 2005."

Nobility of that magnitude is inconceivable to me.

A Name on a Scrap of Paper

Several weeks after Yonatan's death, I sat at a meeting in my office when suddenly Dafna Harari, the head of the IDF Casualties Department, received a note. She showed it to me and asked to be excused. According to the note, a soldier had been killed in a complicated parachuting accident.

I knew that complex parachuting maneuvers were performed almost only in Ilan's unit. Dafna, who had met Talilah after Yonatan's death, had become acquainted with the rest of Ilan's squad. I let her go to gather more details and resumed the discussion in the meeting, even though my mind was somewhere else.

The discussion ended. I walked out of the meeting and saw Dafna coming toward me with a scrap of paper in her hand. On it was a name: Yosef Goodman. Goodman, a member of Ilan's crew, was a soldier whose name came up around our Shabbat dinner table now and again. We all laughed heartily from stories about his naivete. Though he might have been naive, he was one of Ilan's top soldiers and was considered the best fighter.

One Saturday night, we had been on our way back home from friends, when we decided to go and visit Ilan's friends. Ilan himself was no longer with the squad, since he had been sent several days earlier to Bahad 1 for officer training. We called Yosef and asked him if we could bring some food, and Goodman said, "Yes, thanks. And bring a lot because the guys are starving and they could use a good meal."

We stopped on the way at a restaurant owned by our friend Yoav Edward. Whenever Yoav hears that someone is on his way to visit soldiers he opens his heart and his kitchen. He was familiar with the squad from earlier visits, and after he learned for whom we were buying the food, we left with crates of pita, and all kinds of meat, salads, and beverages.

When we arrived at the base it started to rain. I called Goodman and asked him to come to the parking lot to pick up the food. He took the bags and we turned to drive away. Goodman, who was wearing a coat, said, "No, please come in, the guys will be very happy to see you." When we asked him where they were, he said that they were in an operational briefing. We asked him, "And you?" and he said, "The commanders gave me permission to skip the briefings..." He wasn't at his best in briefings, and yet no commander agreed to go out on a mission without him.

We were about to get out of the car, but Goodman told us to wait inside, ran, and returned after a few seconds with an umbrella that he opened above Dorit's head. We met the guys, had a good time, and when we went back to the car, Goodman hurried to escort us with the umbrella over Dorit's head again. We entered our car, and Goodman said good-bye and disappeared into the darkness, gone to arrange his gear for another night in Jenin. At our next meeting, he was already classified as "a casualty of a parachuting accident."

Preserving Honor and Preventing Pain

Nimrod Segev, from Rosh Pina, was killed during the Second Lebanon War when his tank was hit by a roadside bomb and an anti-tank missile. I visited his family while they sat mourning in his Ramat Gan apartment. As often happened when I met a bereaved family, I formed an instant, strong, personal connection with the family.

Weeks after Nimrod's funeral, a few additional body parts were identified. Due to the sensitivity of the issue, I direct the personnel of the Casualties Department to return to the families in such cases and offer one of three options: to bury the additional parts in a collective military grave; to open their child's grave by military authorities without the parents present and bury the new parts with the body; or to open the grave and hold a full military ceremony during the reburial process. I asked the officer whose job it was to present the options to the families to do everything she could to convince them to forfeit the third option, which was like holding a second funeral, and that if a family insisted on this option to have them meet me before it takes place.

I was on my way home when the officer called me and said that the Segev family was insisting on holding a second funeral, and they wanted it to be held tomorrow. She also told me that the media had already been informed. I called Dorit from the car and told her that my plans had changed. I suggested uneasily that she join me on a trip to Rosh Pina. Dorit knew well enough that we weren't going to Rosh Pina for dinner but that her presence was needed in order to help me talk to the parents.

We reached Rosh Pina at 11 p.m. We knocked on the door and went inside. The family was busy saying good-bye to some friends who were leaving. We waited quietly, and while they said good-bye I heard someone say, "See you at the ceremony tomorrow."

I played naive and asked what ceremony they were referring to. The parents answered that they intended to have a funeral tomorrow. "Whose funeral?" I asked them, and they told me that they considered it to be a tribute they owed Nimrod. I asked them about their own pain, and the grief of the widow? Do they really believe that Nimrod would prefer his honor over their pain? We spoke about this, and I told them that I refrained from going to funerals during the war, but I would be willing to go to this funeral and be present there personally, if they would forego attending the burial. I said that this way we would both preserve Nimrod's honor and spare them the pain of having to bury their son a second time.

Slowly but surely, the parents were convinced. When we got up to leave they said that they would still have to consult with Nimrod's widow, because they could not do anything without her consent. I suggested that I also speak with her, and we all discussed the issue. I also managed to convince the family to keep the media away.

The next day I received the family's authorization to perform the ceremony by myself. We agreed that I would not inform them of the exact time of the ceremony so that they wouldn't have to fight the urge to come to the cemetery, and I said that I would inform them after it was all finished. The reburial was set for 10 p.m. I ordered a plane to take me from Tel Aviv to Rosh Pina.

The burial was done that night in the presence of the cemetery authorities and several IDF officers in the most dignified way possible. We were careful not to leave behind any mark that the grave was ever reopened.

I promised Hezi, Nimrod's father, that I would complete the burial by Shabbat. He called me the next day, which was Friday, and told me that he didn't know if we had performed the ceremony yet but that if we had, we didn't leave any visible trace on the grave and that for him this means it was done honorably. I told him that he had beaten me to the phone and that I appreciated his family's nobility. I hoped that we had started a new framework for similar future incidents that, I prayed, would never happen.

Which of the Two?

The Sheinbrom family lost their son Yaniv during the Second Lebanon War. Due to the ongoing fighting, I unfortunately could not find the time to come to their house during the shiva, the traditional seven days of Jewish mourning. They lived in a small Moshav called Mei-Ami.

Mirta and Sergio had come to Israel from South America and raised two sons, Yaniv and Tal, both of whom served in the Nahal Brigade. When I was able to come to the family's home, Sergio told me about the day Yaniv was killed.

"I was worried. I had two sons and both were in Lebanon. I wanted to speak to someone who knew what was happening so I managed to get the phone number of Sarit, the Nahal Brigade's casualties officer. I called her around three in the afternoon and asked her what the standard procedure was when a soldier was injured. How was the family informed? Sarit said that if a soldier is lightly wounded, they let him contact his family and inform them. When his wound is more complicated, other officers make the call. If it is a very serious wound, or if the soldier is dead, officers come to the family's home and personally deliver the tragic news.

"But we have a gate in our moshav," Sergio said to the officer, "and it is usually locked."

"We have the list of all the security officers in all the moshavim in the country and their phone numbers and they open the gates for us," she said.

"And what if someone is not home?"

"We have all the work addresses as well, and if necessary we go there."

"But my wife and I work in two different parts of the moshav."

"We check this in advance and come simultaneously to both places."

"Several hours later," continued Sergio, "a little past eight o'clock, we were sitting in the living room, and through the window I saw the car of the director of the moshav's factory coming down the road, followed by a cab. Now this is a village of simple folk, and we don't usually hire cabs, so I kept looking curiously at the cars until they came to a stop right in front of our house. Since the shutters were partly closed, I couldn't see the people who came out of the taxi. All I could see were their military boots. I didn't want them to knock on the door so I went out to meet them.

We entered the house, and Mirta only asked, "Which of the two is it – Tal or Yaniv?"

Afterwards we were naturally very worried about Tal. The people who came to inform us managed to get him on the phone, and he told us that he knows about his brother's death and that his commanders had moved him to a safer location. He said that their wounded soldiers were scheduled to be evacuated soon and that Tal would be on the helicopter with them. At 4 a.m. Tal called and said he had arrived with the transport of wounded soldiers at a hospital in Rehovot. I asked him how he intended to get home, and he said that the military would take care of it.

After I heard his voice from Israeli territory, Sergio said, I closed my eyes for the first time and slept. He came home at 6:30 in the morning and sat on my bed. I immediately woke up and tears began streaming from my eyes. This was the first time I had cried since I was told that Yaniv was killed. I asked Tal who had arranged for his transport, and he said that her name was Sarit, the casualties officer. I asked him to call her and tell her that I was the father who had bothered her with questions about wounded soldiers a few hours earlier.

Two hours later Sarit stood at the door of our house.

Visiting Shlomo Three Times a Day

I came to visit the Buchris family in the middle of the war. Shlomo, the son of Sarah and Rafi, was killed at the age of thirty-six. He was a reserve soldier from the Northern Paratroopers Brigade, a unit that I had once commanded. He lived with his parents and worked in the greenhouse next to their home.

My immediate impression was that this was a stable and strong family. The father – with deep blue eyes and strong farmer hands – greeted every visitor with a shining face. He told me at length about his own adventurous days as a paratrooper in the era of Ariel Sharon and Motta Gur. He sat with his wife and their many children and grandchildren. I was more and more assured this was a family that would be back on its feet fairly quickly.

Several months later I was informed by the casualties officer who had taken care of the parents that there were troubles with the Buchris family and that they had asked if I could stop by for another visit. I sat again in their living room with the parents, one of the sisters, and several of their grandchildren. The problem, they told me, was that Rafi visited Shlomo's grave too often, and as a result he had trouble moving on with his own life.

I told them about my very dear friend, the famous Israeli actor Shlomo Vishinski, whose son Lior was killed in 2004 in the Gaza Strip. I had a big fight with him after he told me that he visited his son's grave twice a week. I tried to convince him that once a week was enough, and used as proof Dorit's parents, who used to go to Ilan's grave only once a week; we managed to convince them that even that was too much, and now they go to the grave even less. Vishinski explained to me that he had to visit the grave twice a week, since on Fridays he would meet other parents there as well, and that on Tuesdays he would come to spend some private time with his son. And he added, "I know what's under the stone there, but I invest time in Dana, my other child – how can I stop investing time in Lior? I know I am a little crazy, but hey, that's me."

At this point Shlomo's sister interrupted, "Why bring us Vishinski's example and his visits twice a week? My father goes there every single day!"

Now the mother intervened. "Once a day? I wish he went there once a day! He goes to the grave three times a day!"

I stared at the poor father, and he chose to speak openly: "Not only do I visit the grave three times a day. I also get up every morning to prepare Shlomo his usual cup of tea!"

I took a deep breath and embraced the man, and he said with his head reclined, "Yes, I know that I'm a little crazy, but what can I do?"

And to think that I had considered myself an expert on bereaved families just because I had made thousands of visits like this in the past!

I decided to pull out my ultimate weapon. I told them about Penina Kenishbach and her only son, Captain Mucky, who served with me as a company commander in the Paratroopers Brigade and was killed in an operation in southern Lebanon in 1980. I then told them about her only brother, Lieutenant Tzvika Kenishbach, who also was killed when his reconnaissance aircraft crashed in 1959 in the Judean Desert. I told them that I had been in contact with Penina for more than thirty years and that I admired her for her ability to simply get out of bed every morning.

I told Rafi Buchris that the last time I had met my good friend Mucky was on my honeymoon that had lasted precisely three days. On one of those three days, we visited the battalion headquarters and I met Mucky there getting ready for an operation inside the Lebanese territory. He said to me, "Not all of us will return from this mission."

And he didn't return.

Ever since, when I hear a commander tell his soldiers that if someone gets killed during an operation the whole thing was a waste, I stop him and say that in that case maybe we shouldn't be doing the operation to begin with. We always went into the battlefield with the knowledge that nobody can guarantee us a safe return.

I asked Rafi to look around him and observe the number of reasons he has for being happy. I suggested that he go visit Penina and talk to her. Later I was pleased to see that he had followed my advice.

Two weeks after I finished my term as the head of the Human Resources Directorate, the phone rang. "Elazar, this is Buchris speaking. I am sorry that I didn't have an opportunity to speak with you sooner, but I want you to know that you saved me. Thanks to your visit, everything seems different and there's even happiness. And please give my best regards to Penina. She certainly is a magnificent woman!"

Every bereaved family – and each member of those families – is forced to go through unimaginable and difficult situations. One of issues they always have to struggle with is the question of how much attention they plan to pay their dead loved one and, as a direct consequence, how much attention they will be able to pay to those who remain alive.

How much time, money, and attention will they invest in the memory of their dead child or sibling, and how much will they invest in the living ones, or even in themselves? There isn't one single formula; there are no simple answers to these tragic questions. Every family has to find their own formula. No one can find it for them.

As for me, I always believed in giving the major part of yourself to those who are living around you.

Another difficult phase that many families go through is the wish – which in many cases turns into an obsession – to know as many and as exact details as possible about how their loved one died. This is often interwoven with a search for someone to blame. On the other hand, there usually is a wish to remain in close and friendly relations with those who were there when the child or sibling died.

There aren't simple formulas or answers for these dilemmas. Though I was always careful not to trespass into families' personal mourning, I felt obligated at times to discuss these issues out in the open with the families as part of a modest effort to help them. I hope that those families accepted my prying into their intimate feelings with understanding.

Udi and Eldad

On July 12, 2006, Eldad Regev and Ehud (Udi) Goldwasser were abducted by Hezbollah in a cross border attack on an IDF patrol along the Lebanese border. The attack took place a few weeks after Gilad Shalit was abducted by Hamas in the Gaza Strip. In both cases, we followed the guidelines we had set from the kidnapping of three soldiers along the Lebanese border in October 2000.

In line with those guidelines, I decided to personally visit the soldiers' families the day after the kidnapping in order to share with them everything we knew, and especially to design from a very early stage the relationship between these families and the army throughout the hard days that still awaited us.

Based on initial information, we thought that there were three missing soldiers: Udi, Eldad, and Wasim Nazel. On my way to the North, I was forced to stop on the side of the highway and wait until the Military Rabbinate finished identifying the corpses and concluded that Wasim, who drove the Hummer jeep, was one of the kidnapped soldiers.

First I went to the Druze village Kfar Yanouch, to see Wasim's parents. I started my visit by telling them that Wasim was missing, which left the parents and the widow with hope he was alive. While I was sitting in the house, I got another call from the chief military rabbi, who asked me to step out of the house for a moment. Wasim's corpse had been identified.

I went to a gas station on the outskirts of the village and instructed my men to arrange the formal notification team. It was around midnight. The house was packed with family and friends, and all the nearby villages and the streets were crowded with friends of the deceased soldier and his family. I decided that since I was the one who brought them the false message that their son was only missing, I should also be with them when they were informed that he had been killed. I waited for the delegation to arrive and we gathered outside the village. They entered the house and I was right behind them. Hope was gone. This one was certainly one of the hardest.

From there I went to Nahariya, to the house of the Goldwasser family. I suggested to them earlier that we postpone the visit by a few days, but the family insisted that I come at any hour, as did the Regevs. I arrived at the Regevs' house at three in the morning.

During the first days after the kidnapping, I was told by the families that if, God forbid, their beloved ones were dead, they didn't think that Israel should free terrorists in exchange for their bodies. I admired them for saying that. I didn't lose my admiration toward them when months later, events drove them to revise their position.

After the full inquiry was finished, when we knew the severity of the two soldiers' wounds, I met the families and presented them our findings. Those meetings were very complicated. After I presented the findings to the Goldwassers, Udi's mother asked me: "If you knew that you were going to tell us what you just did, how come you came without a doctor?" I said that I had one waiting outside and called him into the house. That was the severity of the situation.

Months passed and the families launched a public campaign to influence the government (which I consider completely legitimate) to get their sons back in the quickest way possible. One day the families came to my office for a meeting with several American officials and representatives from the Foreign Ministry. Udi's mother told me that she had received hundreds of signatures from members of Congress, all calling for the immediate release of the two soldiers. I asked her if she had asked all those congressmen who signed her petition why they never sign similar petitions for kidnapped American soldiers. Mickey Goldwasser thought for a moment and said that it must be because unlike in Israel, the US military is not considered the army of the people and therefore our commitment to soldiers is far greater then theirs.

I said that from what I know about the Americans, the reason is completely different. Americans bluntly refuse to negotiate with terrorists. I must admit that when I observe our conduct and compare it to American policy, I am much closer to the American standpoint.

When Udi's mother heard what I said, she replied, "But you must remember that you are my son's commander and therefore you have the obligation to bring him back!" I answered that it is true that I am his commander, but I am also the commander of many other soldiers, and some of them might get hurt, kidnapped, or even killed if we are willing to pay the price to bring Udi and Eldad back home – be they dead or alive.

After obtaining more information that confirmed our assessment that Eldad and Udi were dead, I asked the chief military rabbi to check if according to Jewish law they could be declared as dead soldiers whose final resting place is unknown. One of the reasons for my inquiry was that this would counter Hezbollah's dirty game. The guerilla group deliberately didn't reveal any information regarding the soldiers' physical condition. I thought that such an announcement would force them to reduce their demands in the ongoing negotiations. I also remembered the agony of the families of the three MIA (missing in action) soldiers from the battle of Sultan Yacoub. In that affair, the information was quite clear, but for different reasons the announcement was delayed. When finally, after twenty-two years, the authorities decided to announce that the soldiers were dead, the families objected and even petitioned the High Court of Justice to prevent it. It is much simpler to announce the death of an MIA soldier during the first couple of years after he has disappeared.

Therefore, as the information accumulated regarding Eldad and Udi, I gave the military rabbi instructions to begin the exchange process. It was several weeks before the "deal" for the exchange was concluded, and the pressure began to mount on the political echelon to approve the deal. The rabbi who started the exchange process had to drop it due to this pressure and due particularly to the media, which supported the deal. The exchange was concluded as planned.

A few days before the exchange was carried out, we had a meeting in my office to decide on the nature of the ceremony that would take place after the bodies were returned to Israel. The Defense Ministry favored a full government ceremony, as was done when the bodies of soldiers from the 2000 kidnapping were returned. I objected to the idea and said that once the bodies were returned to Israel they would be to us exactly like all other casualties from the Second Lebanon War and should be treated exactly the same way. We shouldn't let a one-time mistake become a general rule. The chief of staff and the prime minister accepted my position, and instead of an official ceremony, a hall was arranged for the families at a base in the north to have a few moments with their dead sons, and anyone who wanted to show their respect would come there.

I waited at the Rosh Hanikra Border Crossing on the Lebanon border together with OC Northern Command Major General Gadi Eizenkot during the entire exchange process, which was done through the Red Cross. I wasn't among the many Israelis who were tricked by Hezbollah leader Sheikh Hassan Nasrallah into thinking until the very last minute that maybe the kidnapped soldiers would return alive.

Afterward, I hurried to the Goldwasser family to inform them officially that their beloved son and husband, Udi, had been killed in battle, and Major General Gadi Shamni, head of the Central Command at the time, went to the Regev home at exactly the same moment. In the evening, when the families came to take their private leave of the two soldiers, Udi's widow, Karnit, said to me that the families deeply appreciated the dignified way they were treated and accompanied by the IDF throughout the entire ordeal. She also approved of my decision that all dead soldiers should receive equal treatment and consequently that there should not be an official government ceremony.

When I was invited a month later to a memorial service in honor of Udi and Eldad in Toronto, I said that I would come on condition the ceremony was not held exclusively in honor of Eldad and Udi, but in honor of all IDF casualties from that war. I also made it clear that my speech would be in a similar vein.

Prime Minister Ehud Olmert, who came to the hall at the military base in the north to pay his respects, took me aside, embraced me, and told me that he appreciated the courage that I showed during the process. Since I knew very well his opinions on the question of the price we were required to pay and his compassion toward the families on the one hand and his broader understanding of the significance of surrendering to Hezbollah's demands on the other, I told him that the courage he showed was greater than mine.

At Any Price?

In different discussions in which I participated in the IDF, I often heard the popular claim that IDF soldiers expect that their country will do everything for them and pay any price to free them from captivity. In my opinion, a majority of soldiers want to know that their state will make every effort to rescue them, but they are also aware that these efforts will have limits.

"We will rescue a wounded soldier at all costs" and "We will pay any price to bring back our POWs" are slogans that we should use for educating our soldiers, but they must stop at the platoon commander, or at most with the company commander.

Battalion commanders must consider what they would deem an exaggerated price for saving a wounded soldier. Prime ministers and ministers of defense must consider what "at any price" will do not only to our motivation, but also to the motivation of our enemy, and not only in the battle that we conduct right now, but also in future battles.

Slogans such as "the government will do everything to free a soldier" are misleading. A good example to demonstrate the falsehood is a procedure called the "Hannibal Procedure," which is essentially a set of guidelines for when soldiers are abducted. According to this procedure, soldiers are directed to shoot at the kidnapping vehicle's wheels in order to stop it from getting away, and if that doesn't work they must shoot the engine, and if that still doesn't work they are instructed to shoot at the passengers in the vehicle. Everybody understands that from such a shooting, the kidnapped soldier might also get hit, but the instructions were accepted by field commanders without hesitation. When I myself gave those orders to soldiers, I checked carefully and discovered that all of the soldiers were strongly against trading soldiers for large numbers of terrorists if they themselves ever became prisoners of war.

Soldiers should be ready at any given moment to pay with their lives to save a wounded soldier, but we shouldn't close our eyes to the fact that there are also other responsibilities. Imagine a situation where a commander sends soldiers to bring back a wounded soldier who is completely exposed to enemy gunfire. In the first rescue attempt, nine other soldiers are killed and the attempt is unsuccessful; then the commander sends a second rescue team and this time fifteen are killed, and they are still unsuccessful. Where should he draw the line? I guess it is fairly obvious that there is a limit. So when we say "at any price" it might be perfectly true as an educational principle, but that doesn't allow us to ignore the broader picture.

When I voiced this opinion before a mother of one of the soldiers who had been abducted in recent years, she responded by saying that she expected me, her son's military commander, to do everything possible to return him. I told her that she was right but that at the same time she needed to understand that I was also the commander of dozens of other soldiers who could pay with their lives in the future if archterrorists were released.

As a state that was once known for not surrendering to terrorism, we have become a country that leads the world in giving in to terrorist demands. This type of surrender emboldens terrorists and undermines our own national security, since instead of standing strong in face of their demands, we demonstrate dangerous weakness and oversensitivity.

Open Letter to Gilad Shalit

Shalom Gilad,

We know each other, but we don't know each other. After five years in captivity and the extensive public campaign for your release, every citizen of Israel can say those words – "We know each other, but we don't know each other." I know you a little bit better than most citizens. I came to your house on the day you were kidnapped, after your parents had already received the message that you were missing. While I was at your house, thanks to the information gathered in the interim, we were able to inform your parents that indeed you had been kidnapped and not killed. We could also encourage them that according to the information, you were observed being taken into captivity on your own two legs, so that despite a light injury, you were in a reasonably sound state.

As the days, months, and years passed, I got to know you well, through your parents as well as through the stories in the media. I also got to know you as a result of various efforts made in the IDF to estimate your ability to endure captivity, especially the conditions of isolation we assumed you were in. Along with the entire Jewish people, on the day of your release I rejoiced at your return home to your family. I was especially glad to see that, at least according to the photos and interview clips broadcasted on television, considering the long period of captivity, you returned home safely and in a reasonable medical state. I wish for you and pray with all my heart that your condition will only improve.

But I admit, that compared to all the expressions of joy here, mine was incomplete, and it remains so. I also admit that if I had been the one who had to make the decision that the Israeli government made, I can reasonably assume that the day of your release would have been postponed by days, weeks, and probably even months – not because I want your return less than anyone else, but because of the severity of the price.

Do not be angry with me or with those who think like me. I believe that in the end, positions such as the one I expressed in public convinced Hamas to show flexibility. Several times, in meetings and on the phone, I told your parents that I believed my opposition to the deal at exaggerated prices contributed to your return home more than all the demonstrations and marches. I knew, not on the basis of estimation alone, that every time a wave of marches broke out, the Hamas toughened its position. But I was wrong on one point: the demonstrations did contribute to your return, in that they weakened the prime minister. To the best of my evaluation, at the end of the day he gave in not only to the terrorist demands of the Hamas, but mainly to public opinion in the State of Israel. His capitulation led to your release on the day you returned home.

This capitulation was the result of a public relations campaign that was not afraid to regularly place its credibility in doubt, if not prove it completely false. For example, as part of the campaign for your return, they argued over and over that if the Israeli government would not agree to pay any price for your release, this would undoubtedly cause a drop in the motivation of the youth to serve in the IDF, most certainly in combat units.

To me, this argument was infuriating and insulting to the youth, their maturity, and the level of sacrifice they are at any rate required to make, with clear judgment. Furthermore, this argument, composed by the campaign members as an axiom, was simply wrong. The day you returned from captivity, after the emotional photographs of your arrival in Israel were broadcast, I sat in the studio of Channel 2. The principal of the high school where you studied in the Western Galilee was interviewed live on the screen. Yair Lapid asked her for the school's latest draft statistics, and how your long captivity had influenced the desire of your comrades to serve the country, which seemingly did not do enough to bring you home earlier. The principal of your school, with great pride, reported the very high percentages of school graduates who were drafted into combat units, with no decline in motivation or in the draft statistics at all during the period of your captivity. I was not surprised that those who stuck to those slogans throughout the years of your captivity refused to "eat their hats," arguing that such processes take years, and that we would yet witness the fulfillment of their threat.

They also belittled the soldiers, saying that if the IDF did not "pay any price," their combat spirit would be damaged. This saying contains within it not only an affront to the soldiers, but also a real blow to the strength of Israeli society. This strength is based, among other things, on the knowledge that the IDF soldiers are willing to sacrifice themselves in order to protect Israel's civilians. True, in the second Lebanon War we were a bit confused. We related to the lives of our soldiers with exaggerated sensitivity. We gave the fighters a flood of instructions and orders to ensure they would protect themselves as far as possible, at the very moment that civilians on the home front were being injured. How can it be that we can relate to such a lofty value with "exaggerated sensitivity"? In a world with no painful dilemmas or conflicting values, apparently the value of the lives of our soldiers was higher than anything else. But unfortunately, when our nation is obliged to stand up and fight, like in every civilized society, the value of civilians is higher than that of the fighters who are protecting them. It hurts, but this is what I was taught, and this is what I taught thousands of fighters and officers. Like the behavior in the second Lebanon War, the deal that led to your release endangers many civilians in order to protect the life or reduce the days of suffering of one soldier.

Furthermore, if there is any suspicion of harming the fighting spirit of IDF fighters, then it exists because of this deal. I know more than one bereaved family of fighters who sacrificed their lives during an operation to catch terrorist murderers, some of whom were released in exchange for your release. In the future, fighters might say to their commanders: What are we being asked to endanger our lives for, when at any rate those very same murderers will be released in the future?

You have most certainly noticed, Gilad, that immediately following your return, the public debate was again raised regarding "the Hannibal procedure." Many years ago, when we understood the price of kidnappings, a "Hannibal" order was written in the IDF. This procedure defined the series of actions we had to take when one of our fighters, or we ourselves, were kidnapped. The last stage in this procedure was shooting into a car in order to stop it. We gave this order even when it was clear to us that this would definitely endanger the life of the kidnapped soldier. At the foundation of this procedure lies the assumption that it is better for us to die than for the

State of Israel to give in to terror and pay highly exaggerated prices. Most Israeli soldiers and their commanders, especially those who belong to the combat ranks, are not willing to be kidnapped, and prefer to endanger themselves or sacrifice their lives, especially if their kidnapping might lead to the endangering or death of so many civilians.

Capitulation to terror contributes to its growth and represents a serious blow to national strength, as instead of strength and resilience, we are demonstrating over-sensitivity (as differentiated from great sensitivity, which is essential and characterizes the spirit of the IDF), and dangerous weakness.

Could we describe a situation in which the Americans released one of the planners of the attack on the Twin Towers in a prisoner release deal? For among the candidates for release in the Shalit deal appeared murderers who acted in a comparable manner, relative to Israel. In the United States, although it is spread across borders that are much more exposed than ours, there are no kidnappings. Their policy against negotiating with terrorists makes an important contribution to this fact. They did not negotiate with terrorists even when a sharp knife was placed across the neck of a kidnapped civilian, in the case of Daniel Pearl.

Most of the individuals and bodies that participated in the demonstration that preceded your return asserted to me after the deal, that they had joined the struggle – for reasons that I also think are justified – but they did not call for the government to pay the price that the Hamas demanded. Their intention was for the Israeli government to end the freeze and do something significant with the Hamas in order to change the situation. This could mean increasing pressure on Hamas leaders by worsening the conditions of the prisoners in jail in Israel, or by moving the targeted eliminations to their chiefs.

Unfortunately, they did not correctly estimate the significance of their action in the public atmosphere that washed over the nation, and their justified protest was lost in the unified stream that led to a deal at any price.

To my sorrow, the tragedy of the disappearance of Ron Arad was also used for the campaign to bring you home. In truth, the case of Ron Arad illustrates exactly the consequences after we pay exaggerated prices. Ron Arad fell into captivity months after the Jibril deal. Believe me, Gilad, that I have who and what to lean on when I say that Ron Arad paid the price of the Jibril deal, which broke records in the price that the Israeli government was willing to pay to give in to terror. Following that deal, the government and its head avoided paying a price, even a lower one, shortly afterward, in exchange for Arad's return. I must point out that the record determined by the price of the Jibril deal was broken with your release. I hope, Gilad, for all of us but especially for you, that you will not carry the burden that sits on the shoulders of those released in the Jibril deal. They have to carry not only the fate of Ron Arad, particularly considering the circumstances of his falling into captivity, as well as the lives of dozens and hundreds of Israelis who paid with their lives the price of that deal and were murdered by those released in it.

But the precedent of the Jibril deal and its implications did not interest public opinion in Israel in the five years before your release. The rousing campaign to bring you back "at any price" was adopted with no objections by the majority of the media, even the government ones. It silenced any debate, and at times seemed to have become true brainwashing. I do not know if your captors permitted you to listen to the radio in the terrible place where they held you. I do not know if you know that our military radio station, Galei Zahal, opened its broadcast every day by counting the days you had been held in captivity. As if they could not trust our memory, they repeated it on the afternoon news as well.

The public relations campaign for your release did not exclude any possible channel: billboards, marches, staged simulation of the kidnapping and imprisonment, cloning you in dozens of cardboard likenesses. Out of respect for you, I will not mention those programs in which actors played you in prison. I was humiliated for you, and to some extent for them as well. Brick by brick, a consensus was built up from which we were forbidden to deviate, oppose, or debate in principle or substance. Anyone who dared to question the logic of capitulation to the demands of Hamas was silenced, and worse than that, presented as one who decreed your fate. Not only me. Serious people like the previous chief of the General Security Services, Yuval Diskin, and the previous chief of the Mossad, Meir Dagan, who came out against the deal while still in their positions of responsibility. Several ministers and members of Knesset also opposed it. Anyone who dared to express another point of view was mocked in the orchestrated campaign managed in the media.

While you were in prison, public relations offices presented your life, and I can understand that, as more valuable than punishment of any terrorist. There was no talk whatsoever of the deterrent inherent in keeping the murderers in jail for their entire lives. In the last five years, as a society we have been reeducated. Today, not only the terrorists have learned to mock the severity of the punishments they are given, knowing that in the next deal they will go out free. We also have become used to relating to the life imprisonment given murderous terrorists as if it is given to them with a wink of an eye.

But I do not want to stop only with the question of deterrence, with all of its importance. Rather, I want to share with you, despite all, the question of whether punishment itself has any value. Is there no meaning to the suffering of those dozens and hundreds of bereaved families who opposed the deal, and who were forced to watch in frustration as the murderers of their loved ones were released and received like heroes? Can we understand, for example, the feelings of the family of the soldier who was murdered in the lynch in Ramallah, as they watch the murderer with blood on his hands waving repeatedly to the crowds, a broad smile on his face? Before your release, Gilad, we could not discuss this price. Do you think we can discuss it now?

In the five years of your captivity, I must emphasize, your family was not part of the media circus. On a number of opportunities, I said to your noble parents that if the parents of other kidnapped soldiers and their families had behaved like they did, you would have been at home a long time ago. You would have been at home, because if the terrorist organizations knew that we did not pay exaggerated prices for kidnapped soldiers, their motivation to kidnap would be much lower. I imagine that this would also have saved the lives of many who were killed during the various kidnapping attempts. In such a reality, I assume that you would not have been kidnapped at all, and even if so, the price demanded for your release would have been inestimably lower, and we could have paid it close to the time that you were kidnapped.

After you returned safely, I was told that your family was very angry at me because of things I said about the behavior of Ye'ara Winkler, among other reasons. I met Ye'ara only after you returned from captivity. She came into the picture years and months after you fell captive, as the partner of your brother

Yoel. The Israeli people met her shortly before you did. She burst into our consciousness on the eve of Israel's 63rd Independence Day, in a provocation she led at the torch-lighting ceremony.

We, the Israeli public, have perhaps three sacred ceremonies that are dedicated to memorial, pain, and revival. Never, but never, have these ceremonies been exploited for demonstrations, no matter how sacred the goal. The ceremony at Yad Vashem was never exploited, not even for advancing the treatment of Holocaust survivors, who for years suffered from neglect at the national level. The opening ceremony on Yom Hazikaron, Israel's Memorial Day, was never exploited, not for advancing the construction of heritage sites or for correcting injustices in our treatment of bereaved families. With all due respect to Ye'ara Winkler, she was no more than the girlfriend of the brother of a captured soldier. This certainly did not permit her to desecrate the sacred occasions of Israeli nationhood and turn the torch-lighting ceremony into her private demonstration. I write this not only as a criticism of her, even though I heard recently that she has had second thoughts about her act. I mention this event also as evidence of the brainwashing that Israeli society was undergoing at that time, that it accepted her outburst with understanding.

The reception given you upon your return to Israel did not honor you either. To me, everyone wanted to hitch a ride on that ceremony. You certainly must have noticed that consideration of you and your family was not the focus of the ceremony. They did not consider you, and certainly not all those families of terror victims, who melted into the background of the ceremony, watching but not visible. If it had been up to me, when you returned to Israel you would have been received by the commander of your unit, who had perhaps completed his mission with that. All those VIP's who crowded around you would have been in the homes of those who paid the price of the deal. Perhaps, if they had done so, it would have been faithful testimony that they indeed understood the pain of all those terror-victim families who objected to the deal, and certainly an expression of identification or appreciation for terror-victim families who supported the deal. Unfortunately, they chose a way that was planned to the smallest detail, to arouse the excitement of the masses and direct its attention from the heavy price, which was also part of the deal. If I had any doubts up to that moment, this final chord completely undermined the faith in the true motivations and sensitivity of the decision-makers who authorized the deal that enabled your return.

Gilad, I write these words, but know that neither you, nor your parents or family members, bear responsibility for the deal, nor for the ridiculous character of the campaign that led to it. You were caught in an impossible situation. You did everything in order to survive, and your family acted with great nobility in doing everything possible in order to bring you home. But the decision-makers who behaved as they did, and the media, which instead of stopping and asking questions, fanned the most immediate gut feelings, will have to do some serious soul-searching when they finally discover that we have only just begun to pay the true price of this deal. Though I hope, Gilad, with all my heart, that this day will never come.

With all my heart, I wish you a speedy rehabilitation and full return to life,

Elazar

Along with the Memory

The day after Eldad's and Udi's bodies were returned to Israel, I attended Udi's funeral in Nahariya and a few hours later Eldad's funeral in Haifa. From the second funeral I drove directly to the official farewell ceremony that was being held in honor of my discharge from the IDF.

People had suggested that I postpone my ceremony. But since I didn't want a chain of farewell ceremonies and parties, as sometimes happens, I had scheduled my event on the last day possible before the beginning of the "three weeks" – a period of mourning leading up to the ninth day of Av – so there was no way the ceremony could be postponed.

Soon after the event started, I asked for a permission to say a few words. Dorit told me later that when the chief of staff saw me go to the stage he turned to the minister of defense and said, "I wonder what Stern prepared for us today...."

I said to the people in the crowd that I would like to remind them of the day's events. "We buried Eldad and Udi today. We have here in the audience several bereaved families who 'with their death have bequeathed us our lives' so that our lives won't be only weeping and mourning, but also lives of construction. Along with the memory, lives of joy, lives of creation."

I know the defense minister and the chief of staff breathed a sigh of relief.

Chapter 16

Lone Soldiers: A Gift and a Responsibility

An Unrevealed Secret

Throughout my years as a combat soldier and commander, I came across soldiers who decided to make aliyah on their own and serve in the IDF. We call them *chayalim bodedim,* "lone soldiers." Their loneliness comes from being far from their families, the daily difficulties of adjusting to a new country, language barriers, and being culturally different from their fellow soldiers in the IDF.

It was not easy to understand their problems. While serving as head of the Education Corps and later as head of the IDF's Human Resources Directorate, I occasionally spoke with some of the lone soldiers so that we could anticipate their needs and update them about privileges we offered as some compensation for their loneliness.

On one such occasion I met with about three hundred lone soldiers in Netanya. On my way out a young officer in Golani named Dima approached me. "Commander," Dima said, "do you really think you know what it means to be a lone soldier? In my opinion you do not understand."

Dima continued, "I will tell you what it is to be a lone soldier. I was a cadet in the infantry officers' course. On Friday morning we all went home for Shabbat. I arrived in Tel Aviv around noon. I took my dirty wash and looked for a Laundromat, then I ran to buy some food for Shabbat so I would have something to eat, and then I ran back to fetch my washed clothes. On Saturday night I packed my stuff so that it would be ready for my return to the base on Sunday. We arrived at the base, threw our bags on our beds and changed into training clothes as quickly as possible. At night, after training, we got back to our rooms and each of us opened our bags to take out what we brought from home and set it in our little cabinet. Eran, whose bed was next to mine, suddenly screamed and cursed. He was almost hysterical. I asked him what happened, and finally he told me, 'Don't ask.' I did ask. Eran said, 'My mother forgot to pack a towel for me.'"

"Did you understand?" Dima asked me with a smirk on his face.

Yes, but only now did I understand.

Another new friendship was started. Today Dima teaches in a high school and volunteers in Keren Heseg, instructing and assisting young soldiers in a "big brother" program he initiated. The lone soldiers and their families are still a bit of an unrevealed secret to me. This goes for all lone soldiers, but more so with regard to lone soldiers who have joined IDF units with difficult training.

I was privileged to command two lone soldiers in the paratroopers, Danny Singer and his older brother Alex, *z"l*, who fell in battle in Southern Lebanon. Despite the age and rank difference between us – I was a battalion commander and they were young recruits who had recently joined the paratroopers – the Singer boys drew my attention. I was startled by their character and their beauty.

Why I Asked Suzanne Singer to Write about Alex, *z"l*

When deciding to make aliyah, like any choice to leave one's birthplace, two forces act together. One pushes; one pulls. Each force contains both material elements and ideals.

Often the material elements dominate the immigrant's decision. I have no doubt that if material concerns had been most important to Alex Singer, he would have decided to remain in the United States. But anyone who knew him or has read his letters and journals collected in *Alex: Building a Life*, realizes that it was the idea of Israel as the homeland of the Jewish people that pulled him to make aliyah.

Until today I cannot fully comprehend the impact on Alex's life of his experiences and of his family that led him not only to immigrate to Israel and serve in the IDF, but also to volunteer in a combat unit. Thankfully, throughout the years, many other young men and women have made Alex's decision to become lone soldiers, each leaving family to respond to the pull of Israel.

I asked Alex's mother, Suzanne, to help me understand the mystery that amazes me: Why did Alex choose to make Israel his home, and how did he accomplish so much in his twenty-five years?

Alex's Story in My Words and His

Elazar Stern asked me, what brought our son Alex to Israel to serve as a lone soldier in the IDF? I think what Elazar wants to know is what went on in our family that led Alex to leave us, his friends, abundant possibilities for his future, and the ease and familiarity of life in Washington, DC? As I tell about our family and Alex, some of that story will also explain why our other three sons now live in Israel with their eleven sabra children whom Alex never knew. But some of the answer to Elazar will be Alex's own words – from his letters to friends and family and from his journals during his two and a half years in the IDF.

Each of the more than two thousand young men and women from abroad who serve in the IDF each year as lone soldiers has his or her own story.

But that is jumping ahead.

The event that changed everything for our family was moving to Jerusalem in 1973 when Alex was eleven and his brother Saul, twelve, Daniel, eight, and Benjy, six. We intended to remain for a year, but that year became four. My husband, Max, took leave from Hudson Institute that he had helped start twelve years earlier, to work at an Israeli policy research center. It was our answer to Saul's approaching bar mitzvah year. We realized that we had nothing much to give him Jewishly from ourselves or from the charming but Jewishly impoverished New York City suburb where we lived. But surely a year in Israel would give Saul and his brothers something importantly Jewish.

We arrived in Israel not knowing anyone, enrolled the boys in Jerusalem schools, and when the Yom Kippur War began two months later Max volunteered and was assigned to ride with an Arab fuel truck driver on his deliveries. Not an easy time but an intense introduction to Israeli solidarity. Our new friends made the difference. When the opportunity came, we extended our time in Israel. During the fourth year, Saul and Alex lived at Kibbutz Kissufim in the Negev and attended the regional high school. During those years, almost every Shabbat Alex walked the land with us and his brothers.

We thought about aliyah, but reluctantly decided to return to the US, to Washington, DC. We carried back with us a deep connection to the historic land we had explored together, participation in the cycle of the Jewish year, and commitment to kashrut and Shabbat with all our family together.

Alex finished public high school in Chevy Chase, Maryland, and in 1980 entered Cornell University. Accepted to their College Scholar program, he could build an academic program from whatever interested him. That became economics, print making, and Jewish and Russian studies, with a senior thesis required at the end of the senior year.

Alex spent his junior year in Europe enrolled at the London School of Economics. During holiday breaks he traveled to Italy, Spain, Greece, and to Russia, which was still under the Communists. On his trip to Leningrad (today again St. Petersburg) he secretly brought gifts needed by refuseniks, those Jews who were denied the opportunity to leave or to practice their Judaism and who lived in great hardship. With difficulty he managed to locate all the Jews on the list he had been given and not only to bring the gifts but to teach some Hebrew and to tell them about the life of freedom in Israel. All the while Alex was writing letters to friends and family and drawing wherever he was.

When he returned to Cornell, the experiences Alex wrote about, his drawings made all over Europe, and the Jewish history of the countries where he traveled became the heart of his senior thesis, *Letters from the Diaspora*.[1] Here is what he wrote to a friend in a letter included in *Alex: Building a Life*, the collection of his letters, journals, and drawings: "Consider the year [in Europe] a modern pilgrimage – not to a place but to a readiness to move on to the place – Israel. My wanderings took me in the end to Israel...but the year was not directed towards Israel as a whole. The trip to Russia was the biggest factor in bringing my thinking back toward Jewish issues. When I heard my brother Daniel had decided to join the Israeli army it came even closer."[2]

Letters from the Diaspora ended with these words in a letter Alex wrote to Saul: "The irony is that living here and traveling in the least Jewish of places has pushed me closer to Israel than Israel itself could have done... If you want to learn about Israel, Europe is the world's best classroom."

Awarded recognition as the best senior thesis of that year, it also led to Alex's degree being granted *summa cum laude*. But more important was the clarity that it brought to him. After studying intensive Arabic at Hebrew University during the summer and then traveling alone in Jordan to practice his Arabic, Alex made aliyah on the last day of 1984. In February 1985 he was drafted as a lone soldier and passed the grueling field test to join the IDF paratroops.

Already more than four years older than Israeli recruits, Alex was invited to rush to officer school and to extend his eighteen-month obligation by a year. While at the officer training base, Bahad 1 in the Negev, he wrote to an American friend who was skeptical about his military service: "[The IDF] officer craves to create from his group of kids a force which will be mature and humane as much as it will be effective. For they (we) know that as each soldier is, so will be his unit, and as each unit is, so will be

---

[1] Now available in full at www.alexsinger.org.

[2] *Alex: Building a Life* (Jerusalem: Gefen Publishing House, 1996), p. 68.

the armed forces. And as those forces are, so will be Israel which is our home." [3]

In October 1986 he received his rank as a Second Lieutenant in the IDF and was sent to the air force to run short courses for cadets in infantry skills. While there Alex wrote of his attachment to Israel:

> This country is my home emotionally, religiously, and in every other way except for the location of my family. When I say that Israel is my home religiously, I mean that as a Jew I should live in the Jewish state, the only Jewish state, which Jews for 2,000 years prayed to return to, and died for, and dreamed of.
>
> You know my family and you know that I was not brought up in an Orthodox home. I think that I could not live anywhere else permanently. I feel more at home here than I can describe. This is not an intellectual feeling. It is just the way it is.
>
> My connection to this country is only strengthened as my knowledge of and commitment to Judaism grows.
>
> Home is home and it will take more than irritations to force me to leave. I want to make this place better.[4]

Frustrated at not having a platoon to command, Alex eventually succeeded by switching to the Givati brigade in May 1987. He wrote from the Syrian border: "I'm finally a platoon commander and I couldn't be more pleased.... I have so much more to deal with than when I was a training officer (rather than one with soldiers completely under my supervision as I am now). I've made plenty of mistakes.... But I am learning how to deal with people, to improve them, to train them, and much more."[5]

---

[3] Ibid., p. 188.

[4] Ibid., p. 222.

[5] Ibid., p. 240.

At dusk on September 15, 1987, Alex's twenty-fifth birthday, he, his commander Ronen Weissman, and ten other soldiers were dropped by helicopter onto the boulder-strewn Christofani Ridge in the foothills of Mt. Hermon in Lebanon. Their mission was to set an ambush to intercept terrorists on their way into Israel. Unexpectedly, about thirty terrorists were already there, hidden in shadows among boulders. In the battle that began when the first helicopter landed, Alex's commander was killed. Alex, the deputy commander, landed under fire. Knowing that there was silence from Ronen, he ran to find him. Alex was killed on the same spot. A short time later, Oren Kamil went to find his commanders and he, too, was killed at the same place. Outnumbered and under fire, with several wounded and without their commanders, the young soldiers continued fighting with help from helicopters until the terrorists retreated.

In Alex's last unfinished letter found in his pack, he wrote that he had decided to stay on for two more years to become the commander of a new company of soldiers during their first two years in the IDF.

Alex was buried in the military cemetery at Mt. Herzl in Area Dalet (D), Section 10. As most of the family still lived in Washington, Alex's *shloshim* took place at the Embassy of Israel. Saul read a letter he had written to his dead brother in which he said: "Your message to me is one word. 'Do.' Do as you believe and people will follow you. Do not just *know* what is right, *do* what you know is right. Only then will other people follow you. Only then will you have the power to affect the world."

It is twenty-five years since Alex was killed. A new generation of Jews was born since that day and still, each year, some strong souls leave family and home abroad and come to serve in the IDF. Their influence is greater than their numbers. They bring idealism, Zionism, independence, leadership, and inspiration to their service side by side with those born in Israel. They are examples whose devotion to Israel outshines those who seek ways to avoid their obligation to their nation, an obligation that *chayalim bodedim* take upon themselves.

Sadly, some of these lone soldiers, like Alex, have given their lives throughout the years since the founding of the State. I want to speak of two others, Yoan Zarbiv, *z"l*, and Michael Levin, *z"l*. Both fell in battle during the Second Lebanon War in the summer of 2006.

Yoan, the eldest of four brothers, was born in the outskirts of Paris to a large close family of Moroccan origin. When he was nineteen he made aliyah on his own and entered the army in the Nahal combat unit. Before Hezbollah began its attack against Israel that led to the war in Lebanon, the IDF offered to shorten Yoan's service so that he could begin university. Due to the outbreak of the war, Yoan refused. The war against Hezbollah terrorists embedded among and within civilian villages in southern Lebanon and sending rockets into Israeli cities continued for thirty-four days. During the last twenty-four hours before the cease-fire, on August 12, Yoan was killed. Devoted to Israel, Yoan was among the almost three hundred *chayalim bodedim* from France serving in the IDF.

Elazar Stern met Yoan Zarbiv's family when Yoan's parents arrived in Israel after Yoan's death. Later Elazar visited the Zarbiv family. "Sitting in their home," Elazar recalled, "I knew that the aliyah stories and the foundation of the State of Israel are not just historical anecdotes about the pioneers who created the State; their devotion continues to beat in the hearts of youth all over the Diaspora. I admire their parents, the education, and the values they instill in their children, whether explicitly or by way of showing them the path."

Michael ("Mikey") Levin came from a different world from Yoan, but with the same passion for Israel and commitment to living there and serving in Israel's defense. After Mikey's aliyah at age 19 in 2003, he volunteered for the paratroops and passed its difficult test. His huge determination made up for his small stature. When the war began in Lebanon in July 2006, Mikey was on thirty-day leave in Philadelphia with his family. He immediately returned to Israel and, despite the army's reluctance, he rejoined his unit in the 890th battalion of the paratroops in Lebanon. On August 1, Mikey was killed by a Hezbollah sniper in the village of Aita al-Shaab. Two days later, Tisha b'Av, thousands of people who never knew Mikey, but were inspired by his story, came to honor him at his funeral at the military cemetery at Mt. Herzl. Elazar Stern met Mikey's family while they were sitting shiva in Israel.

Today, the Lone Soldier Center in Memory of Michael Levin provides advice, guidance, Shabbat meals, educational programs, and furniture to the 5,700 lone soldiers serving in the IDF.

We honor Alex, Yoan, and Michael, who gave their lives to protect the people of Israel, and we honor all the lone soldiers who serve in the IDF without the warm support of their families. They remind us that Israel will be ours only if we love and protect it.

Suzanne F. Singer
June 2012

Chapter 17

Instead of an Epilogue: We Are All Brothers

Several months after the death of Uri Grossman – the son of the famous Israeli novelist David Grossman – during the Second Lebanon War, I received a call from Rabbi Aharon Bina, head of the Netiv Aryeh yeshiva, located in the Old City of Jerusalem, and the son of my late rabbi, Aryeh Bina. In addition to serving as a full-time rabbi and head of a large yeshiva, Rabbi Bina is also the representative of Jewish philanthropists Ira and Ingeborg Rennert for all their charity work. Their collaboration has helped innumerable people in a variety of ways, including easing their misery and grief.

Every year the Rennerts donate ten Torah scrolls in memory of fallen IDF soldiers. Often the scrolls are dedicated to the memory of specific soldiers, and this time, Rabbi Bina suggested that one of them should be dedicated to the memory of Uri Grossman.

My instinctive response was that from my very short acquaintance with the Grossman family, I did not believe that they would appreciate the gesture. I said so because just before their son was buried, the family contacted me and asked for permission to bring a female rabbi from their congregation to participate in the funeral ceremony of their son alongside the military rabbi, and allow her to say a prayer while standing over the open grave. I replied that it shouldn't be a problem. At almost every military funeral different people speak on the family's behalf and we never interfere or ask what they intend to say. Since the ritual was conducted by the Military Rabbinate, I informed the chief IDF rabbi about the family's request and he did not object.

I told Rabbi Bina about this request so that he would also know in advance that there was a chance the Torah would be donated to a Conservative or Reform synagogue with a female rabbi. I was happy to hear that he does not ask where the Torah will be placed or about the affiliation of a particular synagogue. Rabbi Bina said that for him, Uri Grossman, who died defending the Land of Israel, was holy in every respect.

After Rabbi Bina gave his recommendation for the dedication of the Torah scroll, I still anticipated that it would be difficult to persuade Michal and David Grossman to accept the scroll. It wasn't. They were extremely grateful and appreciative and only asked that the Torah be placed in the synagogue within their community, which is not Orthodox. When I answered that this would not pose a problem, they asked for some time to come to a final decision.

We spoke again after a few weeks. The Grossmans had two issues they wanted to discuss with me. First, they wanted to ensure that the scroll would be small enough that girls could hold and dance with it during their Bat Mitzvahs. Knowing Rabbi Bina, I agreed immediately to this request. Their second concern was about the motivation behind the decision to donate a Torah in Uri's memory. They wanted to make sure that Uri was not receiving the Torah since he was the "son of David Grossman, the famous novelist." They also wanted to make sure that David would not have to make any special public appearances because of the donation.

I told them about the Rennert family and how they had already donated dozens of Torahs to bereaved families from across the country.

The celebration during which the writing of the Torah scrolls would be completed was supposed to be held on the eve of the Sukkot holiday in 2008. On Friday before the event, I received a call informing me that David Grossman did not plan on personally attending the event. I was asked to try and convince him to come. I explained to the caller that first, I hadn't even mentioned in my conversations with David any celebrations in which he would be expected to take part; and second, I didn't know how he would feel about a celebration inside a yeshiva in the Old City of Jerusalem. I also explained that I conducted all my conversations with David with utmost discretion and prudence, and I didn't have any intention of abusing the open door that I have to him as head of the Human Resources Directorate for any purpose, especially something of a religious nature.

Soon after the Shabbat ended I received another call, but I didn't change my mind. An hour later, Rabbi Bina himself called me. This indicated that the situation was more complicated than I had realized. Rabbi Bina said to me that as a representative of the donors they had gone "as far as they could" by agreeing for the Torah to be placed in a non-Orthodox synagogue and for a female rabbi to represent the Grossmans at the ceremony. I knew that as an Orthodox rabbi, Rabbi Bina had really done more than could have been expected. All they wanted now was that David Grossman respect the evening with his attendance. I knew that the attendance of David Grossman held a great symbolic significance for Rabbi Bina and Ira Rennert since it symbolized our unity as a nation, and that his absence would reflect the opposite. I realized that I could no longer remain passive.

Since I knew that the families of the other soldiers killed with Uri Grossman were close to David and Michal, I decided first to try and recruit Hagit Rhein, mother of Benaya Rhein, the tank commander. Hagit explained to me that this was not something she could take upon herself.

I realized that I had no choice, and I called the Grossman house. David answered the call and after a few usual niceties I told him that I was calling about the Torah dedication ceremony; I asked him whether he'd rather that I speak to his wife, or if he and I should continue discussing the matter. He said, "Let's give it a try!"

I described the exact location of the yeshiva and its proximity to the Kotel, and then I described the hall in which the ceremony was going to take place. On a large table, I told him, would be the five Torah scrolls, each nearly finished, and in front of each scroll would sit the *sofer* – the scribe – who wrote it, and whose task it would be to carefully supervise the relatives and friends who would be honored with writing the last few letters in each scroll. When this was done, all the participants would go dance with the scrolls in their arms.

At a certain point David asked me what I thought. I replied that I was not willing to take sides, but I humbly pointed to the fact that there are two central elements of dedicating a Torah scroll for a fallen IDF soldier. First, there is the religious aspect of writing the holy scroll. The second element is the dedication: the commemoration and tribute paid to the fallen soldier and his or her family. Every time the Torah will be brought out from the ark or when bar mitzvah boys or bat mitzvah girls will read from it or dance with it in their arms, they will see and remember Uri's name. I added that if he was concerned that he would feel out of place at the ceremony, I would be honored to personally drive his family there and accompany them throughout the evening. David accepted.

The following day I met David, Michal, and Michal's parents, and we drove together to the Old City. On our way we spoke a bit about one of David's recent books and about his large number of readers. Grossman told me that many religious Israelis were among those readers and that he often receives reactions from people who live over the Green Line in settlements in the West Bank.

When we entered the Old City through the Zion Gate and approached the Kotel, I told them about the many fascinating archeological findings at the City of David. Grossman admitted that it had been a while since he had visited the place, and we agreed to set up a joint tour in the future.

We entered the yeshiva and together approached the Torah scroll dedicated in Uri's memory. Next to the Torah sat the scribe, and at his side stood the female rabbi of the Grossman family's congregation. I took a look at the cover of the scroll. They usually have a quote from the Torah but this one had several lines from a poem, by the poet Rachel, that read: "Uri, I will call him, my Uri. Gentle and lucid is his name, like a fragment of light." David wrote a letter and I added one after him. We learned that Ehud Barak, the defense minister, who is a friend of the Grossmans, was about to join the celebration. David, with his delicate manners, asked Barak that he approach the other families before coming over to him.

I stood next to the Grossmans and reminded them that I was at their service and whenever they wanted to leave they should just let me know. An hour passed and I reminded them again. We left the yeshiva after two hours and began driving to the King David Hotel for the celebratory banquet. As we entered my car, David called his daughter Ruti and told her that they had just been through one of the most exhilarating and emotional experiences of their lives.

Dorit was a full partner of mine throughout the entire process that led up to the Torah dedication ceremony. I told her everything and consulted with her before every step I took. Now I felt obliged to share with her the response I had heard from the Grossmans. I called Dorit with them in the car and told her what David had just said to his daughter. I wouldn't say in those tragic circumstances that she was happy to hear it, but she was, like me, relieved. Michal and David took the phone and continued the conversation with Dorit, who like them knew what it was like to lose a loved one.

When we arrived at the King David Hotel, Grossman turned to me and said, "At the end of the day, we really are the same people. If things were just a little different I could have been the scribe and he could have been me."

I knew then that despite the sadness that surrounds us there is some hope. Despite the differences, there is sometimes unity.